# THE BIG BOOK OF
# SOUPS & STEWS

# THE BIG BOOK OF

SOU

MARYANA VOLLSTEDT

CHRONICLE BOOKS
SAN FRANCISCO

**262** recipes for serious comfort food

'EWS

LIBRARY OF CONGRESS
CATALOGING-IN-
PUBLICATION DATA:

VOLLSTEDT, MARYANA.
THE BIG BOOK OF SOUPS AND STEWS :
262 RECIPES FOR
SERIOUS COMFORT FOOD / BY
MARYANA VOLLSTEDT.
P. CM.
INCLUDES INDEX.
ISBN 0-8118-3056-X (PBK.)
SOUPS. 2. STEWS. I. TITLE.

TX757 .V65 2001
641.8'13-DC21

PRINTED IN THE
UNITED STATES OF AMERICA

DESIGNED BY VIVIEN SUNG
FOOD AND PROP STYLING BY
DARIENNE SUTTON

DISTRIBUTED IN CANADA BY
RAINCOAST BOOKS
9050 SHAUGHNESSY STREET
VANCOUVER, BC V6P 6E5

10 9 8 7 6 5
CHRONICLE BOOKS LLC
85 SECOND STREET
SAN FRANCISCO,
CALIFORNIA 94105

WWW.CHRONICLEBOOKS.COM

## DEDICATION

To my husband, Reed, without whose advice, patience, support, and many, many hours on the computer, this book would never have happened. It was truly a joint venture. He was also a good tester.

## ACKNOWLEDGMENTS

To Bill LeBlond, senior editor, Chronicle Books, who encouraged me to write my second Big Book, *The Big Book of Soups & Stews,* following *The Big Book of Casseroles;* to Rebecca Pepper for her thorough and precise copy editing and helpful suggestions; and to Amy Treadwell, editorial assistant, for all of her help.

And special thanks to Jim Herbold, computer consultant; Margi Herbold and Donna Addison for their testing and contributions; and to friends, family, and neighbors who willingly sampled many of the recipes.

# CONTENTS

# INTRODUCTION

Soups and stews are a universal food, found in almost every part of the world. All countries have their own traditional ingredients, but all soups and stews have one thing in common—they make you feel good! No wonder they are often called "comfort food," or food for the soul.

Today's approach to making soups and stews calls for fresh ingredients and high-quality meat. They are no longer considered a budget meal or a way to use leftovers. Soups and stews are great for family meals but can also be served for casual, informal gatherings, such as tailgate parties, luncheons, buffets, and suppers.

In *The Big Book of Soups and Stews*, you will find a variety of practical, savory soups and stews for all occasions. Many of the traditional and classic soups and stews have been revised, updated, and streamlined for today's home cook. Also included, along with the old favorites, are some well-known ethnic-inspired and international soups and stews, plus other original and exciting new combinations and fresh ideas. All recipes have been home tested.

Soups and stews are similar in that both are a combination of complementary ingredients cooked in one pot in a flavorful broth or sauce. However, they also have some differences.

Soups are appealing and usually agree with almost everyone. What is more welcome than a steaming bowl of soup on a cold, stormy night, or a refreshing cold soup on a hot summer day? Soups are for all seasons.

Homemade soups are easy to make and are generally more nutritious and more flavorful than the canned or packaged variety. Soups can be thick, thin, smooth, hot, cold, light, or heavy. Creamy soups are often served as a first course to stimulate the appetite. Hearty, chunky soups are served as the main course for lunch or a light supper. Fruit soups can be served any time of the day: breakfast, brunch, lunch, supper, dinner, or a late-night snack.

- Some stoves are hotter than others. If medium-low is too hot for gentle simmering, reduce the temperature to low, or alternate between medium-low and low.

- If you like more seasonings, add more, especially salt and pepper. Always taste the soup or stew before serving. If you are a garlic or onion lover, you can always add more than the recipe calls for.

- If there is an ingredient that you don't like, leave it out or use a substitute. Vegetarians can use vegetable broth instead of chicken or beef broth.

- If the soup or stew is too thick, add more liquid (this is especially true when reheating). If the soup is too thin, add more ingredients or a thickening agent.

- If necessary, most soups and stews can simmer longer than is called for in the recipe on very low heat until ready to serve.

- Be flexible, use common sense, and have fun!

Soups are usually served in individual bowls or from a fancy tureen or decorative bowl for an elegant occasion. They are often garnished with various toppings for extra flavor and eye appeal (see page 40).

Stews are prepared by a method called stewing. The ingredients are cooked in a small amount of liquid in a covered pot for several hours. The long cooking period tenderizes the meat and allows the flavors to blend with other ingredients. Stews are chunkier and thicker than soups and have more substance. They can be served in bowls or alongside pasta, grains, potatoes, or polenta. Stews can be cooked on top of the stove in a heavy pot or in an ovenproof pot or casserole in a medium oven.

Stews are usually served as the main course—the proverbial one-dish meal—for lunch or dinner. They are especially popular in the fall and winter when there is a chill in the air.

All that is needed to complete the meal is a green salad and crusty bread.

# SOUPS & STEWS:

# a PRiMER

## ADVANTAGES OF SOUPS AND STEWS

- Add variety to the menu.

- Easy to make.

- Great for make-ahead meals. Most soups and stews improve when reheated; the exception is seafood.

- No-fuss meal—all in one pot.

- Easy serving and easy cleanup (one bowl).

- Satisfying and wholesome—soothes the appetite.

- Minimum special equipment needed.

- Economical (depending on ingredients).

- Little attention required while cooking.

- Flexible—ingredients can vary with availability and cook's preference.

- A fun way to entertain for a casual, informal party or a nutritious family meal.

- Can play a role in weight watching.

- Slow cooking builds flavor.

- Canned products such as tomatoes, broth, and beans can be used for convenience.

- Frozen vegetables can be used.

## COOKING TERMS

**BEAT:** To mix vigorously with a spoon or mixer.

**BÉCHAMEL:** A white sauce made by stirring milk into a butter-flour roux.

**BISQUE:** A rich, thick soup usually consisting of seafood (sometimes poultry and vegetables) and cream.

**BLANCH:** To partially cook very briefly in boiling water.

**BOUILLON:** A broth made by cooking vegetables, meats, poultry, or fish in water. Available canned (concentrated) and in cubes (dehydrated).

**BOUQUET GARNI:** A bundle of herbs and spices in a metal tea ball, spice ball, or tied in a cheesecloth sack to flavor soups and sauces. Remove before serving.

**CAYENNE:** A hot, pungent powder made from tropical chiles, also called red pepper.

**CELERIAC:** The root of a special type of celery, also called celery root.

**CHIFFONADE:** To cut leafy herbs and vegetables into thin strips.

**CHOP:** To cut into small, irregular pieces.

**CHOWDER:** A thick, chunky seafood or vegetable soup, as in clam chowder; usually includes potatoes.

**CLARIFY:** To clear a cloudy liquid by removing sediment (see page 32).

**CONSOMMÉ:** Clarified stock, often sold in condensed form.

**CRÈME FRAÎCHE:** A thickened cream with a nutty flavor and velvety rich texture (see page 27).

**CROUTONS:** Bread cubes lightly browned in oil or melted butter and sautéed or baked, used to garnish soups and salads. Toasted baguette slices are also referred to as croutons.

**CUBE:** To cut into ½-inch or larger cubes.

**DEVEIN:** To remove the intestine from the curved back of a shrimp.

**DICE:** To cut into tiny cubes smaller than ½ inch.

**FILÉ:** A powder used to thicken and flavor gumbos and Creole dishes. Made from sassafras leaves.

**FLAKE:** To separate cooked fish and other foods into sections with a fork.

**FLAMEPROOF:** A pan such as a Dutch oven that can withstand stovetop, broiler, and oven temperatures.

**FLORET:** The tender blooms or crown of broccoli or cauliflower.

**GARNISH:** An edible accompaniment to finish dishes and add eye appeal and flavor.

**GRATE:** To cut into thin strips using a hand grater or food processor fitted with a grating blade.

**GREMOLATA:** A garnish made of minced parsley, lemon peel, and garlic. Sometimes crumbs are added (see page 43).

**JULIENNE:** To cut into matchstick-sized strips.

**LEEK:** A vegetable that is related to both garlic and onion, though its flavor and fragrance are milder and more subtle.

**MINCE:** To cut into very fine pieces, as in minced garlic.

**MIREPOIX:** A mixture of diced carrots, celery, and herbs sautéed in butter. Bacon or ham is sometimes added. Used to season soups and sauces or as a bed to braise food.

**PANCETTA:** Italian bacon that is cured with salt and spices, not smoked.

**PARE:** To remove an outer covering, such as potato or apple skin, with a knife.

**PEEL:** To strip off an outer covering, such as banana or orange skin, by hand.

**PESTO:** A sauce or paste made from uncooked basil (or other ingredients), olive oil, nuts, garlic, and Parmesan cheese (see page 41).

**PREHEAT:** To heat the oven to the temperature specified in a recipe.

**PURÉE:** To reduce food to a smooth, thick consistency with a food processor, blender, or food mill.

**ROUILLE:** A garnish for fish soups and stews made of chiles, garlic, and oil (see page 44).

**ROUX:** A mixture of flour and fat cooked over low heat. Used to thicken soups and sauces.

**RUSSET:** A potato low in moisture and high in starch that is good for cooking. Also called Idaho potato.

**SAUTÉ:** To cook food in a small amount of fat on top of the stove for a short period of time, stirring often.

**SHALLOT:** A large, garlic-shaped member of the onion family with a mild onion flavor. Less pungent than garlic.

**SKIN:** To remove skin from poultry or fish.

**SLICE:** To cut into flat pieces.

**STIR:** To mix ingredients in a circular motion.

**VELOUTÉ SAUCE:** A stock-based white sauce thickened with a roux.

**WHISK:** To stir ingredients together with a wire whip to blend.

**ZEST:** The outermost skin layer of citrus fruits (usually lemons or oranges), which is removed with the aid of a citrus zester, paring knife, or vegetable peeler.

## COOKING TIPS FOR MAKING AND SERVING SOUPS & STEWS

- Read the recipe carefully. Shop for all needed ingredients.
- Assemble all ingredients and equipment before starting.
- Do the preparation work (chopping, grating, opening cans, and so on) ahead of time.
- Simmer soups and stews over medium-low or low heat, depending on the stove. Do not boil, just keep them at a gentle ripple. Gas stoves are hotter and faster than electric ones.
- Add vegetables that require a short cooking time (mushrooms, green beans, summer squash, spinach, and so on) at the end of the cooking period to prevent overcooking.
- Add fresh herbs at the end of the cooking time. They lose their flavor and intensity when cooked for a long period of time. Most recipes call for dried herbs or a combination of fresh and dried. Crush dried herbs between your fingers to release flavor.
- Use sea salt or kosher salt for more intense flavor (see page 26).
- Rinse frozen vegetables under hot water before measuring.
- Chop whole canned tomatoes in the can with stainless steel scissors.
- Trim excess skin and fat from chicken with stainless steel kitchen scissors.
- Use a food processor to chop vegetables if uniform pieces for visual purposes are not required. Cut vegetables in large, uniform pieces before placing them in the food processor.

- Use a food processor or blender to make purées to thicken some soups. Purée 1 cup vegetables with a small amount of broth, then blend with the remaining soup in the pan.

- Thicken stews by adding a paste of flour, cornstarch, or arrowroot blended with water to the liquid. Grains, legumes, and tapioca are also used to thicken soups and stews.

- Use a chilled stainless steel bowl to make cold soups.

- Serve hot soups in warmed bowls and cold soups in chilled bowls. (To warm bowls, place in a warm oven for 30 minutes, or pour hot water into the bowls and let them stand for 10 minutes. To chill bowls, place in the freezer for 1 hour.)

- Soups can be served in tureens; large, interesting heatproof bowls; or, for a special occasion, a hollowed-out pumpkin or a hollowed-out round loaf of peasant bread. To prepare a loaf of bread to use as a container for soup, slice off the top quarter. Hollow out the loaf, leaving about 3/4 inch around the edge, being careful not to cut through the bottom. Brush the insides and top with vegetable or olive oil. Bake at 350°F for 10 minutes. Ladle the soup into the bread container and serve immediately. Individual loaves can also be used.

- Store soups and stews, covered, in the refrigerator for up to 3 or 4 days. (Fish soups do not store well.) Leave the fat layer that accumulates on top until ready to serve (it seals the soup), or freeze in tightly covered containers for 1 to 2 months.

- Reheat soups or stews that have been made ahead over low heat, stirring constantly and adding more liquid if necessary. If using a microwave oven, watch carefully and do not overcook.

## HELPFUL EQUIPMENT

- Large stockpot for making stock. The high sides help the stock circulate for even cooking and reduce evaporation.

- Large, stainless steel (nonreactive) or enamel-lined soup pot, with a heavy bottom. Do not use aluminum or iron because tomato products react to these materials.

- Dutch oven. A large, heavy, flameproof pot with a lid, made of cast iron, enamel-lined cast iron, or stainless steel. It retains heat and can be used for browning, sautéing, stewing, braising, or baking. Perfect for making stews and soups.

- Skimmer. A stainless steel tool with a fine mesh used to skim off foam that rises to the top.

- Three or four good knives. A stainless steel chef's knife for chopping, a utility or boning knife, a paring knife, and a serrated knife for slicing bread.

- Food processor or blender for chopping and puréeing. For a velvety-smooth, puréed soup, the blender does the best job. Blend in batches (not more than one third full, with lid on).

- A stick (hand) blender is convenient to use, with less cleanup, but is not as efficient.

- Food mill. Used to strain fiber, seeds, and skin, and to mash and purée. Comes with interchangeable disks. To purée in a food mill, use the fine disk. Convenient but not essential.

- Measuring cups and spoons, whisk, vegetable peeler, wooden spoon or heavy-duty plastic spoon, spatula, slotted spoon, tongs, and timer.

- Stainless steel mesh sieve and colander for draining, or chinois (conical French sieve with an extremely fine mesh) for straining.
- Kitchen scale. Convenient when a recipe calls for an ingredient by weight.
- Cheesecloth for straining stocks or to make a bouquet garni.
- Spice holder or tea caddy for holding spices.
- Soup bowls, soup spoons, and a ladle. Deep bowls keep soup hotter, but wide bowls are more suitable for hearty soups and stews. Mugs work for sipping thin soups. Ovenproof ramekins for baked soups.
- Soup tureen for elegant serving.
- A crockpot or pressure cooker can also be used in making stews and soups. Follow the manufacturer's directions.

# TECHNIQUES
# & HELPFUL HINTS

### ROASTING RED BELL AND CHILE PEPPERS

Preheat the broiler. Cut peppers in half lengthwise and remove seeds and ribs. Make several 1-inch slashes around the edge of each half. Place skin-side up on a foil-lined baking sheet. Press peppers down with the palm of your hand to flatten them. Broil until skin is charred, about 10 minutes. Remove from broiler, fold foil tightly over peppers, and let steam for 15 minutes. Unwrap peppers and peel off skin.

Whole peppers can also be roasted over a gas flame. Spear them with a long-handled fork and turn them as they become charred, or place on a grill and turn them with tongs.

### COOKING WITH FRESH TOMATOES

To remove the skin from fresh tomatoes, drop the tomatoes into boiling water to cover for 30 seconds. Remove immediately with a slotted spoon and rinse under cold water; then peel. The skins will slip off easily.

To remove the seeds from fresh tomatoes, cut tomato in half crosswise. Hold a half over the sink and squeeze gently, or use a finger to scoop out the seeds along with some of the juice. To remove all of the seeds after cooking, use a food mill or strain through a strainer.

### COOKING WITH CANNED TOMATOES AND OTHER TOMATO PRODUCTS

Canned tomatoes are often used in soups and stews. They are available in a variety of forms—peeled, whole, crushed, stewed, diced, in a sauce, plain or puréed, with herbs and spices, or as a paste. Roma (Italian plum) tomatoes are preferred because they are meatier, have fewer seeds and less juice, and hold up well during canning. Canned organic tomato products are also available.

Sun-dried tomatoes are packed in oil or dry-packed. They are intensely flavored and chewy, and are used in sauces and soups. Reconstitute dry-packed sun-dried tomatoes by soaking them in hot water, then drain.

**Leftover Tomato Paste** Often a recipe calls for a small amount of tomato paste, available in cans and tubes. What do you do with leftover paste? Place the paste remaining from a can in a small jar and freeze it, or freeze the tube. Or measure out 1-tablespoon amounts and freeze on a piece of foil, then seal them in a plastic bag and store in the freezer, ready to use.

### COOKING WITH ONIONS

There are two main classifications of onions—dry and green (also called scallions)—and many varieties. The yellow onion is the most common and least expensive and is used in many of the recipes in this book. White onions are slightly more expensive but can also be used. Red onions are stronger. Pearl onions are very tiny and can be used as a garnish or in drinks.

Boiling onions are about 1 inch in diameter. They are mildly flavored and are commonly used in stews. To peel boiling onions, drop them in boiling water for 30 seconds. Remove, peel, and trim the ends.

Chives have a mild onion flavor. Add to soups and stews at the end of the cooking time, or sprinkle sliced chives on top as a garnish before serving for added color and taste.

Leeks are related to both garlic and onions but have a milder flavor. They look like giant scallions and are available year round. Use the white and light green parts only in cooking.

### COOKING WITH HERBS

Fresh herbs lose their flavor and intensity when cooked for a long time. Add them at the end for a last-minute burst of fresh flavor. Dried herbs are available year-round in bulk or jars. They are often more convenient and hold up better during a long cooking period. Crumble dried herbs between your fingers to release the flavor before adding them to a recipe. To substitute dried herbs for fresh herbs, the general rule is to use 1 teaspoon dried for 1 tablespoon fresh.

**Parsley** is a fresh-tasting herb. Flat-leaf or Italian parsley is preferred because the flavor is more intense, but curly parsley can be used (just use more). Sprigs of curly parsley make an attractive garnish.

Sprinkle minced fresh parsley on soups to add color and flavor.

**Cilantro** is the bright green leaves and stems of the coriander plant (also called Chinese parsley). Some people object to the flavor, claiming it tastes "soapy." It is used in Mexican dishes and as a garnish.

**Chiffonade** is strips of fresh leafy herbs (basil) and vegetables (spinach). Stack 5 or 6 washed and dried leaves. Tightly roll the stack into a tube, and then thinly slice crosswise.

### SKINNING CHICKEN PIECES

With a paper towel, pull the skin away from the meat. Remove any excess fat with stainless steel kitchen shears.

### POACHING CHICKEN BREASTS

Use either skinned and boned chicken breasts or breasts with the bone in and skin on. (The bones and skin add extra flavor.) Put chicken breasts in a saucepan. Add enough water or chicken stock to cover. For 4 chicken breast halves, add ¼ teaspoon salt, 1 sprig parsley, 1 piece of onion, and several peppercorns. Bring to a boil over high heat, immediately reduce the heat to low, and simmer (the liquid should barely bubble), covered, until chicken turns white, 10 to 15 minutes. Remove chicken to a plate to cool until ready to use, or cool in the liquid if time allows. Remove any skin and bones, if necessary. The cooking broth can be strained and refrigerated or frozen.

**NOTE:** *Add 2 tablespoons dry white wine to the poaching water, if desired.*

### CRISPING TORTILLAS STRIPS

Preheat oven to 400°F. Brush or lightly spray both sides of tortillas with vegetable oil. Stack 4 tortillas together. With a sharp knife, cut into 1/2-inch strips. Place in a single layer on a baking sheet and bake for 3 to 4 minutes. Sprinkle with salt or other seasonings, if desired. Tortillas can also be fried in oil or grilled on a grill or griddle until crisp.

### TOASTING NUTS AND SEEDS

For most nuts, preheat the oven to 350°F. Place nuts on a baking sheet and bake until lightly browned, 7 to 10 minutes for whole nuts, 4 to 5 minutes for sliced nuts or chopped nuts. You can also toast nuts in the microwave by cooking them for 3 to 4 minutes. Watch carefully, as they burn easily. Cool before using.

If using pine nuts, place them in a nonstick skillet over medium-high heat. Stir with a wooden spoon until nuts are golden, 4 to 5 minutes.

To toast sesame seeds, place them in a small, nonstick skillet and cook over medium-high heat, stirring until golden, about 2 minutes.

### CHOOSING SALT

Salt enhances the flavor of foods. Sea salt and kosher salt are coarse-grained salts that are free of additives. They are preferred over table salt because of their superior texture and flavor.

### COOKING WITH MILK PRODUCTS

Use whole milk in a recipe that calls for milk. To reduce calories you can substitute 2 percent or nonfat milk. The richer the milk, the creamier and richer the soup.

Canned skim milk, fat-free half-and-half, buttermilk, or nonfat yogurt can also be used to reduce calories. Buttermilk works well in cream soups; it adds an extra tangy taste that most people like.

Half-and-half is half milk and half cream. Heavy cream is whipping cream.

**Sour Cream** is available in regular, light, and nonfat varieties. A dollop of sour cream is often added on top of soups as a garnish for eye appeal and extra creaminess.

**Yogurt** is used as a calorie saver in soups or as a topping. Pour off the excess liquid from the carton and then stir. If using yogurt in soups, heat gently after adding it; do not boil.

**Yogurt Cheese** is drained nonfat yogurt that is very thick with no fat. It is good as a topping for soups or as a vegetable dip.

To make yogurt cheese, place 2 cups plain nonfat yogurt in a sieve lined with cheesecloth or a coffee filter. Suspend over a deep bowl, cover tightly with plastic wrap, and refrigerate for 24 hours or longer. Discard the liquid whey in the bottom of the bowl. Store refrigerated in an airtight container for up to 10 days. Makes about $3/4$ cup.

**Crème Fraîche** is a thickened cream with a nutty flavor and a velvety, rich texture. It is used in sauces or soups because it will not curdle. Flavored with vanilla and slightly sweetened, it is also delicious on fruits and desserts. It can be purchased but is easy to make.

To make crème fraîche, place 1 cup whipping cream and 2 tablespoons buttermilk in a glass jar. Cover and let stand at room temperature (70°F) until thick, 8 to 24 hours. Stir well and refrigerate, covered, up to 10 days.

### CHEESE

Cheese is added to soups as a topping or a main ingredient, as in cheese soups. It enriches the soup and acts as a thickener. Cheese used in soups should have good melting qualities, such as Monterey Jack, Cheddar, Swiss, fontina, mozzarella, and cream cheese. Freshly grated Parmesan cheese is called for as a topping in many soups. It is a hard, dry cheese with a sharp flavor that grates well. The primo Parmesan cheese is Italy's Parmigiano-Reggiano, one of the world's great cheeses. It has a nutty-sweet, slightly salty, spicy flavor and a granular texture that melts in your mouth. It is more expensive than domestic Parmesan, but well worth it.

### COOKING WITH OILS

There are two categories of oil: salad oil and cooking oil.

Cooking oils have a high smoking point, which means they can take the heat without smoking. Corn oil, safflower oil, canola oil, sesame oil, and vegetable oil are common cooking oils. Peanut oil has a slightly lower smoking point but can also be used for cooking. Pure olive oil can be used for cooking, especially in Mediterranean dishes. Sautéing vegetables in oil or butter seals in the juices and flavor and keeps them firm.

Salad oils have a low smoking point but are more flavorful than cooking oils. They are used to flavor dressings, sauces, and marinades. Salad oils are olive oil, nut oil, Asian sesame oil, avocado oil, and other flavored oils.

To cut back on oil when cooking, use a nonstick vegetable spray.

### COOKING WITH LEGUMES

Legumes are beans, peas, soybeans, lentils, and peanuts. They are an important ingredient in soups and stews because they add nutrients, body, fiber, and flavor and are also inexpensive. They are available dried or canned. Dried beans keep their texture and flavor better than canned ones, but canned beans can be used for convenience. Drain and rinse canned beans to reduce sodium.

Presoak beans and dried peas to soften them and shorten the cooking time. First wash dried beans thoroughly in cold water. Pick over and sort the beans, discarding any foreign matter or discolored beans. Split peas and lentils are softer and do not need presoaking.

There are two methods for presoaking beans.

**OVERNIGHT SOAKING METHOD:** In a large soup pot, place beans and enough cold water to cover by 2 inches. Let stand overnight. Drain and proceed with the recipe.

**QUICK-SOAK METHOD:** In a large soup pot, place beans and cold water to cover. Bring to a boil over high heat and boil for 2 minutes. Skim off foam that rises to the surface. Remove from heat, cover, and let stand, covered, 1 hour before using. Drain and proceed with the recipe.

**TO COOK PRESOAKED BEANS:** Drain beans and add fresh water or broth to cover by 2 inches. Bring to a boil over high heat, skimming off any foam that rises to the surface. Reduce heat to low, cover, and simmer until beans are tender. Add more liquid if needed. Don't add salt until after cooking; adding salt during the cooking period toughens the beans. Dried beans will at least double in volume after cooking.

The following are the most popular beans for the home cook:

- White beans: navy, Great Northern, and cannellini (white kidney beans). They are interchangeable.
- Black beans, native to South America, used in soups and side dishes.
- Black-eyed peas, used in Southern cooking.
- Chickpeas (garbanzos), used in Mexican and international cooking.
- Pinto and pink beans, used in Mexican and Spanish cooking.
- Red kidney beans, used in soups, chilis, and salads.

# BASIC STOCKS & BROTHS

A rich, flavorful stock is the foundation of most soups and stews. Homemade stocks are preferred because they are richer and more flavorful and the sodium is controlled. Commercial broths are often more convenient, however. They are available canned, bottled, in cubes, granulated, and in concentrated paste form in a jar. If using a commercial broth, choose a fat-free, low-sodium variety. To enrich a commercial chicken stock or broth, simmer two or three chicken pieces and some vegetables in it for 30 minutes. Although you can use bouillon cubes, be aware that they are often quite salty.

Making stock is a simple procedure. It involves simmering bones and inexpensive cuts of meat, fish and fish bones, or bony pieces of chicken with vegetables and seasonings in liquid in a stockpot (a high-sided pot) for several hours to extract the flavors. The bones should first be rinsed thoroughly in cold water or blanched to remove any trace of blood. Use cold water or bottled water for making stock. As the ingredients cook, a foam rises to the top that should be skimmed off to prevent cloudiness in the stock. When using stock in cooking, taste stock for saltiness before adding more salt.

Vegetables used in making stock are onions, celery, carrots, leeks, shallots, and garlic. Do not use strong-flavored vegetables such as broccoli, cauliflower, and cabbage (except in vegetable stock). Cut vegetables into large pieces.

After cooking, strain the stock through a very fine sieve or a sieve lined with several layers of cheesecloth, into a bowl. After you've removed the solids you can reduce the stock by boiling it rapidly to concentrate and enrich the flavor. Discard the solids and transfer the stock to storage containers, let it cool, and store it, covered, in the refrigerator for up to 3 days or freeze it for up to 3 months. If you need to keep stock in the refrigerator for longer than 3 days, bring it to a boil, cool, and refrigerate again. Vegetable and fish stock can be frozen for up to 2 months. Remove the fat layer that rises to the top before using or freezing the stock.

Consommé is meat, poultry, or fish stock that has been clarified. To clarify a stock, in a large stockpot combine 2 crushed eggshells and 2 egg whites with the stock. Bring to a boil, lower the heat, and simmer, uncovered, until the egg whites collect any particles and sediments, 10 to 15 minutes. Cool for 1 hour, then pour the mixture through a sieve lined with cheesecloth. To make double-strength consommé, boil the stock until it is half the original volume. It will have twice the flavor of regular consommé and can be served hot or cold.

**NOTE:** *Many recipes in this book call for chicken stock or broth; use either homemade stock or fat-free, low-sodium canned broth. If the recipe calls for 2 cups of broth and you are using canned (14½ ounces, approximately 1¾ cups), add water to make 2 cups.*

# CHICKEN STOCK

**Freeze the raw, bony parts of a chicken that you don't use in cooking until you have about 3 pounds, or use a whole chicken to make stock.**

1 yellow onion, quartered

2 stalks celery, cut into chunks

2 carrots, cut into chunks

One 3-pound chicken, or 3 pounds chicken parts (backs, wings, necks, and giblets; do not use the liver; it will make the stock cloudy)

10 cups water

4 cloves garlic, unpeeled

1 teaspoon salt

1 bay leaf

10 peppercorns

3 sprigs parsley

$\frac{1}{2}$ cup dry white wine

$\frac{1}{2}$ teaspoon dried thyme

In a large stockpot over high heat, place all ingredients except thyme and bring to a boil. Skim off foam. Add thyme, reduce heat to low, and simmer, partially covered, for 2$\frac{1}{2}$ to 3 hours. Pour stock through a very fine sieve or a sieve lined with a double thickness of cheesecloth. Discard solids. (Save chicken meat for another use, if desired.) Degrease stock with a fat separator or store, covered, in the refrigerator overnight and then remove and discard the layer of fat that forms on the top. Use within 3 days, or freeze in airtight containers for up to 3 months.

**MAKES ABOUT 8 CUPS**

# TURKEY STOCK

**Put the carcass of your holiday turkey to good use by making this stock.**

1 turkey carcass

Water to cover (about 8 cups)

2 carrots, cut into chunks

3 sprigs parsley

2 yellow onions, quartered

½ cup celery leaves

2 teaspoons salt

8 peppercorns

1 bay leaf

Remove the meat from carcass and set meat aside. Place carcass and water in a large stockpot. Bring to a boil, uncovered, and skim off foam. Add remaining ingredients. Reduce heat to medium-low, cover, and simmer for 1½ hours. Skim off foam as it forms. Remove carcass. Pour stock through a very fine sieve or a sieve lined with a double thickness of cheesecloth. Discard solids.

**MAKES ABOUT 8 CUPS**

# TURKEY GIBLET STOCK

**This can be made two days ahead to use in making gravy and soups. Cool and refrigerate.**

6 cups water

4 cups chicken stock or broth

1 stalk celery, coarsely chopped

1 carrot, chopped

1 yellow onion, quartered

Neck and giblets from turkey

1 bay leaf

Sprigs of parsley, thyme, sage, and rosemary, or ½ teaspoon of each dried

1 teaspoon peppercorns

In a large stockpot, bring water, stock, celery, carrot, onion, and turkey parts (excluding liver) to a boil. Skim off foam. Add remaining ingredients. Reduce heat to medium-low and simmer, uncovered, until liquid is reduced to about 5 cups, about 2 hours.

In a small pan, simmer the liver in water for 15 minutes and add to the stock. Pour stock through a fine sieve into a large bowl. Cut up giblets, including liver, to use in gravy. Discard remaining solids.

**MAKES ABOUT 5 CUPS**

# BEEF STOCK

**Roasting the bones in the oven develops flavor and makes a richer, browner stock. This step is optional. You can also roast the vegetables along with the bones.**

3½ to 4 pounds meaty beef bones
1 pound stew meat
2 carrots, cut into chunks
2 stalks celery, cut into chunks
1 yellow onion, quartered
2 cloves garlic, halved

1 teaspoon salt
6 peppercorns
3 whole cloves
3 sprigs parsley
1 bay leaf
8 cups water

Preheat oven to 400°F. Rinse bones thoroughly in cold water. Place bones in a roasting pan and brown for about 30 minutes. Transfer to a large stockpot, add remaining ingredients, and bring to a boil over high heat. Skim foam from stock, reduce heat to low, and simmer, covered, 3 to 4 hours. Remove bones.

Strain stock through a very fine sieve or a sieve lined with a double thickness of cheesecloth. Discard solids. Degrease with a fat separator, or cover and refrigerate overnight and then remove and discard the layer of fat that forms on the top. Use immediately or freeze in airtight containers for future use. Will keep in the refrigerator for 3 or 4 days, and up to 3 months in the freezer.

**MAKES ABOUT 8 CUPS**

4

# FISH STOCK

**Fish stocks are used as a base for soups, stews, sauces, and poaching liquid. Use bottled clam juice as a substitute for fish stock if you do not want to make your own.**

2 pounds fish bones, heads, and trimmings, preferably white fish (available at fish markets)

2 stalks celery, sliced ¼ inch thick

1 yellow onion, sliced ¼ inch thick

1 carrot, sliced ¼ inch thick

1 clove garlic, unpeeled

8 cups cold water

1 cup dry white wine

1 tablespoon fresh lemon juice

1 teaspoon salt

1 teaspoon peppercorns

½ teaspoon dried thyme

4 sprigs parsley

1 bay leaf

Rinse fish bones and trimmings several times to remove any trace of blood. In a large stockpot over high heat, bring all ingredients to a boil. Skim off foam. Reduce heat to medium-low or low and simmer, covered, for about 30 minutes. Strain through a very fine sieve or a sieve lined with a double thickness of cheesecloth. Discard solids. Use immediately or freeze in airtight containers for up to 2 months.

**MAKES ABOUT 8 CUPS**

# VEGETABLE STOCK

**Use mature vegetables for the best flavor, but clean and scrape out any bad areas. Leave the onion skins on to add flavor and color. Scrub vegetables, but it is not necessary to peel them. Vegetable stock can be substituted for chicken or beef stock when making soups and stews.**

3 yellow onions, unpeeled, quartered

6 carrots, cut into chunks

2 parsnips, cut into chunks

2 stalks celery, cut into chunks

3 cabbage leaves, cut up

1 red bell pepper, seeded and coarsely chopped

2 bay leaves

2 cloves garlic, chopped

6 peppercorns

2 whole cloves

8 cups water

1 teaspoon fresh thyme leaves, or ½ teaspoon dried thyme

6 sprigs parsley

Salt (optional)

In a large stockpot over high heat, combine all ingredients except salt. Bring to a boil and skim off foam. Reduce heat and simmer, uncovered, for about 2 hours. Strain through a very fine sieve or a sieve lined with a double thickness of cheesecloth. Discard solids and add salt, if desired. Use immediately or freeze in airtight containers for future use. Will keep in the refrigerator for 3 or 4 days, or up to 2 months in the freezer.

**MAKES ABOUT 8 CUPS**

# FINISHING TOUCHES:
# TOPPINGS & GARNISHES

## GARNISHES

Garnishes are used especially on soups and occasionally on stews. They add color, flavor, texture, interest, and eye appeal. The more complex the soup, the simpler the garnish should be. Often a small amount of an ingredient that suggests the soup's flavor, such as a few sliced mushrooms for a cream of mushroom soup, are sprinkled on top.

Thin soups can be garnished with small herb sprigs or a sprinkling of fresh-snipped herbs that float on top. Light cream soups improve in appearance when sprinkled with finely chopped parsley or chives or a dash of paprika.

## SUGGESTED GARNISHES AND TOPPINGS

Choose garnishes that are complementary to the dish: chopped parsley, chopped cilantro, chopped watercress, chopped celery leaves, chopped green onions, onion rings, minced onions, chopped mushrooms, sliced chives, toasted nuts, crumbled bacon, grated cheese, sliced stuffed olives, thin lemon slices, grated carrots, sliced radishes, diced fresh tomato, chopped hard-cooked eggs, small shrimp, orange chunks, croutons, crushed chips, broken pretzels, garlic crumbs, sour cream, crème fraîche, yogurt, yogurt cheese, and edible flowers. Appropriate garnishes are called for in specific recipes.

# BASIL PESTO

**This classic, fresh-tasting sauce originating in Italy is a favorite to use with vegetables and soups, especially minestrone, and with seafood.**

2 cups firmly packed fresh basil leaves, washed and dried

2 sprigs parsley

2 cloves garlic, cut up

3 tablespoons pine nuts or chopped walnuts

¼ cup freshly grated Parmesan cheese

¼ teaspoon salt

Freshly ground pepper to taste

3 to 4 tablespoons olive oil

In a food processor or blender, place all ingredients except oil. Process until minced. With motor running, slowly pour oil through the tube and blend. Scrape down sides of bowl with spatula. Transfer to a bowl, cover, and refrigerate until ready to use, or freeze for several months. Bring to room temperature before using.

**MAKES ABOUT ½ CUP**

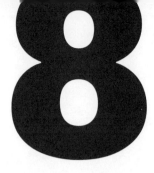

# FRESH TOMATO SALSA

**Salsa appears on the Mexican table at every meal, to complement almost any dish. You can make it as hot as you like by varying the amount and variety of chiles you use. It is best when freshly made. You can also purchase salsa in jars and cartons.**

2 cups coarsely chopped tomatoes, peeled or unpeeled, seeded and drained

¼ cup chopped green bell pepper

2 jalapeño chiles, ribs and seeds removed and finely chopped (see Note)

½ cup finely chopped white onion

1 tablespoon lime or lemon juice

¼ teaspoon ground cumin

1 to 2 tablespoons chopped fresh cilantro or parsley

Salt and freshly ground pepper to taste

In a small bowl, mix together all ingredients. Serve immediately, or cover and refrigerate for several hours.

**NOTE:** *When working with chiles, wear gloves or wash hands thoroughly afterward, and keep hands away from face and eyes.*

**MAKES ABOUT 3 CUPS**

# GREMOLATA

Sprinkle this garnish over meat soups and stews to add a fresh, sprightly flavor.

$\frac{1}{4}$ cup dry bread crumbs

$\frac{1}{4}$ cup chopped parsley

1 teaspoon chopped fresh rosemary, or $\frac{1}{2}$ teaspoon dried rosemary

1 tablespoon grated lemon zest

1 clove garlic, minced

Salt and freshly ground pepper to taste

In a small bowl, mix all ingredients.

**MAKES ABOUT $\frac{1}{2}$ CUP**

# ROUILLE

**Rouille is a French sauce used as a garnish with fish and fish stews such as bouillabaisse. It is very hot.**

1 red bell pepper, roasted (see page 23) and cut up

1 small, hot, red chile pepper, cored, seeded, and cut up

1 large clove garlic, cut up

1 egg yolk

½ teaspoon salt

Freshly ground pepper to taste

¾ cup olive oil

¼ teaspoon lemon juice

Place all ingredients except olive oil and lemon juice in food processor and process until blended. Slowly add oil and process until thick and smooth. Transfer to a bowl and stir in lemon juice.

**MAKES ABOUT 1½ CUPS**

10

# BREADS

## BREADS

Breads and other bread items, such as cheese bread, garlic bread, herb bread, bread sticks, and cornbread are a good accompaniment to soups and stews. A good bread adds substance and interest to a simple meal of soup or stew. A wide selection of specialty breads is now available in bakeries and some supermarkets.

# THREE-CHEESE BREAD

1 loaf sourdough French bread,
  halved lengthwise

Dijon mustard, for spreading on bread

1 cup grated Cheddar cheese

1 cup grated Monterey Jack cheese

½ cup grated mozzarella cheese

½ cup chopped parsley

Preheat oven to 350°F. Place bread on baking sheet and spread mustard evenly on cut sides. In a bowl and using a fork, toss together cheeses and parsley. Sprinkle cheese mixture on top of bread.

Bake until bread is warm and cheese is melted, 10 to 12 minutes. Cut into 1½-inch slices.

**MAKES ABOUT 24 SLICES**

# FRESH HERB GARLIC BREAD

½ cup (1 stick) butter or margarine, at room temperature

2 cloves garlic, minced

3 tablespoons finely chopped mixed fresh herbs (basil, rosemary, oregano, thyme, parsley, or any combination)

1 loaf French bread, halved lengthwise

Preheat oven to 375°F. In a small bowl, mix all ingredients except bread until blended. Spread herb mixture on cut sides of bread. Place bread, buttered-side up, on a baking sheet and bake until warmed through and crispy, 12 to 15 minutes. Cut into 1½-inch slices.

**MAKES ABOUT 24 SLICES**

12

# CLASSIC GARLIC BREAD

½ cup (1 stick) butter or margarine,
   at room temperature

2 or 3 cloves garlic, minced

1 teaspoon paprika

1 loaf French bread, cut into
   ¾-inch slices

Preheat oven to 350°F. In a small bowl, mix butter, garlic, and paprika. Spread on one side of each bread slice. Stack bread slices together to form a loaf. Wrap tightly in foil. Bake until warmed through, 15 to 20 minutes.

**MAKES ABOUT 24 SLICES**

# FRENCH BREAD WITH GARLIC SPREAD

½ cup (1 stick) butter, at room temperature

½ cup freshly grated Parmesan cheese

¼ cup mayonnaise

3 large cloves garlic, minced

2 tablespoons chopped parsley

¼ teaspoon dried oregano

¼ teaspoon paprika

1 loaf French bread, halved lengthwise

Preheat oven to 375°F. In a bowl, mix all ingredients except bread. Spread mixture on cut sides of bread. Place bread on a baking sheet, cut-side up. Bake until golden, 12 to 15 minutes. Cut into slices to serve.

**MAKES ABOUT 24 SLICES**

# HERBED BUTTERMILK STICKS

**These biscuitlike sticks go with all soups. They're best when freshly baked; serve warm.**

2 cups all-purpose flour

1 tablespoon sugar

Dash of salt

2 teaspoons baking powder

$\frac{1}{4}$ teaspoon baking soda

2 teaspoons snipped fresh tarragon, or $\frac{1}{2}$ teaspoon dried tarragon

2 teaspoons snipped fresh rosemary, or $\frac{1}{2}$ teaspoon dried rosemary

$\frac{1}{2}$ cup (1 stick) butter

1 egg

$\frac{1}{2}$ cup buttermilk, plus extra to brush on top

Preheat oven to 425°F. In a medium bowl, stir together flour, sugar, salt, baking powder, baking soda, and herbs. With 2 knives or a pastry blender, cut butter into flour mixture until coarse crumbs form. In a small bowl, beat egg with buttermilk. Make a well in center of flour mixture and pour in egg-buttermilk mixture. Stir with a fork until moistened. Turn dough out on a lightly floured surface and knead 10 to 12 times. Lightly roll dough into a 6-by-12-inch rectangle. With a sharp knife, cut into 24 six-inch strips. Place strips $\frac{1}{2}$ inch apart on a lightly sprayed or oiled baking sheet. Brush with buttermilk. Bake until golden, about 10 minutes. Cool on a rack.

**MAKES 24 STICKS**

15

# IRISH SODA BREAD

**This classic peasant bread is one of the specialties of Ireland and is still baked in countless farmhouses and homes all over the country. It is best served fresh or toasted the next day. It's very easy to make.**

2 cups all-purpose flour

1½ teaspoons baking powder

1 teaspoon salt

¼ teaspoon baking soda

1 cup buttermilk

Preheat oven to 350°F. In a large bowl, mix flour, baking powder, salt, and baking soda. Stir buttermilk into flour mixture until the dough is moistened evenly.

On a floured surface, knead dough 5 or 6 times. Form dough into a ball. Transfer to a buttered baking sheet and shape into an 8-inch mound. With a sharp knife, cut a shallow cross in the top. Bake until golden brown, about 40 minutes. Remove from pan and wrap in a clean kitchen towel and cool on a rack for 1 hour. Slice and serve.

**MAKES ONE 8-INCH ROUND LOAF**

# COMPANY CORNBREAD

**This buttery cornbread is baked in a loaf pan and served in slices instead of squares.**

1 cup all-purpose flour

1 cup yellow cornmeal

$\frac{1}{4}$ cup granulated sugar

1 tablespoon baking powder

$\frac{1}{2}$ teaspoon salt

1 cup milk

1 large egg

$\frac{1}{2}$ cup (1 stick) butter or margarine, at room temperature

Preheat oven to 400°F. In a large bowl, stir together dry ingredients. In a small bowl, whisk together milk and egg until just combined. Add butter to flour-cornmeal mixture and beat with an electric mixer until mixture resembles coarse meal. Add milk-egg mixture and beat until combined. Pour batter into lightly sprayed or oiled 9-by-5-by-3-inch loaf pan. Bake until a tester comes out clean, about 40 minutes. Cool on a rack for 10 minutes. Run a knife around the edges of the pan and turn out on rack to cool. Cut into thick slices to serve.

**MAKES 1 LOAF**

# CHEESE WAFERS

**These light snacks can be made ahead and are perfect to serve with soups or drinks.**

½ cup (1 stick) butter or margarine, at room temperature

1 cup firmly packed grated Cheddar cheese (4 ounces)

½ teaspoon Worcestershire sauce

2 drops Tabasco sauce

¼ teaspoon salt

1 cup all-purpose flour

In a bowl, blend together butter and cheese. Stir in Worcestershire sauce, Tabasco sauce, and salt. Add flour and mix well. Divide dough in half and form into logs 1½ inches in diameter. Wrap in waxed paper or plastic wrap. Chill for 3 hours or overnight.

Preheat oven to 375°F. Cut dough into slices ⅜ inch thick. Place 2 inches apart on a baking sheet lined with parchment paper. Bake until golden, 10 to 12 minutes.

**MAKES ABOUT 24 WAFERS**

18

# FLAKY CHEESE BISCUITS

**These "melt in your mouth" biscuits complement all soups and stews (and they're good for breakfast, too).**

2 cups all-purpose flour
1 tablespoon baking powder
1/2 teaspoon salt
1/4 teaspoon sugar

1/3 cup shortening
3/4 cup milk
1 cup grated Cheddar cheese

Preheat oven to 450°F. In a bowl, combine dry ingredients. With 2 knives or a pastry blender, cut shortening into dry ingredients until crumbs form. Add milk all at once. Add cheese and stir with a fork just until dough leaves side of bowl and forms a ball.

On a lightly floured surface, knead dough 10 to 12 times. Roll or pat dough to 1/2 inch thick. Cut with a floured 2 1/2-inch biscuit cutter.

Place 1 inch apart on an ungreased baking sheet. Bake until golden, about 10 minutes.

**MAKES 10 BISCUITS**

# PESTO BISCUITS

**These special biscuits go especially well with Winter Tomato Soup (page 237) and Seafood Stew with Clams and Mussels (page 208).**

2 cups all-purpose flour

2 teaspoons baking powder

¼ teaspoon baking soda

½ teaspoon salt

⅓ cup shortening

¼ cup Basil Pesto, homemade (page 41) or purchased

¾ cup buttermilk

Preheat oven to 450°F. In a bowl, combine dry ingredients. With 2 knives or a pastry blender, cut shortening and pesto into dry ingredients until crumbs form. Add buttermilk all at once. Stir with a fork just until dough leaves side of bowl and forms a ball.

On a lightly floured surface, knead dough 10 to 12 times. Roll or pat dough ½ inch thick. Cut with a floured 2½-inch biscuit cutter.

Place 1 inch apart on an ungreased baking sheet. Bake until golden, about 10 minutes.

**MAKES 10 BISCUITS**

# BAKED GARLIC CROUTONS

Croutons are toasted bread cubes that float on top of soups. They add a crisp texture and extra flavor. Add croutons just before serving, or pass them separately. Croutons can also be whole pieces of toasted bread topped with cheese or other ingredients. These croutons can also be added to tossed salads.

2 tablespoons butter or margarine

1 tablespoon olive oil

3 cloves garlic, halved

2 cups cubed French bread (1-inch cubes), day-old or air-dried for 2 hours

Freshly grated Parmesan cheese, minced herbs, or seasoned salt for sprinkling on top (optional)

Preheat oven to 325°F. In a nonstick skillet over medium heat, melt butter with oil. Add garlic and sauté for 2 minutes. Remove garlic and discard. Add bread cubes and toss until coated. Place on a baking sheet and bake until crisp and golden, 10 to 12 minutes. Sprinkle with any of the toppings while warm, if desired. Use immediately or store in an airtight container for up to 1 week.

**MAKES ABOUT 2 CUPS**

# GARLIC CRUMBS

**Sprinkle these crisp, garlic-flavored bread bits on top of soup for added texture.**

4 or 5 slices sourdough bread (depending on size), to make about 2 cups coarse crumbs

2 tablespoons butter

1 tablespoon vegetable oil

1 large clove garlic, minced

Tear bread into large chunks and let air-dry for several hours, or place in a 300°F oven for 1 hour.

Place bread in a food processor and process slightly. Crumbs should be very coarse. In a small, nonstick frying pan over medium-high heat, melt butter with oil and garlic and sauté briefly. Add crumbs and toss to coat. Stir constantly until crumbs are golden and crisp, 2 to 3 minutes.

**MAKES ABOUT 2 CUPS**

# BASIC CROSTINI

**Crostini are thin, toasted baguette slices to serve with soups or as a base for hors d'oeuvre toppings.**

¼ cup olive oil

2 large cloves garlic, quartered

1 baguette, cut into ¼- to ⅓-inch slices

In a small jar, combine oil and garlic. Let stand to allow oil to absorb flavor, about 30 minutes.

Preheat broiler. Arrange bread slices on a baking sheet and broil on one side until lightly browned, about 2 minutes. Turn slices over and brush with garlic oil. Broil about 1 minute longer.

**NOTE:** *You can bake the bread slices instead of broiling them. Arrange bread slices on baking sheet and place in a preheated 350°F oven. Brush one side with garlic oil. Bake until lightly browned and crisp, about 10 minutes.*

**MAKES ABOUT 30 SLICES**

# GARLIC CROSTINI

**Float these garlic toasts on top of soups or serve as an accompaniment.**

¼ cup olive oil

2 cloves garlic, minced

2 teaspoons minced parsley

2 teaspoons finely chopped fresh basil leaves

½ baguette, sliced ½ inch thick

Coarse salt

Preheat oven to 350°F. In a small bowl, combine olive oil, garlic, parsley, and basil; mix well. Place bread on a baking sheet and spread with olive oil mixture, sprinkle lightly with salt. Bake until golden, about 15 minutes.

**MAKES ABOUT 12 SLICES**

# RYE OR PUMPERNICKEL CROSTINI

**These are good served with Sauerkraut Soup (page 227).**

¼ cup olive oil

1 clove garlic, minced

¼ teaspoon salt

⅛ teaspoon freshly ground pepper

1 tablespoon chopped fresh dill, or
1 teaspoon dried dill weed

1 loaf sliced cocktail rye bread (use
as much as you need)

Preheat oven to 350°F. In a bowl combine oil, garlic, salt, pepper, and dill. Brush one side of bread with mixture and arrange on a baking sheet. Bake until golden and crisp, 10 to 15 minutes.

**MAKES ABOUT 20 SLICES**

# PARMESAN CROSTINI

**Serve with Italian soups. Substitute another type of cheese, if you like.**

¼ cup butter
¼ cup olive oil
1 clove garlic, minced

1 baguette, cut into ¼-inch slices
¾ cup freshly grated Parmesan cheese

Preheat oven to 350°F. In a small pan over medium heat, melt butter with oil and garlic. Remove from heat. Brush bread slices with butter mixture on both sides. Arrange bread on baking sheets. Sprinkle cheese on top. Bake until bread is golden and crisp, 12 to 15 minutes.

**MAKES ABOUT 25 SLICES**

# HERBED TOASTS

**These croutons complement cream soups. Use fresh herbs, if available, but dried herbs can also be used.**

¹⁄₄ cup olive oil

¹⁄₄ cup chopped fresh herbs
(rosemary, basil, oregano, etc.), or
2 teaspoons mixed dried herbs

2 cloves garlic, minced

10 to 12 slices French bread

Preheat broiler. In a small pan over medium-low heat, simmer oil, herbs, and garlic until fragrant, about 1 minute. Place bread on a baking sheet. Broil until golden, about 1 minute. Turn toasts over and brush with oil mixture. Broil until golden and crisp, about 1 minute.

**MAKES 10 TO 12 SLICES**

# BAGEL STRIPS

**These crispy strips make a good accompaniment for soups.**

2 plain bagels, split
Olive oil for brushing on bagels

Coarse salt or Parmesan cheese or both for topping

Preheat oven to 350°F. Brush bagel halves with oil and sprinkle with salt and/or Parmesan cheese. Cut into ½-inch strips. Place on a lightly sprayed or oiled baking sheet. Bake 10 minutes. Cool and serve.

**MAKES ABOUT 20 STRIPS**

# PITA BREAD WEDGES

**Serve with Greek soups or stews, or as an hors d'oeuvre.**

¹/₄ cup olive oil
2 cloves garlic, sliced

3 pita breads

In a small bowl, mix olive oil and garlic and let stand for 30 minutes.

Preheat oven to 300°F. Halve pita bread, and cut each half into 4 wedges. Open wedges, split them into 2 triangles, and place, smooth-side down, on a baking sheet. Brush with garlic oil and bake until slightly browned, about 10 minutes.

**MAKES 24 WEDGES**

29

# FOCACCIA

**This popular bread is quickly mixed in the food processor. It goes well with Italian soup or stew.**

1 package (¼ ounce) active dry yeast
¾ cup warm water (105 to 115°F)
2 cups all-purpose flour
1 teaspoon salt

3 tablespoons olive oil, plus oil for brushing
½ teaspoon coarse salt for sprinkling on top
½ teaspoon dried rosemary for sprinkling on top

In a small bowl stir yeast with water until dissolved. Let stand 5 minutes. In a food processor combine flour and salt. Add olive oil and process until mixed, about 30 seconds. Add yeast mixture and process until dough forms a ball. Process 1 minute longer. Turn out onto a lightly floured surface. Knead until smooth, 10 to 15 times. Place dough in an oiled bowl. Turn dough over to oil top. Cover with a clean towel and let rise in a warm place, about 1 hour. Punch dough down and let rest 5 minutes.

Preheat oven to 425°F. Fit dough into an oiled 10-inch deep dish pie plate. Dimple the dough with your fingertip in about 12 places and brush with olive oil. Sprinkle with coarse salt and dried rosemary. Bake until golden and a tester when inserted in center comes out clean, 18 to 20 minutes. Remove from pie plate and cool on a wire rack.

**SERVES 6 TO 8**

Hearty and chunky meat soups and stews are substantial and satisfying. They are often a "meal in a bowl" and serve as the main course. Vegetables provide additional nutritional value as well as flavor.

Many meat soups and stews can be made ahead and reheated at serving time. In fact, they often improve in flavor when served the next day.

In this chapter, you will find some of the old soup favorites like vegetable beef, with orzo added for a new twist; Hamburger-Vegetable Soup with Tortellini; Taco Beef Soup, a favorite with kids; spicy chili; hearty chowders; and many more to suit any occasion.

The stews include a variety of vegetable-meat combinations. Oven Beef Beer Stew is baked in the oven with a bold beer sauce, and Pork Stew with Prunes and Apples is perfect for a crisp fall day. Classic Lamb Stew has been updated but has the same delicious flavor.

**SOUPS & STEWS**

# BEEF AND ONION SOUP

## SERVES 6 TO 8

**This is similar to a French onion soup with meat and mushrooms added. The beef and onions simmer in rich beef broth with just a hint of Dijon mustard. It makes a substantial and filling meal.**

In a large Dutch oven over medium-high heat, warm oil. Add beef cubes and brown, about 5 minutes. Remove to a plate. Reduce heat to medium-low. Add butter and onions and toss until onions are slightly limp, 6 or 7 minutes.

Add stock, Dijon mustard, wine, salt, and pepper. Return beef cubes to Dutch oven. Bring to a boil. Reduce heat to medium-low and simmer, covered, until meat is very tender, about 1 hour. Add mushrooms and simmer 30 minutes longer. Add parsley. Ladle into bowls and sprinkle with cheese.

1 tablespoon vegetable oil

1 pound round steak, cut into 1-inch cubes

1 tablespoon butter or margarine

3 medium yellow onions, sliced into rings

6 cups beef stock or broth

1 tablespoon Dijon mustard

¼ cup dry red wine

1 teaspoon salt

Freshly ground pepper to taste

6 ounces medium mushrooms, sliced

¼ cup chopped parsley

1 cup grated Swiss cheese for topping

**Minestrone means "big soup" in Italian and refers to a thick soup that generally includes a variety of vegetables and pasta, with or without meat (see Vegetarian Minestrone, page 234). This one with meat makes it a complete meal. A wedge of Parmesan cheese slowly melts into the soup as it cooks for extra flavor. Serve with Classic Garlic Bread (see page 49).**

1 cup dried Great Northern or navy beans, presoaked (see page 29), or substitute canned beans (see Notes)

1 can (16 ounces) plum tomatoes, coarsely chopped, with juice

6 cups beef stock or broth

1 pound beef stew meat

1 small yellow onion, chopped

2 cloves garlic, minced

2 carrots, sliced

1 stalk celery, sliced

1 cup shredded cabbage

1 tablespoon chopped fresh thyme, or ³/₄ teaspoon dried thyme

1 bay leaf

2¹/₂ teaspoons salt

¹/₄ teaspoon freshly ground pepper

1-by-1-inch wedge Parmesan cheese

1¹/₂ cups cut-up green beans (1-inch pieces)

1 small zucchini, unpeeled, halved lengthwise and then sliced

¹/₂ cup small uncooked macaroni

Freshly grated Parmesan cheese for topping (optional)

In a large soup pot or Dutch oven, combine drained beans, tomatoes, stock, beef, onion, garlic, carrots, celery, cabbage, thyme, bay leaf, salt, and pepper. Bring to a boil. Immerse the Parmesan cheese wedge in the soup. Reduce heat to medium-low and simmer, covered, until beans and meat are tender, about 1 hour and 15 minutes. Add green beans, zucchini, and macaroni. Cover and simmer until vegetables are tender-crisp and macaroni is al dente, about 20 minutes longer.

Remove bay leaf and discard. Ladle into large bowls and sprinkle with Parmesan cheese, if desired.

**NOTES:** *You can use 1 can (15 ounces) white kidney beans (cannellini), rinsed and drained, instead of the presoaked beans. Add them when you add the macaroni.*

*For a thicker soup, at the end of the cooking time, purée 1 cup of the vegetables in a food processor or blender. Return to soup, mix well, and reheat.*

**32**

# BEEF VEGETABLE SOUP WITH ORZO

**SERVES 6**

**This homey soup derives its flavor from the long simmering of vegetables and beef. Orzo provides starch and texture.**

In a large soup pot over high heat, combine beef, carrots, celery, onion, garlic, stock, tomato juice, Worcestershire sauce, salt, and pepper. Bring to a boil. Reduce heat to medium-low and simmer, covered, 1 hour and 15 minutes.

Add mushrooms and orzo and simmer, covered, 10 minutes longer. Stir in peas and cook, uncovered, until all ingredients are tender, about 10 minutes longer. Ladle into bowls and sprinkle with Parmesan cheese.

12 ounces beef stew meat

2 carrots, sliced

2 stalks celery, sliced

1 cup chopped yellow onion

1 clove garlic, minced

5 cups beef stock or broth

1 can (11½ ounces) spicy tomato juice

1 teaspoon Worcestershire sauce

¾ teaspoon salt

Freshly ground pepper to taste

6 ounces medium mushrooms, thickly sliced

¼ cup uncooked orzo

1 cup fresh or frozen peas

Freshly grated Parmesan cheese for topping

33

**There's lots of flavor in this wholesome, delicious vegetable beef soup. It's always a favorite. You'll never eat the canned version again!**

1 tablespoon vegetable oil

1½ pounds round steak, cut into 1-inch cubes

1 yellow onion, chopped

2 cloves garlic, minced

2 stalks celery, chopped

2 carrots, chopped

½ green bell pepper, chopped

3 cups beef stock or broth

3 cups tomato juice

1 can (14½ ounces) whole tomatoes, coarsely chopped, with juice

1 cup water

1 teaspoon chili powder

1 teaspoon soy sauce

1 teaspoon Worcestershire sauce

½ teaspoon dried thyme

1 bay leaf

1¼ teaspoons salt

Freshly ground pepper to taste

1 cup corn kernels, fresh or frozen

1 cup peas, fresh or frozen

Freshly grated Parmesan cheese for topping

In a large Dutch oven over medium heat, warm oil. Add meat, onion, and garlic and sauté until meat is no longer pink, about 10 minutes. Add celery, carrots, and bell pepper and mix well. Add stock, tomato juice, tomatoes, water, chili powder, soy sauce, Worcestershire sauce, thyme, bay leaf, salt, and pepper. Reduce heat to medium-low and simmer, covered, 1 hour and 15 minutes.

Add corn and peas and simmer, uncovered, until flavors are blended and meat is tender, about 15 minutes longer. Remove bay leaf and discard. Ladle into bowls and sprinkle with Parmesan cheese.

**SERVES 6**

# MEATY VEGETABLE-BEAN SOUP

**SERVES 6 TO 8**

# 35

**Real men eat this soup—it has lots of meat and lots of flavor. Serve with a loaf of warm, crusty bread.**

In a large Dutch oven over medium heat, cook bacon until crisp. Remove to a plate, leaving 1 tablespoon bacon drippings in the Dutch oven. Add onion and garlic and sauté until tender, about 5 minutes. Add meat shanks and stock and bring to a boil. Reduce heat to medium-low and simmer, covered, until meat is tender, about 1½ hours. Remove shanks to a plate and cool. Cut meat from bones.

Add beans, carrots, zucchini, sausage, salt, oregano, and pepper. Return meats, including bacon, to pot and simmer, covered, until vegetables are tender and flavors are blended, about 30 minutes. Ladle into large bowls and sprinkle with parsley.

6 slices bacon, diced

1 large yellow onion, sliced

2 cloves garlic, minced

1 meaty beef shank (about 1 pound)

1 meaty ham shank (about 1 pound)

4 cups beef stock or broth

3 cups chicken stock or broth

2 cans (15 ounces each) garbanzo beans, drained and rinsed

2 carrots, chopped

1 zucchini, coarsly chopped

½ pound kielbasa sausage, cut into ⅜-inch slices

½ teaspoon salt

½ teaspoon dried oregano

⅛ teaspoon freshly ground pepper

¼ cup chopped parsley for topping

**Looking for a tasty soup that can be made in minutes? This combination of hamburger, salsa, and beans is so easy, even the kids can make it. The avocado gives a cooling touch.**

1 pound lean ground beef

1 cup chopped yellow onion

1 teaspoon vegetable oil, if needed

Salt and freshly ground pepper to taste

1 can (15 ounces) pinto beans, drained and rinsed

3 cups beef stock or broth

1 cup Fresh Tomato Salsa (page 42) or purchased salsa

Corn chips or crushed tortilla chips for topping

Sliced avocado for topping

In a large Dutch oven over medium heat, cook meat and onion until meat is no longer pink, about 5 minutes. Add oil if needed to keep meat from sticking. Season with salt and pepper.

Add remaining ingredients except toppings. Reduce heat to medium-low and simmer, uncovered, until flavors are blended, 10 to 15 minutes. Ladle into bowls and top with chips and avocado slices.

# HAMBURGER-VEGETABLE SOUP WITH TORTELLINI

**SERVES 6 TO 8**

**Here is a healthful soup that will appeal to the whole family. Frozen mixed vegetables are used for convenience and variety.**

In a large Dutch oven over medium heat, brown meat with onion until meat is no longer pink, about 5 minutes. Add oil if needed to keep meat from sticking. Add tomatoes, stock, tomato juice, thyme, salt, pepper, Worcestershire sauce, and Tabasco sauce. Bring to a boil. Reduce heat to medium-low and simmer, uncovered, for 30 minutes. Increase heat to medium-high. Add vegetables and tortellini and cook, uncovered, until vegetables and tortellini are tender, about 10 minutes. Ladle into bowls and sprinkle with Parmesan cheese.

1 pound lean ground beef

1 cup chopped yellow onion

1 teaspoon vegetable oil, if needed

1 can (14 1/2 ounces) tomatoes, coarsely chopped, with juice

6 cups beef stock or broth

2 cups tomato juice

1/4 teaspoon dried thyme

1 teaspoon salt

Freshly ground pepper to taste

2 teaspoons Worcestershire sauce

2 or 3 drops Tabasco sauce

1 package (10 ounces) frozen mixed vegetables, rinsed

1 package (9 ounces) cheese-filled tortellini

Freshly grated Parmesan cheese for topping

**This main-course soup with vegetables and barley is a favorite for a family supper. For a simple menu, add a fruit salad and chocolate cookies.**

1 pound lean ground beef

1 cup chopped yellow onion

2 stalks celery, chopped

2 medium russet potatoes (about 1 pound), peeled and cubed

1 zucchini, unpeeled, cut into ½-inch slices

1 can (14½ ounces) whole tomatoes, coarsely chopped, with juice

2 cups beef stock or broth

3 cups tomato juice

¼ cup pearl barley, thoroughly rinsed

1 bay leaf

1 teaspoon salt

Freshly ground pepper to taste

Chopped parsley for topping

In a large soup pot over medium heat, cook meat, breaking it up with a spoon, until it is no longer pink, 6 to 8 minutes. Add remaining ingredients except parsley, reduce heat to medium-low, and simmer, covered, until vegetables are tender and flavors are blended, about 1 hour. Remove bay leaf and discard. Ladle into large bowls and sprinkle with parsley.

# SPAGHETTI SOUP

### SERVES 6

**On a cold winter day, this hearty soup of meat, tomatoes, and spaghetti is a meal in itself. Kids love it, and you will too! Serve with Classic Garlic Bread (page 49) and spumoni ice cream.**

In a large soup pot over medium-high heat, cook beef, sausage, onion, and garlic, stirring and breaking up meat with a spoon. Cook until meat is no longer pink and vegetables are tender, about 10 minutes, stirring occasionally.

Pour off any excess grease from pan. Reduce heat to medium-low and add tomatoes, stock, tomato juice, salt, oregano, basil, bay leaf, pepper, parsley, and spaghetti. Cover and simmer until flavors are blended, about 30 minutes. Add olives, if desired, and cook, uncovered, 10 minutes longer or until ready to serve. Remove bay leaf and discard.

Ladle into bowls and sprinkle with cheese.

½ pound lean ground beef

½ pound bulk sausage

1 cup chopped yellow onion

2 cloves garlic, minced

1 can (28 ounces) Italian-style tomatoes with basil, coarsely chopped, with juice

2 cups beef stock or broth

1 cup tomato juice

1 teaspoon salt

¼ teaspoon dried oregano

¼ teaspoon dried basil

1 bay leaf

Freshly ground pepper to taste

¼ cup chopped parsley

1 cup broken spaghetti (1-inch pieces)

½ cup sliced black olives (optional)

Freshly grated Parmesan or Asiago cheese for topping

**Need dinner in a hurry? This soup goes together quickly and will satisfy a hungry family. Serve with an avocado salad and warm tortillas.**

1 pound lean ground beef

$1/2$ cup chopped green onions, including some tender green tops

2 cups beef stock or broth

1 can ($14^{1}/_{2}$ ounces) diced tomatoes, with juice

1 can (8 ounces) tomato sauce

1 can (4 ounces) chopped green chiles, drained

1 can (15 ounces) pinto beans, drained and rinsed

$1/2$ teaspoon salt

Freshly ground pepper to taste

$1/2$ teaspoon chili powder

1 teaspoon ground cumin

$1/4$ teaspoon dried oregano, crumbled

**TOPPINGS**

Grated cheese

Sour cream

Crushed tortilla chips

Salsa

Sliced olives

In a large soup pot over medium heat, cook meat and green onions, breaking up meat with a spoon. Cook until meat is no longer pink and vegetables are tender, 6 to 7 minutes.

Reduce heat to medium-low. Add remaining ingredients except toppings and simmer, uncovered, until flavors are blended, about 30 minutes. Ladle into bowls and pass the toppings separately.

**40**

# HAMBURGER, MACARONI, AND BEAN SOUP

**SERVES 6**

**The combination of hamburger, macaroni, and beans in this thick tomato-based soup improves in flavor as it simmers. It's good to serve on a night when the family is on the go with different activities and eating schedules.**

In a large Dutch oven over medium heat, combine meat, onion, garlic, and bell pepper. Cook, breaking up meat with a spoon, until meat is no longer pink and vegetables are tender, about 10 minutes. Add oil if needed to keep mixture from sticking. Add remaining ingredients. Bring to a boil. Reduce heat to medium and simmer, uncovered, stirring several times, until macaroni is tender and flavors are blended, 15 to 20 minutes. Cover and keep warm over low heat until ready to serve.

1 pound lean ground beef

1 cup chopped yellow onion

1 clove garlic, minced

$\frac{1}{2}$ green bell pepper, seeded and chopped

1 teaspoon oil, if needed

1 can (14 $\frac{1}{2}$ ounces) diced tomatoes, with juice

6 cups beef stock or broth

1 can (8 ounces) tomato sauce

1 teaspoon Worcestershire sauce

$\frac{1}{2}$ teaspoon dried basil

1 teaspoon salt

Freshly ground pepper to taste

1 cup uncooked elbow macaroni

1 can (15 ounces) kidney beans, drained and rinsed

41

**This is an easy chili that I make in the winter when we have guests at our cabin on Oregon's McKenzie River. Pass the toppings separately in small bowls, and serve with Three-Cheese Bread (page 47).**

1 pound lean ground beef

1 yellow onion, chopped

1 can (28 ounces) whole tomatoes with juice, cut up

1 can (15 ounces) tomato sauce

3 cans (15 ounces each) kidney beans, drained

3/4 teaspoon salt

2 teaspoons chili powder, or more to taste

1/2 teaspoon ground cumin

1/4 teaspoon freshly ground pepper

**TOPPINGS**

Grated Cheddar cheese

Chopped green onions

Sour cream

In a large pot over medium heat, combine beef and onion, breaking up meat with a spoon. Cook until meat is no longer pink and onion is tender, about 10 minutes. Reduce heat to medium-low and add remaining ingredients except toppings. Simmer for 20 to 30 minutes. Ladle into bowls and pass the toppings separately.

# MEXICAN MEATBALL SOUP (ALBÓNDIGAS)

**43**

*Albóndigas* **is the Spanish word for meatballs. In this version, spicy bite-sized meatballs are studded with pine nuts and simmered in a clear beef broth.** *¡Muy bueno!*

In a large soup pot over high heat, combine all ingredients except meatballs and sherry. Bring to a boil. Reduce heat to medium-low and simmer, uncovered, 15 minutes. Strain and discard solids. Return stock to pan. Bring to a boil and drop meatballs, a few at a time, into stock. Reduce heat to medium-low and simmer, covered, until meatballs are cooked through, 10 to 15 minutes. Add sherry just before serving.

8 cups rich beef stock or broth (homemade preferred)

1 bay leaf

1 yellow onion, quartered and separated

3 cloves garlic, halved

$\frac{1}{2}$ teaspoon salt

Freshly ground pepper to taste

Mexican Meatballs (recipe follows)

$\frac{1}{4}$ cup dry sherry or dry white wine

# MEXICAN MEATBALLS

1 pound lean ground beef

½ teaspoon salt

1 teaspoon chili powder

¼ teaspoon ground cumin

1 cup crushed saltine crackers

1 egg, beaten

¼ cup pine nuts

In a bowl, mix all ingredients together and shape into firm, small balls about ¾ inch in diameter. (Press pine nuts inside the meat as much as possible.)

# HAMBURGER-BARLEY SOUP

**SERVES 6**

**This home-style soup is always welcome for a family meal. Make it ahead to allow the flavors to develop, then reheat it at serving time. Barley is highly nutritious and adds a chewy bite.**

In a Dutch oven over medium heat, warm oil. Add meat, onion, garlic, celery, and carrots, and cook, breaking up meat with a spoon, until meat is no longer pink, about 5 minutes. Add remaining ingredients and bring to a boil. Reduce heat to medium-low and cook, covered, until vegetables and barley are tender, about 1 hour. Remove bay leaf and discard.

1 teaspoon vegetable oil

1 pound lean ground beef

1 large yellow onion, chopped

1 clove garlic, minced

2 stalks celery, chopped

2 carrots, chopped

1 can (14½ ounces) whole tomatoes, coarsely chopped, with juice

½ cup pearl barley, thoroughly rinsed

4 cups beef stock or broth

1 cup water

¼ teaspoon dried thyme

¼ teaspoon dried marjoram

1 bay leaf

1 teaspoon salt

Freshly ground pepper to taste

44

**This great soup combines all of the tastes of a Reuben sandwich. Serve it with a glass of ice-cold beer.**

2 tablespoons butter or margarine

1/2 cup chopped yellow onion

1 tablespoon all-purpose flour

4 cups beef stock or broth

1 cup sauerkraut, drained and rinsed

1 bay leaf

1/2 teaspoon salt

1/2 teaspoon dried thyme

Freshly ground pepper to taste

1/2 pound thinly sliced deli corned beef, shredded

10 to 12 slices cocktail rye bread

2 cups grated Swiss cheese

In a large soup pot over medium heat, melt butter. Add onion and sauté until tender, about 5 minutes. Sprinkle flour over onion and mix well. Add stock and stir in sauerkraut. Add remaining ingredients except bread and Swiss cheese and simmer for 15 to 20 minutes. Remove bay leaf and discard.

Preheat broiler. When soup is ready to serve, place bread on a baking sheet and broil for 2 minutes. Turn and sprinkle with Swiss cheese. Broil until cheese melts, about 1 minute.

Ladle soup into bowls, and float 1 piece of toast on top of each bowl. Pass remaining toast as an accompaniment.

# SAUSAGE, VEGETABLE, AND RAVIOLI SOUP

**SERVES 4**

**Make this soup ahead (except for the ravioli) and serve to celebrate a victorious football game. Add the ravioli just before serving. Serve with chips and dips.**

In a large Dutch oven over medium heat, brown sausage, onion, carrots, and garlic until meat is no longer pink, 6 to 7 minutes. Add oil if needed to keep mixture from sticking. Add remaining ingredients except ravioli. Bring to a boil. Reduce heat to medium-low and simmer, covered, 15 minutes. Add ravioli and bring to a boil. Cook, uncovered, until ravioli is tender, about 6 to 9 minutes.

1 pound bulk Italian sausage

1 cup chopped yellow onion

2 carrots, chopped

1 clove garlic, minced

1 teaspoon vegetable oil, if needed

6 cups beef stock or broth

1/2 teaspoon dried basil

1/2 teaspoon salt

Freshly ground pepper to taste

1 can (8 ounces) tomato sauce

1 can (14 1/2 ounces) whole tomatoes, coarsely chopped, with juice

1/4 cup chopped parsley

1 zucchini, quartered lengthwise and sliced

8 ounces medium mushrooms, sliced

1 package (9 ounces) fresh cheese ravioli

**This stewlike soup is easy to make because everything is dumped into one pot and the flavors develop as it simmers away. This makes a large batch and will keep, refrigerated, for several days.**

6 cups chicken stock or broth

1 yellow onion, chopped

3 cloves garlic, chopped

1 pound kielbasa sausage, cut into bite-sized slices

2 medium russet potatoes (about 1 pound), peeled and diced

1 can (15 ounces) kidney beans, drained and rinsed

1 can (14$\frac{1}{2}$ ounces) whole tomatoes, coarsely chopped, with juice

2 tablespoons tomato paste

$\frac{1}{2}$ head (1 pound) cabbage, shredded

1 carrot, diced

2 stalks celery, diced

$\frac{1}{2}$ green or red bell pepper, seeded and chopped

1 turnip, peeled and diced

$\frac{1}{4}$ cup chopped parsley

In a large soup pot, combine all ingredients except parsley. Bring to a boil. Reduce heat to medium-low and simmer, covered, 1 hour, stirring occasionally. Uncover and simmer until flavors are blended, about $\frac{1}{2}$ hour longer. Stir in parsley before serving.

47

# CORN AND RED BELL PEPPER CHOWDER WITH KIELBASA

**SERVES 4**

**This thick soup is a standout and easy to make. Kielbasa is a fully cooked sausage, also called Polish sausage. It is ready to eat but improves in flavor when heated.**

In a large Dutch oven over medium heat, combine sausage, onion, garlic, and bell pepper and sauté until vegetables are tender, 6 to 7 minutes. Add oil, if needed. Add stock, potatoes, salt, and white pepper. Bring to a boil. Reduce heat to medium-low and cook, covered, until potatoes are tender, about 20 minutes. Add corn, half-and-half, and parsley and simmer, uncovered, until flavors are blended, about 10 minutes longer.

**NOTE:** *To add more body to the soup, mash a few potato pieces with the back of a spoon against the side of the pan.*

¹⁄₂ pound kielbasa sausage, cut into ³⁄₈-inch slices and then halved

1 cup chopped yellow onion

2 cloves garlic, minced

1 cup chopped red bell pepper

¹⁄₂ tablespoon olive oil, if needed

2 cups chicken stock or broth

3 medium red potatoes (about 1 pound), unpeeled, cubed

¹⁄₂ teaspoon salt

¹⁄₈ teaspoon white pepper

1¹⁄₂ cups corn kernels, fresh or frozen

1 cup half-and-half

¹⁄₄ cup chopped parsley

48

## 49

**A warm-up soup that is just right for a stormy winter night. Serve with Herbed Buttermilk Sticks (page 51) and a wedge of iceberg lettuce with blue cheese dressing.**

$\frac{1}{2}$ pound bulk pork sausage

1 teaspoon vegetable oil, if needed

1 yellow onion, chopped

$\frac{1}{2}$ green bell pepper, seeded and chopped

2 cups chicken stock or broth

2 cups beef broth

1 can (15 ounces) kidney beans, drained and rinsed

1 can (14$\frac{1}{2}$ ounces) diced tomatoes, with juice

1 medium russet potato (about $\frac{1}{2}$ pound), peeled and chopped

$\frac{1}{4}$ teaspoon chili powder

$\frac{1}{4}$ teaspoon dried thyme

1 teaspoon salt

Freshly ground pepper to taste

1 bay leaf

In a large soup pot over medium heat, brown sausage. Add oil if needed to keep meat from sticking. Break up sausage with a spoon as it cooks. Add onion and bell pepper and sauté until meat is no longer pink and vegetables are tender, about 5 minutes. Add remaining ingredients. Reduce heat to low and simmer, covered, until flavors are blended, about 45 minutes. Remove bay leaf and discard.

# SAUSAGE, CORN, AND TOMATO SOUP

SERVES 4

**Spicy sausage adds flavor to this colorful and appealing soup. Sprinkle crushed tortilla chips on top for extra crunch. Serve with warm Company Cornbread (page 53).**

In a large Dutch oven over medium heat, brown sausage for about 5 minutes, breaking it up with a spoon as it cooks. Add onion, bell pepper, celery, and garlic, and sauté until vegetables are tender, about 5 minutes. Add tomatoes, stock, corn, salt, and pepper.

Reduce heat to low and simmer, covered, until flavors are blended, about 20 minutes. Simmer, uncovered, 10 minutes longer or until ready to serve. Ladle into bowls and top with crushed tortilla chips.

$^3$/4 pound bulk pork sausage

$^1$/2 cup chopped yellow onion

$^1$/2 cup chopped green bell pepper

1 stalk celery, sliced

2 cloves garlic, minced

1 can (14$^1$/2 ounces) whole tomatoes, coarsely chopped, with juice

2$^1$/2 cups chicken stock or broth

1 cup corn kernels, fresh or frozen

$^3$/4 teaspoon salt

Freshly ground pepper to taste

Crushed tortilla chips for topping

My German grandfather used to make a sauerkraut soup for the family that tasted similar to this one. At a young age I wasn't interested in recipes, but I think he used leftover mashed potatoes. I like the cubed potatoes better. Serve with Pumpernickel Crostini (page 61) and a glass of beer.

2 tablespoons butter or margarine

1 pound kielbasa sausage, cut into $\frac{1}{4}$-inch slices

1 cup chopped yellow onion

1 large russet potato (about $\frac{3}{4}$ pound), peeled and cubed

4 cups beef stock or broth

$\frac{1}{2}$ cup beer, allowed to go flat

$\frac{1}{2}$ teaspoon salt

$\frac{1}{4}$ teaspoon freshly ground pepper

1 bay leaf

1 teaspoon caraway seeds

2 cups sauerkraut, drained

In a saucepan over medium heat, melt butter. Add sausage and cook, turning frequently, until well browned, about 5 minutes. Remove with a slotted spoon to a plate.

Add onion to same pan and sauté until tender, about 5 minutes. Add potato, stock, beer, salt, pepper, bay leaf, and caraway seeds. Bring to a boil. Reduce heat to medium-low and simmer, covered, until vegetables are tender, about 20 minutes. Add reserved sausage and sauerkraut and simmer, uncovered, until flavors are blended, stirring once, about 10 minutes longer.

Remove bay leaf and discard.

51

# SAUSAGE, MUSHROOM, AND RED PEPPER SOUP

**SERVES 4**

**Red pepper imparts a sweet flavor and adds color to this spicy soup with sausage and vegetables. Serve for lunch with a cheese sandwich.**

In a large soup pot over medium heat, cook sausage for 2 minutes, breaking up meat with a spoon. Add oil if needed to keep sausage from sticking. Add onion, celery, mushrooms, and bell pepper and sauté until meat is no longer pink and vegetables are tender, about 7 minutes longer. Add stock, rice, salt, and pepper and bring to a boil. Reduce heat to medium-low. Cover and simmer until rice is tender, about 20 minutes. Ladle into bowls and sprinkle with parsley.

½ pound bulk pork sausage

1 teaspoon vegetable oil, if needed

1 cup chopped yellow onion

2 stalks celery, chopped

8 ounces medium mushrooms, sliced

½ red bell pepper, seeded and chopped

3 cups chicken stock or broth

½ cup long-grain white rice

½ teaspoon salt

Freshly ground pepper to taste

¼ cup chopped parsley for topping

**This substantial and satisfying Mexican soup featuring pork (often a pig's head) and hominy is traditionally served at Christmastime. This version calls for a tender cut of pork and a shorter cooking period. A variety of toppings are usually added at the table.**

1 tablespoon vegetable oil

1 pound pork tenderloin, cut into ³⁄₄-inch pieces

1 to 2 tablespoons chili powder

1 cup chopped yellow onion

2 cloves garlic, minced

1 can (15 ounces) white hominy, drained and rinsed

1 can (16 ounces) tomato sauce

2 cups chicken stock or broth

1 can (14¹⁄₂ ounces) diced tomatoes, with juice

¹⁄₂ teaspoon dried oregano

¹⁄₂ teaspoon ground cumin

¹⁄₂ teaspoon salt

Freshly ground pepper to taste

**TOPPINGS**

Sliced radishes

Cubes of cream cheese

Diced avocado

Chopped green onions

Shredded lettuce

Lime wedges

In a large Dutch oven over medium heat, warm oil. Add pork and chili powder and sauté for 2 minutes. Add onion and garlic and sauté until tender, about 5 minutes longer. Add remaining ingredients except toppings. Reduce heat to medium-low and simmer, uncovered, until flavors are blended, about 15 minutes. Ladle into bowls and pass the toppings separately.

**SERVES 4**

# PORK AND HAM SOUP (POSOLE)

# HAM, CABBAGE, AND BEAN SOUP

**SERVES 8 TO 10**

# 54

**This big batch of soup with ham, vegetables, and beans is perfect for a cold, stormy night. It's very filling and satisfying. Leftovers are good, too.**

In a large soup pot, combine vegetables, stock, marjoram, thyme, bay leaf, salt, and pepper. Bring to a boil. Reduce heat to medium-low and simmer, covered, until vegetables are tender, about 30 minutes. Add ham and beans and simmer until flavors are blended, 30 to 40 minutes longer. Remove bay leaf and discard.

$^1/_2$ head cabbage (about $1^1/_2$ pounds), cut into $^1/_2$-inch strips

1 cup chopped yellow onion

2 cloves garlic, minced

2 carrots, chopped

1 medium russet potato (about $^1/_2$ pound), peeled and cubed

8 cups chicken stock or broth

$^1/_2$ teaspoon dried marjoram

$^1/_4$ teaspoon dried thyme

1 bay leaf

$1^1/_2$ teaspoons salt

Freshly ground pepper to taste

2 cups cubed ham

2 cans (15 ounces each) Great Northern beans, drained and rinsed

**Here is a tasty way to use up leftover ham from a holiday dinner. Potatoes and ham with cheese make a good combination. Serve with crusty bread and a fruit salad.**

2 tablespoons butter or margarine

1 cup chopped yellow onion

1 cup cubed ham

¼ teaspoon dried thyme

3 large russet potatoes (about 2¼ pounds), peeled and sliced

3 cups chicken stock or broth

1 cup grated Gruyère cheese

¼ to ½ cup milk

Salt and freshly ground pepper to taste

Chopped parsley for topping

In a saucepan over medium heat, melt butter. Add onion and sauté until tender, about 5 minutes. Stir in ham, thyme, potatoes, and stock. Cover and simmer over medium-low heat until potatoes are very tender, about 20 minutes. Potatoes should be broken up and slightly mushy.

Add cheese and milk and stir until cheese melts and soup is heated through, about 5 minutes. Season with salt and pepper. Ladle into bowls and sprinkle with parsley.

SERVES 4

55

# OVEN BEEF BEER STEW

### SERVES 6

**This is one of the best beef stews! It's easy and quick to make because browning is not necessary. The meat slowly bakes in a bold sauce of beer, stock, and seasonings until it is fork tender. Serve with noodles.**

Preheat oven to 325°F. In a large, lightly sprayed or oiled, Dutch oven, combine meat, salt, pepper, thyme, marjoram, flour, mustard, vinegar, Worcestershire sauce, onion, garlic, and beer and mix well. Cover and bake for 1 hour. Add stock, carrots, and mushrooms and bake, covered, until meat is very tender, about 1 hour longer.

2 pounds beef stew meat

1 teaspoon salt

¼ teaspoon freshly ground pepper

½ teaspoon dried thyme

½ teaspoon dried marjoram

3 tablespoons all-purpose flour

1 tablespoon Dijon mustard

1 tablespoon red wine vinegar

2 teaspoons Worcestershire sauce

1 cup chopped yellow onion

3 to 4 cloves garlic, minced

1 cup beer, allowed to go flat

2 cups beef stock or broth

4 carrots, cut into 1-inch slices

8 ounces medium mushrooms, halved

58

**57**

**This delicious stew is full of good ingredients simmered in a full-flavored stock with wine that fills the air with a tempting aroma while it cooks. Serve in bowls with French bread.**

1/4 cup all-purpose flour

1/2 teaspoon dried thyme

1/4 teaspoon dried rosemary

1 teaspoon dried basil

1 teaspoon garlic powder

1 1/2 teaspoons salt

1/4 teaspoon freshly ground pepper

2 pounds beef round steak, cut into bite-sized pieces

2 to 3 tablespoons olive oil

1 large yellow onion, chopped

4 carrots, cut diagonally into 1-inch slices

4 cloves garlic, minced

2 cups beef stock or broth

1 cup dry red wine

4 medium potatoes (about 2 pounds), peeled and quartered

8 ounces medium mushrooms, halved

1/2 green bell pepper, cut into 1-inch pieces

1/4 cup chopped parsley

In a large bowl, mix flour, thyme, rosemary, basil, garlic powder, salt and pepper. Add beef and mix thoroughly, using all of the flour mixture.

In a Dutch oven over medium heat, warm 1 tablespoon of the oil. Add half of the meat and brown, about 10 minutes. Add more oil as needed. Remove to a plate and brown the rest of the meat. Return meat to pan and add onion, carrots, and garlic; stir. Add stock and wine, reduce heat to medium-low, and simmer, covered, 1 hour. Add potatoes, mushrooms, and bell pepper and cook, covered, until meat, potatoes, and vegetables are tender, about 30 minutes longer. Add parsley and serve.

# FAVORITE FAMILY STEW

**SERVES 6**

**This is one of those "no peek" stews that bakes in the oven unattended for 4 hours while the flavors mingle. It will become one of your family favorites. Serve with noodles to absorb the flavorful sauce.**

Preheat oven to 300°F. Combine all ingredients in a large, lightly sprayed or oiled, Dutch oven or 4-quart casserole, stirring to mix well. Cover and bake for 4 hours; do not uncover while baking.

2 pounds round steak, cut into 1-inch cubes

1 yellow onion, quartered

4 carrots, cut into 1-inch slices

4 stalks celery, cut into 1-inch slices

1 green bell pepper, seeded and cut into 1-inch pieces

¼ cup quick-cooking tapioca

½ cup fine dried bread crumbs

1 pound medium whole mushrooms

1¼ teaspoons salt

¼ teaspoon freshly ground pepper

1 can (14½ ounces) plum tomatoes, coarsely chopped, with juice

1 cup dry red wine

Here beef cubes are simmered with onions and tomatoes in a sweet-and-sour stock. To preserve the bright color of the cabbage, add it the last 30 minutes of cooking time. Serve with small, boiled red-skinned potatoes.

1 tablespoon vegetable oil

1¼ pounds beef stew meat

2 yellow onions, sliced

2 cloves garlic, minced

¼ cup fresh lemon juice

2 tablespoons firmly packed brown sugar

1 can (14½ ounces) whole tomatoes, coarsely chopped, with juice

2 cups beef stock or broth

2 cups water

Salt and freshly ground pepper to taste

2 cups shredded cabbage

⅓ cup raisins (optional)

In a Dutch oven over medium heat, warm oil. Brown meat on all sides, about 6 minutes. Add remaining ingredients except cabbage and raisins and mix well. Cover and simmer over medium-low heat until meat is tender, about 1 hour. Add cabbage and raisins, if using, and simmer, covered, 30 minutes longer.

**59**

# OVEN BURGUNDY BEEF STEW

**SERVES 4 TO 6**

**This is a simplified version of the famous French dish, beef bourguignonne. A strip of orange peel imparts a fruity flavor to the meat. Serve with noodles or mashed potatoes.**

Preheat oven to 325°F. In a Dutch oven over medium-high heat, cook bacon until crisp, about 5 minutes. With a slotted spoon, remove bacon to a plate, leaving 2 tablespoons of drippings in pan. Reduce heat to medium. Season meat with salt and pepper. Add to bacon drippings in pan along with shallots and garlic. Sauté until meat is browned and vegetables are tender, about 10 minutes. Stir in flour and blend. Add wine, brandy (if using), stock, thyme, marjoram, bay leaf, carrots, orange zest, onions, and reserved bacon and mix well. Bake, covered, 1½ hours. Add mushrooms and bake, covered, until meat and mushrooms are tender, 20 minutes longer. Remove bay leaf and orange zest and discard.

4 thick slices bacon, diced

2 pounds round steak, cut into 1-inch pieces

Salt and freshly ground pepper to taste

2 shallots, chopped, or 6 green onions, including some tender green tops, sliced

2 cloves garlic, minced

3 tablespoons all-purpose flour

1½ cups burgundy or any good red wine

2 tablespoons brandy (optional)

½ cup beef stock or broth

¼ teaspoon dried thyme

¼ teaspoon dried marjoram

1 bay leaf

3 large carrots, cut diagonally into 1-inch slices

2-inch strip orange zest (use vegetable peeler)

½ pound (about 10) boiling onions, peeled (see page 24)

8 ounces medium mushrooms, halved

**The addition of spices jazzes up this beef stew and creates a tantalizing aroma as it cooks. It is even better reheated the next day.**

1 to 2 tablespoons vegetable oil

1½ pounds round steak, cut into
  ¾-by-2-inch strips

2 cups beef stock or broth

2 tablespoons cider vinegar

1 tablespoon brown sugar

¾ teaspoon salt

Freshly ground pepper to taste

1 bay leaf

⅛ teaspoon ground cloves

¼ teaspoon ground cinnamon

¼ teaspoon ground allspice

1 can (8 ounces) tomato sauce

1 yellow onion, thickly sliced and separated
  into rings

1 small red bell pepper, seeded and cut
  into ½-inch strips

1 small green bell pepper, seeded and
  cut into ½-inch strips

3 medium new red potatoes, unpeeled,
  cut into eighths

2 cloves garlic, minced

¼ cup all-purpose flour

½ cup water

In a large Dutch oven over medium-high heat, warm oil. Add beef strips and brown, about 5 minutes. Add stock, vinegar, brown sugar, salt, pepper, bay leaf, cloves, cinnamon, allspice, and tomato sauce. Bring to a boil. Reduce heat and simmer, covered, 1 hour and 15 minutes. Add vegetables and garlic, and return to a boil. Reduce heat to medium-low and simmer, covered, until meat and vegetables are tender, about 30 minutes longer. In a cup, blend flour and water. Increase heat to medium-high. Stir flour mixture into stew and stir until thickened, 2 to 3 minutes. Reduce heat to low and simmer, uncovered, until flavors are blended, 5 to 10 minutes. Remove bay leaf and discard.

**Although goulash can be made with beef, lamb, or pork, it always includes sweet Hungarian paprika. Hungarian paprika is stronger and more intense than the domestic variety and is available in gourmet shops. If you are using domestic paprika, you may want to increase the amount. Serve this highly seasoned version with buttered noodles.**

On a piece of waxed paper, toss meat with flour to thoroughly coat. Use all of the flour.

In a large Dutch oven over medium-high heat, melt 1 tablespoon of the butter with the oil. Add meat and brown for about 5 minutes. Reduce heat to medium-low. Add remaining tablespoon of butter and stir in onion, paprika, caraway seeds, marjoram, salt, and pepper; mix well. Cook for 2 minutes.

Add stock, vinegar, and tomato paste. Bring to a boil. Cover and simmer until meat is very tender, about 1¹/₂ hours. Serve topped with a dollop of sour cream.

2 pounds beef stew meat

¹/₄ cup all-purpose flour

2 tablespoons butter or margarine

1 tablespoon vegetable oil

2 cups chopped yellow onion

1 tablespoon paprika (preferably Hungarian)

1 teaspoon caraway seeds

1 teaspoon dried marjoram

¹/₂ teaspoon salt

Freshly ground pepper to taste

1¹/₄ cups beef stock or broth

2 tablespoons red wine vinegar

1 tablespoon tomato paste

Sour cream for topping

**The beer gives this stew a tangy flavor and helps tenderize the meat.**

3 tablespoons all-purpose flour

1 teaspoon paprika

1 teaspoon dry mustard

¼ teaspoon salt

Freshly ground pepper to taste

1½ pounds beef stew meat

2 tablespoons vegetable oil

1 cup chopped yellow onion

8 ounces beer, allowed to go flat

1 tablespoon tomato paste

1 bay leaf

1 cup baby carrots

2 medium new potatoes, unpeeled, quartered

¼ cup chopped parsley for topping

On a piece of waxed paper, mix flour, paprika, mustard, salt, and pepper. Add stew meat and turn to coat.

In a large Dutch oven over medium-high heat, warm oil. Add beef and all the flour mixture and brown the meat, about 5 minutes. Add onion and sauté for 2 minutes longer. Add beer and tomato paste. Stir to loosen browned bits. Add bay leaf and carrots.

Reduce heat to medium-low and simmer, covered, 1 hour and 15 minutes. Add potatoes and cook, covered, until meat and potatoes are tender, about 30 minutes longer. Remove bay leaf and discard. Serve sprinkled with parsley.

63

# BISTRO STEW

**SERVES 6 TO 8**

**This is a hearty dish with lots of big vegetable chunks and tender beef cubes. Serve with red wine, a French baguette, and light jazz.**

Mix flour, salt, and pepper on a piece of waxed paper. Roll meat in mixture to coat. Use all the flour.

In a large Dutch oven over medium heat, melt butter with 2 tablespoons oil. Add meat and brown in batches, about 5 minutes for each batch. Remove meat to a plate as it browns. Add onion and sauté until tender, about 5 minutes. Add more oil if needed to keep onion from sticking. Add wine and bring to a boil, scraping up browned bits. Add stock, tomato paste, marjoram, and garlic. Return meat to Dutch oven. Reduce heat to medium-low and simmer, covered, 1 hour and 15 minutes, stirring occasionally. Add potatoes and carrots and bring to a boil. Reduce heat to medium-low and simmer, covered, 30 minutes. Add squash and mushrooms and simmer, covered, until all vegetables are tender, about 15 minutes longer. Taste for seasonings.

5 tablespoons all-purpose flour

1/2 teaspoon salt

Freshly ground pepper to taste

2 1/2 pounds beef stew meat

2 tablespoons butter or margarine

2 to 3 tablespoons vegetable oil

1 large yellow onion, chopped

2 cups red wine

4 cups beef stock or broth

3 tablespoons tomato paste

1 teaspoon dried marjoram

4 cloves garlic, halved

4 medium new potatoes, unpeeled, quartered

3 cups baby carrots

6 baby pattypan squash (about 1 pound), quartered

8 ounces medium mushrooms, halved

**Hungry folks will love this stew with beef cubes, vegetables, and beans cooked in a spicy tomato sauce. Serve with Flaky Cheese Biscuits (page 55).**

2 tablespoons vegetable oil

2½ pounds beef round steak, cut into 1-inch cubes

1 large yellow onion, chopped

2 cloves garlic, minced

4 carrots, cut diagonally into 1-inch slices

2 cups beef stock or broth

1 can (14½ ounces) crushed tomatoes in thick purée

1 can (4 ounces) diced green chiles, drained

1 teaspoon Worcestershire sauce

1 teaspoon salt

¼ teaspoon cayenne pepper

Freshly ground pepper to taste

2 cans (15 ounces each) pinto beans, rinsed and drained

In a large Dutch oven over medium heat, warm oil. Add beef, onion, and garlic and sauté until meat is browned, 8 to 10 minutes. Add remaining ingredients except beans. Reduce heat to medium-low and simmer, covered, 30 minutes. Add beans and simmer, covered, until meat is tender, about 1 hour longer.

# QUICK BEEF STROGANOFF

**SERVES 6**

This classic dish was named after the 19th-century Russian diplomat Paul Stroganoff. This version uses top sirloin beef instead of stew meat, eliminating a long cooking period. You can make it ahead and add the sour cream just before serving. Serve over egg noodles or parsleyed rice for a company dinner.

On a piece of waxed paper, mix together flour, salt, and pepper. Add meat and coat with mixture. Reserve remaining flour mixture.

In a large Dutch oven over medium heat, melt 4 tablespoons of the butter. Add meat and brown on all sides, about 10 minutes. Remove to a plate. Add remaining 2 tablespoons butter and sauté onions, mushrooms, and garlic until tender, about 5 minutes.

Stir in reserved flour and stir until bubbly. Add stock and bring to boil and stir until thickened. Add parsley, mustard, wine, meat, and any collected juices. Reduce heat to medium-low and simmer, uncovered, 10 to 15 minutes. Just before serving, add sour cream and stir until heated through, about 3 minutes.

5 tablespoons all-purpose flour

½ teaspoon salt

¼ teaspoon freshly ground pepper

1¾ pounds top sirloin, cut into ¾-inch cubes

6 tablespoons butter or margarine

6 to 8 green onions, including some tender green tops, sliced

12 ounces medium mushrooms, sliced

2 cloves garlic, minced

2 cups beef stock or broth

2 tablespoons chopped parsley

2 teaspoons Dijon mustard

¼ cup dry white wine

½ cup light sour cream

SERVES 6

**Short ribs and a variety of vegetables will serve a hungry crowd, but leftovers are good too.**

1 to 1½ tablespoons vegetable oil

4 pounds short ribs, fat trimmed

2 cups chopped yellow onion

2 cloves garlic, minced

2 cups baby carrots

2 stalks celery, sliced into 1-inch pieces

½ head cabbage (about 1½ pounds), cut into wedges

3 cups beef stock or broth

2 cans (14½ ounces each) diced tomatoes, with juice

1 teaspoon salt

½ teaspoon dried marjoram

½ teaspoon dried thyme

Freshly ground pepper to taste

4 medium new potatoes, unpeeled, quartered

8 ounces large mushrooms, quartered

1 cup frozen lima beans

1 cup frozen peas

1 cup corn kernels, fresh or frozen

¼ cup chopped parsley

¼ cup all-purpose flour

½ cup water

In a large Dutch oven over medium-high heat, warm 1 tablespoon oil. Add short ribs and brown in batches, 5 to 6 minutes on each side, removing them to a plate when browned. Reduce heat to medium. Add onion and garlic and cook until tender, about 5 minutes. Add more oil if needed to keep mixture from sticking. Return meat to Dutch oven. Add carrots, celery, cabbage, stock, tomatoes, salt, marjoram, thyme, and pepper. Bring to a boil. Reduce heat to medium-low or low and simmer, covered, about 1 hour. Add potatoes and mushrooms and simmer, covered, until vegetables are tender, about 15 minutes. Add beans, peas, corn, and parsley and simmer, uncovered, until heated through, 10 to 15 minutes longer. Blend flour and water in a bowl and stir into stew until thickened, 2 to 3 minutes.

67

# BEEF AND CHILE STEW WITH CORNMEAL DUMPLINGS

**SERVES 6**

**The roasted poblano chile adds heat to this short rib stew. Topped with fluffy cornmeal dumplings, it makes a complete meal. Just add a cool salad.**

In a large Dutch oven over medium-high heat, warm oil. Add short ribs and brown 5 minutes on each side. Add onion and garlic and stir for 2 minutes. Add stock, tomato paste, oregano, salt, pepper, and roasted peppers. Reduce heat to medium-low. Cover and simmer until meat is very tender, 1½ hours. Stir in corn.

In a small bowl, blend flour and water and stir into stew until thickened, 2 to 3 minutes.

Drop about ¼-cup portions of dumpling batter onto top of hot stew. Cook, uncovered, 10 minutes. Cover and cook until a tester inserted in center of dumplings comes out clean, 10 minutes longer. Serve in large bowls with dumplings on top.

2 tablespoons vegetable oil

3 pounds beef short ribs

1 large yellow onion, chopped

2 cloves garlic, minced

4 cups beef stock or broth

1 tablespoon tomato paste

1 teaspoon dried oregano

1 teaspoon salt

Freshly ground pepper to taste

1 poblano (pasilla) chile pepper, roasted (see page 23) and cut into 1-inch pieces

1 large red bell pepper, roasted (see page 23) and cut into 1-inch pieces

1 cup corn kernels, fresh or frozen

¼ cup all-purpose flour

½ cup water

Cornmeal Dumplings (recipe follows)

# CORNMEAL DUMPLINGS

1 cup yellow cornmeal

1 cup all-purpose flour

2 teaspoons baking powder

1 tablespoon sugar

$\frac{1}{2}$ teaspoon salt

$\frac{1}{4}$ cup finely chopped fresh cilantro
or parsley

1 large egg

1 cup buttermilk

In a bowl, combine cornmeal, flour, baking powder, sugar, salt, and cilantro or parsley. In another bowl, whisk together egg and buttermilk. Pour into cornmeal-flour mixture and stir until blended.

# BEEF CORNBALL STEW

## SERVES 6

**Serve this meatball and rice stew any night of the week with Company Cornbread (page 53). Baking the meatballs in the oven removes excess grease; however, you can simmer them in the stew along with the rice if you prefer.**

In a large stew pot over high heat, combine all ingredients except rice and meatballs. Bring to a boil. Stir in rice, reduce heat to medium-low, and simmer, covered, until rice is tender, about 20 minutes.

While stew is simmering, make meatballs. When rice is tender, add meatballs to stew and simmer until flavors are blended, about 10 minutes.

2 cups tomato juice

$^1/_3$ to $^1/_2$ cup Fresh Tomato Salsa (page 42) or purchased salsa (the amount will depend on how hot the salsa is)

$^1/_2$ teaspoon salt

Freshly ground pepper to taste

$^1/_2$ green bell pepper, cut into 1-inch pieces

$^1/_2$ yellow onion, cut into 1-inch pieces

$^1/_2$ cup uncooked long-grain white rice

Meatballs (recipe follows)

# MEATBALLS

1 large egg, beaten

¼ cup milk

¼ cup yellow cornmeal

2 tablespoons finely chopped yellow onion

½ teaspoon chili powder

½ teaspoon salt

Freshly ground pepper to taste

½ teaspoon dry mustard

1¼ pounds lean ground beef

Preheat oven to 400°F. In a bowl, combine all ingredients and mix well. Form into 1-inch balls. Place meatballs on baking sheet and bake until lightly browned and firm, about 12 minutes.

# SPANISH STEW WITH VEGETABLES AND OLIVES

**SERVES 6**

**Pork is popular throughout Spain and is used in many Spanish dishes. The contrasting colors of tomatoes, olives, and green beans with pork make this stew colorful and appealing. Serve it over rice.**

In a large Dutch oven over medium-high heat, warm 1 tablespoon oil. Add pork and brown for about 5 minutes. Add onion, garlic, bell pepper, and mushrooms and sauté about 5 minutes longer. Add more oil if needed to keep mixture from sticking.

Add tomatoes, stock, wine, oregano, thyme, salt, and pepper. Reduce heat to medium-low and simmer, covered, until pork and vegetables are tender, about 30 minutes. Add olives and green beans and simmer, covered, until beans are tender, about 8 minutes. For a thicker stew, mix flour and water and stir into stew until thickened, 2 to 3 minutes.

1 to 2 tablespoons olive oil

1½ pounds boneless pork loin, cut into ¾-inch cubes

1 cup chopped yellow onion

4 cloves garlic, minced

½ red bell pepper, cut into 1-inch pieces

8 ounces medium mushrooms, thickly sliced

2 cans (14½ ounces each) diced tomatoes, with juice

1 cup chicken stock or broth

1 cup dry white wine

¾ teaspoon dried oregano

½ teaspoon dried thyme

1 teaspoon salt

Freshly ground pepper to taste

1 cup pitted kalamata olives or ripe black olives

1 pound green beans, trimmed and halved

¼ cup all-purpose flour (optional)

½ cup water (optional)

**Here the meat slowly simmers in a savory sauce of blended Asian flavors until very tender. Serve with rice or thin noodles.**

1 tablespoon vegetable oil

2½- to 3-pound beef pot roast

3 cups water

6 tablespoons soy sauce

3 tablespoons cider vinegar

6 green onions, including some tender green tops, sliced

3 cloves garlic, minced

2 star anise pods (see Note)

2 slices peeled fresh ginger, ¼ inch thick

¼ cup dry sherry

1 teaspoon Chinese five-spice powder (see Note)

1 cinnamon stick

½ teaspoon salt

Freshly ground pepper to taste

½ teaspoon dark (Asian) sesame oil

Sliced green onions for topping

Toasted sesame seeds (see page 26) for topping

In a large Dutch oven over medium-high heat, warm oil. Brown meat, about 5 minutes on each side. Add all remaining ingredients except toppings. Reduce heat to medium-low and simmer, covered, until meat is very tender, about 1½ hours. To keep the temperature at a gentle roll, you may have to alternate between low and medium-low. Turn beef in Dutch oven every 30 minutes. Remove meat to a plate. Strain stock and discard solids. Return meat and stock to Dutch oven. Keep warm until ready to serve. Slice meat and pour some stock over it. Sprinkle with sliced green onions and sesame seeds. You can use the remaining stock as a cooking liquid for rice or in soups.

**NOTE:** *Star anise is a star-shaped dark brown pod native to China, used in Asian cooking. You can purchase it at Asian food stores. Chinese five-spice powder is available in the spice section of most supermarkets.*

# SPICY CUBAN PORK STEW

**SERVES 4**

**Marinated pork in lime juice and seasonings gives this dish a distinctive Cuban flair. Serve with rice and tropical fruit.**

In a bowl combine pork cubes, lime juice, 2 cloves minced garlic, oregano, cumin, salt, and pepper and mix well. Cover and refrigerate several hours, stirring once.

In a large Dutch over medium heat, warm oil. Add onion, bell pepper, and remaining 2 cloves garlic and sauté until tender, about 5 minutes. Add meat and sauté 5 minutes longer. Add remaining ingredients, reduce heat to medium-low, and simmer, covered, until meat is no longer pink, 20 to 25 minutes. Remove lid and simmer until slightly thickened, about 5 minutes longer. Remove bay leaf and discard.

$1\frac{1}{2}$ pounds boneless pork steak, cut into cubes

2 tablespoons fresh lime juice

4 cloves garlic, minced

$\frac{1}{2}$ teaspoon dried oregano

$\frac{1}{2}$ teaspoon dried cumin

$\frac{1}{2}$ teaspoon salt

Freshly ground pepper to taste

2 tablespoons olive oil

2 cups chopped yellow onion

1 green bell pepper, seeded and cut into 1-inch pieces

$\frac{1}{2}$ cup tomato paste

1 cup dry white wine

1 cup chicken stock or broth

$\frac{1}{4}$ cup sliced pimiento-stuffed olives

$\frac{1}{4}$ cup chopped parsley

$\frac{1}{4}$ teaspoon dried, crushed red pepper

1 bay leaf

**This colorful combination of tender pork chops and three types of peppers makes an impressive dish for a company dinner. Serve with pasta and a green salad.**

1 tablespoon vegetable oil

4 large pork chops, bone in (about 2 pounds)

Salt and freshly ground pepper to taste

1 small green bell pepper, seeded and cut into ½-inch strips

1 small red bell pepper, seeded and cut into ½-inch strips

1 small yellow bell pepper, seeded and cut into ½-inch strips

1 medium yellow onion, sliced

2 cups chicken stock or broth

1 tablespoon balsamic vinegar

2½ teaspoons cornstarch

3 tablespoons cold water

Parsley sprigs for garnish

In a large Dutch oven over medium-high heat, warm oil. Brown pork chops, about 6 minutes on each side. Season generously with salt and pepper. Remove chops to a plate. Add bell peppers and onion and sauté until just tender, 6 to 8 minutes. In a bowl, combine stock and vinegar. Return chops to Dutch oven and pour stock mixture over them. Reduce heat to medium-low and simmer, covered, until chops are done and vegetables are tender-crisp, about 15 minutes. To thicken, blend cornstarch with water and stir into stew until thickened, 2 to 3 minutes. Garnish with parsley sprigs.

# PORK, EGGPLANT, AND RAVIOLI STEW

**SERVES 4**

**Stews don't always have to be a winter dish. Make this in the cool of the morning and serve for a patio dinner to add variety to your summer menus. Serve with Bagel Strips (page 64).**

Spoon flour onto a piece of waxed paper. Roll pork in flour to coat. In a large Dutch oven over medium heat, warm oil. Add pork, onion, and garlic and sauté until meat is browned and onion is tender, 6 to 7 minutes. Add carrots, tomatoes, stock, salt, and pepper. Reduce heat to medium-low and simmer, covered, 1 hour. Increase heat to medium and add eggplant, peas, and ravioli. Cook, uncovered, until meat, vegetables, and ravioli are tender, 10 to 15 minutes longer. Serve in large bowls.

3 tablespoons all-purpose flour

$1^{1}/_{4}$ pounds boneless pork shoulder, cut into 1-inch cubes

2 tablespoons vegetable oil

$^{1}/_{2}$ cup chopped yellow onion

1 clove garlic, minced

2 carrots, cut into 1-inch slices

1 can ($14^{1}/_{2}$ ounces) tomatoes, coarsely chopped, with juice

1 cup chicken stock or broth

$^{3}/_{4}$ teaspoon salt

Freshly ground pepper to taste

2 cups cubed unpeeled eggplant (1-inch cubes)

1 cup fresh or frozen peas

8 to 10 ounces cheese-filled ravioli

74

There are several steps to this stew, but it is really very simple to make. Just get out the timer. You can make it ahead and reheat it at serving time. The tart apples and plump prunes complement the pork and impart a sweet flavor.

1 tablespoon vegetable oil

2 pounds boneless pork shoulder, cut into 1-inch cubes

2 yellow onions, quartered

2 carrots, cut diagonally into 1-inch slices

2 cloves garlic, minced

1 cup chicken stock or broth

1 cup beef stock or broth

1 teaspoon dried sage

$\frac{1}{4}$ teaspoon ground allspice

$\frac{3}{4}$ teaspoon salt

Freshly ground pepper to taste

2 medium russet potatoes (about 1$\frac{1}{2}$ pounds), peeled and quartered

8 ounces medium mushrooms

12 dried prunes

2 apples, peeled, cored, and quartered

2 tablespoons all-purpose flour (optional)

$\frac{1}{4}$ cup water (optional)

In a Dutch oven over medium heat, warm oil. Add meat and sauté until browned, about 5 minutes. Add onions, carrots, and garlic and sauté for 2 minutes. Add stock, sage, allspice, salt, and pepper. Bring to a boil, then reduce heat to medium-low and simmer, covered, 30 minutes.

Add potatoes and mushrooms and bring to a boil. Reduce heat to medium-low and simmer, covered, 20 minutes. Add prunes and apples and simmer until meat, vegetables, and fruit are tender, about 5 minutes longer.

For a thicker stew, blend flour and water in a cup. Stir into stew until thickened, 2 to 3 minutes.

**PORK STEW WITH PRUNES AND APPLES**

SERVES 4 TO 6

# ASIAN STEW WITH PORK, GREEN BEANS, AND MUSHROOMS

**SERVES 4**

# 76

**Here is a combination of pork chops and vegetables simmered in an exotic stock of Asian seasonings. Serve over hot rice for an all-in-one meal.**

On a piece of waxed paper, mix flour and five-spice powder. Add pork and coat with mixture. Reserve any flour mixture not used.

In a large Dutch oven over medium heat, warm 1 tablespoon of the oil. Add pork and sauté until browned, about 5 minutes. Transfer to a plate. Add remaining 1 tablespoon oil, celery, and green onions and sauté until tender, about 5 minutes. Return meat and juices to Dutch oven. Add stock, hoisin sauce, soy sauce, ginger, mushrooms, and beans. Bring to a boil. Reduce heat to medium-low and simmer, covered, until meat and vegetables are tender, about 20 minutes.

Stir in reserved flour mixture and mix well. Serve sprinkled with sesame seeds and sliced green onion tops.

**NOTE:** *Chinese five-spice powder is available in the spice section of most supermarkets.*

2 tablespoons all-purpose flour

2 teaspoons Chinese five-spice powder (see Note)

1½ pounds boneless pork chops, cut into 1-inch cubes

2 tablespoons vegetable oil

2 stalks celery, cut diagonally into 1-inch slices

½ cup sliced green onions, including some tender green tops

1 cup chicken stock or broth

2 tablespoons hoisin sauce

2 tablespoons soy sauce

½ teaspoon ground ginger

8 ounces mushrooms, sliced

8 ounces fresh green beans, trimmed and cut into 1-inch pieces

3 tablespoons toasted sesame seeds (see page 26) for topping

Sliced green onion tops for topping

**Flavors of the islands inspired this stew with pork, fruit, vegetables, and spices. Serve with a tropical fruit plate and rice.**

3 tablespoons all-purpose flour

1 teaspoon salt

Freshly ground pepper to taste

1¼ pounds boneless pork steak, cut into 1-inch cubes

1 tablespoon vegetable oil

1 small yellow onion, chopped

1 clove garlic, minced

½ green bell pepper, seeded and chopped

1 can (14½ ounces) whole tomatoes, coarsely chopped, with juice

2 cups chicken stock or broth

1 large sweet potato, peeled and cubed

1 tablespoon packed brown sugar

½ teaspoon ground cinnamon

¼ teaspoon dried oregano

¼ teaspoon ground cloves

1 cup fresh pineapple chunks

¼ cup sliced pimiento-stuffed green olives

¼ cup chopped parsley

On a piece of waxed paper, mix flour, salt, and pepper. Coat meat in mixture. In a Dutch oven over medium heat, warm oil. Add pork and sauté until browned, about 5 minutes. Remove with a slotted spoon to a plate. Add onion, garlic, and bell pepper and sauté until tender, about 5 minutes. Add tomatoes, stock, sweet potato, brown sugar, cinnamon, oregano, cloves, and reserved pork. Reduce heat to medium-low and simmer, covered, until meat and potatoes are tender, 15 to 20 minutes. Add pineapple, olives, and parsley and simmer, uncovered, until flavors are blended, about 10 minutes longer.

77

# CLASSIC LAMB STEW

## SERVES 6

**Lamb is enjoying a new popularity because better-quality young lamb is readily available. Here is an updated version of an old favorite.**

In a Dutch oven over medium-high heat, warm oil. Add lamb and sauté until browned, about 5 minutes. Reduce heat to medium, add onion and garlic, and sauté until tender, about 5 minutes longer. Add stock and wine, stirring to loosen browned bits. Stir in tomato paste, seasonings, and carrots and bring to a boil.

Reduce heat to medium-low and simmer, covered, 30 minutes. Add potatoes, bell pepper, and lima beans and simmer, covered, until meat and vegetables are tender, about 25 minutes longer. Remove bay leaf and discard.

To thicken sauce, blend water and flour in a small bowl and stir into stew until thickened, 2 to 3 minutes. Sprinkle with parsley and garnish with rosemary sprigs before serving.

2 tablespoons olive oil

2 pounds boneless lamb shoulder, cut into 1-inch cubes

1 yellow onion, quartered

2 cloves garlic, chopped

2½ cups chicken stock or broth

1 cup dry white wine

2 tablespoons tomato paste

1 tablespoon chopped fresh rosemary, or 1 teaspoon dried rosemary

1 tablespoon chopped fresh thyme, or 1 teaspoon dried thyme

1 bay leaf

½ teaspoon salt

¼ teaspoon freshly ground pepper

3 carrots, peeled and cut into 1½-inch slices

4 medium new red potatoes, unpeeled, quartered

1 green or yellow bell pepper, seeded and cut into wedges

1 cup frozen lima beans

¼ cup cold water

2 tablespoons all-purpose flour

¼ cup chopped parsley for topping

Fresh rosemary sprigs for garnish

**This combination of Mediterranean ingredients and seasonings makes a great one-dish meal.**

1 tablespoon olive oil

1 pound boneless lamb shoulder, cut into 1-inch cubes

1 cup chopped yellow onion

3 cloves garlic, minced

$\frac{1}{2}$ teaspoon dried oregano

$\frac{1}{2}$ teaspoon ground cumin seed

$2\frac{1}{2}$ cups chicken stock or broth

$\frac{1}{2}$ teaspoon salt

Freshly ground pepper to taste

$\frac{3}{4}$ cup uncooked orzo

12 ounces cooked fresh spinach, chopped, or 1 package (10 ounces) frozen chopped spinach, thawed and squeezed dry

1 tablespoon lemon juice

$\frac{1}{4}$ cup pitted kalamata olives (optional)

$\frac{1}{4}$ cup crumbled feta cheese for topping

In a large Dutch oven over medium heat, warm oil. Add lamb, onion, and garlic and sauté until meat is browned and vegetables are tender, about 5 minutes. Stir in oregano and cumin and cook for 1 minute. Add stock, salt, and pepper. Bring to a boil. Reduce heat to medium-low and simmer, covered, until meat is tender, about 1 hour.

Add orzo to Dutch oven and bring to a boil. Reduce heat and simmer, covered, until orzo is tender and liquid is absorbed, about 15 minutes longer. Add spinach, lemon juice, and olives, if using, and mix well. Cook until heated through, about 10 minutes longer. Sprinkle with feta cheese.

**SERVES 6**

# LAMB WITH SPINACH AND ORZO

# LAMB STEW WITH APRICOTS AND COUSCOUS

**SERVES 4**

**80**

**In this excellent stew, succulent lamb is simmered with apricots and exotic spices. Serve it with Pita Bread Wedges (page 65).**

On a piece of waxed paper, combine flour, salt, and pepper. Add lamb and coat with mixture. In a large Dutch oven over medium-high heat, warm oil. Add lamb and sauté until browned, about 5 minutes. Reduce heat to medium, add onion and garlic, and sauté until tender, about 5 minutes longer. Stir in wine, cinnamon, allspice, and cloves. Simmer, uncovered, until slightly thickened. Add stock and half of the apricots and bring to a boil. Reduce heat to medium-low and simmer, covered, until meat is tender, about 1 hour. Add the remaining apricots and peas. Cook, uncovered, 10 minutes longer. Serve over couscous.

3 tablespoons all-purpose flour

¾ teaspoon salt

Freshly ground pepper to taste

1½ pounds boneless lamb shoulder, cut into 1-inch cubes

1½ tablespoons vegetable oil

1 cup chopped yellow onion

2 cloves garlic, minced

½ cup dry white wine

½ teaspoon ground cinnamon

½ teaspoon ground allspice

⅛ teaspoon ground cloves

3 cups chicken stock or broth

6 ounces dried apricots, halved (about 1 cup)

1 cup fresh or frozen peas

Couscous (recipe follows)

# COUSCOUS

1½ cups water or chicken stock or broth or a combination

¼ teaspoon salt

1 cup couscous

3 tablespoons chopped parsley

In a saucepan over high heat, bring water and salt to a boil. Remove pan from heat and stir in couscous and parsley. Let stand, covered, for 5 minutes. Fluff the couscous with a fork and serve with the stew.

# "FALLING OFF THE BONES" LAMB SHANKS WITH GREMOLATA

**SERVES 4**

**In this recipe, lamb shanks are cooked slowly in a savory sauce for about 3 hours, becoming very tender and flavorful. A sprinkling of gremolata (parsley, lemon zest, and garlic) adds a sprightly flavor. Veal can also be used. Serve with white beans or mashed potatoes.**

In a large Dutch oven over medium heat, melt butter with oil. Brown lamb shanks in batches, 6 to 7 minutes. Season with salt and pepper. Remove shanks to a plate. Pour off fat in Dutch oven. Add wine, stock, vegetables, garlic, tomato paste, rosemary, parsley, and bay leaf to Dutch oven. Bring to a boil. Return shanks to Dutch oven. Reduce heat to medium-low or low and simmer, covered, until meat is very tender, 2½ to 3 hours.

Transfer shanks to a plate. Strain liquid into a bowl and discard solids. Return liquid to Dutch oven and bring to a boil.

In a small bowl or cup, blend flour and water. Add to liquid and stir until thickened, 1 to 2 minutes. Reduce heat to medium-low. Return shanks to Dutch oven and simmer, uncovered, until ready to serve. Sprinkle meat with gremolata. Garnish with rosemary sprigs.

2 tablespoons butter or margarine

1 tablespoon vegetable oil

4 meaty lamb or veal shanks (about 1 pound each; have butcher cut in half)

Salt and freshly ground pepper to taste

1 cup dry red wine

1 cup chicken stock or broth

1 large yellow onion, quartered

2 stalks celery, sliced

1 carrot, sliced

4 cloves garlic, halved

2 tablespoons tomato paste

1 sprig fresh rosemary, or 1 teaspoon dried rosemary

2 sprigs parsley

1 bay leaf

3 tablespoons all-purpose flour

¼ cup cold water

Gremolata (page 43) for topping

Fresh rosemary sprigs for garnish

**Serve this assertive lamb stew dotted with olives for casual entertaining. Complement the dish with crisp sliced cucumbers.**

2 tablespoons olive oil

1½ pounds boneless lamb shoulder, cut into 1-inch cubes

1 cup chopped yellow onion

2 carrots, chopped

4 cloves garlic, minced

1 teaspoon dried oregano

½ teaspoon salt

Freshly ground pepper to taste

2 bay leaves

1 sprig parsley

2 strips orange zest, 1 inch wide (use a vegetable peeler)

1 cup chicken stock or broth

1 cup dry white wine

1 cup chopped fresh or canned tomatoes

1 cup uncooked orzo

½ cup pitted kalamata olives

In a large Dutch oven over medium-high heat, warm 1 tablespoon of the oil. Add lamb and sauté until browned, about 5 minutes. Remove meat to a plate. Reduce heat to medium, add remaining 1 tablespoon oil, and sauté onion and carrots until tender, about 5 minutes. Return meat to Dutch oven along with garlic, oregano, salt, pepper, bay leaves, parsley, orange zest, stock, wine, and tomatoes. Bring to a boil. Reduce heat to medium-low and simmer, covered, 20 minutes.

Add orzo and olives and simmer, covered, until meat and orzo are tender, about 15 minutes longer. Remove bay leaves and orange zest and discard.

**SERVES 4**

# LAMB STEW WITH KALAMATA OLIVES

**A cookbook of stews is not complete without the original Irish stew. It is cooked in layers and served in bowls at the table. Traditionally, the meat is not browned first and is cooked on top of the stove. Here it is baked in the oven for easier temperature control. Serve with Irish Soda Bread (page 52).**

Preheat oven to 350°F. In a large lightly sprayed or oiled, Dutch oven or casserole, place half the potatoes for the bottom layer. Spread half the onions over the potatoes, followed by all the lamb. Sprinkle with thyme, salt, and pepper. Layer remaining onions and potatoes over lamb. In a small saucepan, bring stock and Worcestershire sauce to a boil. Pour over stew.

Cover and bake until meat is tender, about 1½ hours, or cook on top of the stove over low heat for 1½ hours.

4 medium russet potatoes (about 2 pounds), peeled and cut into ½-inch slices

3 large yellow onions, peeled and cut into ½-inch slices

2 pounds boneless lamb shoulder, cut into 1-inch cubes

½ teaspoon dried thyme

1 teaspoon salt

Freshly ground pepper to taste

Chicken stock or broth or water to cover (about 4 cups)

1 teaspoon Worcestershire sauce

**This hearty Greek stew can be made with beef or lamb. In this version, lamb is used with red wine, herbs, tomatoes, and small boiling onions. Serve with Pita Bread Wedges (page 65).**

3 pounds boneless lamb shoulder, cut into 1-inch cubes

Salt and freshly ground pepper to taste

¼ cup butter or margarine

½ pound small boiling onions, peeled (see page 24)

3 medium new potatoes (about 1 pound), unpeeled, cut into large pieces

4 carrots, cut diagonally into 1-inch slices

2 cloves garlic, minced

½ cup dry red wine

1 tablespoon red wine vinegar

1 tablespoon firmly packed brown sugar

1 can (14½ ounces) crushed tomatoes in rich purée

1 bay leaf

1 cinnamon stick, or ¼ teaspoon ground cinnamon

¼ teaspoon ground cloves

3 tablespoons raisins (optional)

½ cup crumbled feta cheese for topping

Preheat oven to 325°F. Season meat with salt and pepper. In a large Dutch oven over medium heat, melt butter. Add meat and stir to coat but do not brown. Place vegetables on top. In a bowl, mix together remaining ingredients except raisins and feta cheese and pour over stew.

Bake, covered, for 1½ hours. Stir in raisins, if using, and bake, uncovered, 10 minutes longer. Remove bay leaf and cinnamon stick and discard. Spoon into large, warm bowls. Sprinkle with feta cheese.

84

# SAUSAGE AND WHITE BEAN CASSOULET

**SERVES 6 TO 8**

**This variation of the French dish has extra ingredients added. Long simmering in the oven harmonizes the flavors. Serve in large bowls with crusty bread for dunking.**

Preheat oven to 350°F. In a Dutch oven over medium heat, warm oil. Add whole Italian sausages and brown for 15 minutes, turning occasionally. Add kielbasa and brown both sausages about 10 minutes longer. Transfer to a plate and slice Italian sausages into ½-inch rounds. Add leeks and garlic to same pan and sauté until soft, about 5 minutes. Add apple, rosemary, sage, and bay leaf. Stir in tomatoes, Tabasco sauce, beans, stock, and tomato paste. Season with pepper.

Bake, covered, about 1 hour. Remove lid and stir in parsley. Bake, uncovered, 15 minutes longer. Remove bay leaf and discard.

1 tablespoon olive oil

½ pound sweet Italian sausages

1 pound kielbasa sausage, cut into ³⁄₈-inch slices

3 leeks, white and pale green parts only, sliced

3 cloves garlic, minced

1 apple, peeled and chopped

1 tablespoon fresh rosemary, or ½ teaspoon dried rosemary

1 teaspoon dried sage

1 bay leaf

1 can (14½ ounces) diced tomatoes, with juice

2 or 3 drops Tabasco sauce

2 cans (15 ounces each) Great Northern beans, rinsed and drained

1 package (10 ounces) frozen baby lima beans, rinsed

1½ cups chicken stock or broth

2 tablespoons tomato paste

Freshly ground pepper to taste

¼ cup chopped parsley

**This stew actually improves in flavor when made ahead and warmed up. This recipe can be doubled for a crowd.**

1 cup (½ pound) dried Great Northern beans, presoaked (see page 29)

2 cups chicken stock or broth

2 cups water

1 ham shank (about 1½ pounds)

1 cup chopped yellow onion

½ cup chopped celery

½ cup chopped green bell pepper

1 bay leaf

2 cups cubed cooked ham (about ¾ pound)

2 teaspoons Worcestershire sauce

1 tablespoon tomato paste

2 or 3 drops Tabasco sauce

½ teaspoon salt

Freshly ground pepper to taste

In a large soup pot over high heat, mix drained beans with stock, water, ham shank, onion, celery, bell pepper, and bay leaf. Bring to a boil. Reduce heat to medium and simmer, covered, for 30 minutes. Add ham and remaining ingredients and simmer, uncovered, until beans are tender, about 35 minutes longer. Remove bay leaf and ham shank and discard. To thicken, remove 1 cup beans and ¼ cup stock, place in food processor, and purée. Return to pan and reheat.

SERVES 4

# SWEET-AND-SOUR CABBAGE AND SAUERKRAUT STEW WITH SAUSAGE

**SERVES 6 TO 8**

**This fragrant stew is a combination of sweet and sour flavors mingled with sausage and vegetables—very filling!**

In a large, lightly sprayed or oiled Dutch oven over medium heat, brown sausage for about 5 minutes. Add remaining ingredients except sour cream and dill sprigs. Reduce heat to medium-low and simmer, covered, 1 hour. Serve with a dollop of sour cream and garnished with dill sprigs.

1 pound sausage (kielbasa or German), cut into ½-inch slices

1 parsnip, peeled and chopped

2 carrots, peeled and chopped

1 large yellow onion, chopped

2 stalks celery, chopped

1 can (28 ounces) whole tomatoes, coarsely chopped, with juice

2 cups chicken stock or broth

½ head cabbage (about 1½ pounds), sliced

1 teaspoon salt

Freshly ground pepper to taste

2 cups sauerkraut, drained

¼ cup packed brown sugar

¼ cup lemon juice

¼ cup chopped fresh dill, or 1 teaspoon dried dill weed

Sour cream for topping

Fresh dill sprigs for garnish

**An assortment of sausages and peppers goes into this colorful and full-flavored stew. Serve over brown rice.**

1 to 2 tablespoons vegetable oil

1 small yellow onion, chopped

2 cloves garlic, minced

1 green bell pepper, seeded and cut into 1-inch pieces

1 red bell pepper, seeded and cut into 1-inch pieces

1 yellow bell pepper, seeded and cut into 1-inch pieces

1½ pounds assorted sausages (Polish, German, etc.), cut into ½-inch slices

1 can (14½ ounces) crushed tomatoes in thick purée

1 cup chicken stock or broth

1 teaspoon sugar

½ teaspoon dried basil

½ teaspoon salt

Freshly ground pepper to taste

In a large Dutch oven over medium heat, warm 1 tablespoon oil. Add vegetables and sauté until tender, about 5 minutes. Transfer to a plate. Add remaining 1 tablespoon oil, if needed, and sauté sausages until browned, 6 to 7 minutes. Reduce heat to medium-low and add tomatoes, stock, sugar, and seasonings. Return vegetables to Dutch oven and simmer, covered, until flavors are blended, about 30 minutes longer.

88

# ITALIAN MEATBALL AND BEAN STEW

**SERVES 4 TO 6**

**This thick, hearty stew loaded with moist, tender meatballs, vegetables, and beans will please the whole family. You may want to double this recipe for a crowd. Serve with Fresh Herb Garlic Bread (page 48).**

In a large Dutch oven, combine stock, tomatoes, tomato paste, carrot, celery, beans, oregano, salt, pepper, and meatballs. Bring to a boil over high heat, reduce temperature to medium-low, and simmer, covered, until meatballs are done and vegetables are tender, about 45 minutes. Serve in bowls, sprinkled with Parmesan cheese.

2 cups beef stock or broth

1 can (14$\frac{1}{2}$ ounces) Italian-style stewed tomatoes, with juice

2 tablespoons tomato paste

1 carrot, chopped

1 stalk celery, chopped

1 can (15 ounces) cannellini beans or other white beans, drained and rinsed

$\frac{1}{2}$ teaspoon dried oregano

$\frac{1}{2}$ teaspoon salt

Freshly ground pepper to taste

Italian Meatballs (recipe follows)

Freshly grated Parmesan cheese for topping

## ITALIAN MEATBALLS

½ pound bulk country-style sausage

½ pound lean ground beef

½ cup coarse dry bread crumbs

¼ cup finely chopped yellow onion

3 tablespoons milk

1 large egg

2 tablespoons grated Parmesan cheese

¼ teaspoon Worcestershire sauce

¼ teaspoon salt

Freshly ground pepper to taste

2 tablespoons chopped parsley

Preheat oven to 400°F. In a bowl, combine the meats, bread crumbs, onion, milk, egg, Parmesan cheese, Worcestershire sauce, salt, pepper, and parsley and mix thoroughly. Shape into 1½-inch balls. Place on an ungreased baking sheet and bake until browned, about 12 minutes.

# CHOUCROUTE GARNI (SHOO-KROOT GAHR-NEE)

**SERVES 6 TO 8**

*Choucroute* is the French word for sauerkraut. Choucroute garni is sauerkraut served, or "garnished," with a variety of meats, such as sausages, pork, ham, or goose, and potatoes. This version includes bratwurst, knockwurst, smoked pork chops, and baby potatoes all in one pot. This is a great dish for entertaining.

In a large Dutch oven over medium-high heat, cook bacon until crisp, about 8 minutes. Remove bacon, leaving 1 tablespoon of drippings in Dutch oven. Reduce heat to medium. Add onion, garlic, and carrots and sauté until tender, about 5 minutes. Return bacon to Dutch oven. Add stock, wine, sauerkraut, potatoes, bay leaves, herbes de Provence, pepper, and juniper berries, if desired. Reduce heat to medium-low and simmer, covered, about 1 hour. Add meats, submerging some into the stew. Simmer, covered, until sausages have plumped up and flavors are blended, 30 to 35 minutes longer. Remove bay leaves and discard. Serve with an assortment of mustards.

12 ounces bacon, diced

1 yellow onion, diced

3 cloves garlic, chopped

2 carrots, thinly sliced

4 cups chicken stock or broth

1 cup dry white wine

4 cups sauerkraut, drained

12 baby red potatoes, halved

2 bay leaves

1 teaspoon herbes de Provence

Freshly ground pepper to taste

6 to 8 juniper berries (optional)

4 bratwurst, scored (2 or 3 small diagonal slashes a fourth of the way through)

4 knockwurst, scored

3 or 4 smoked pork chops, halved if large

Assorted mustards as an accompaniment

# POULTRY

## SOUPS & STEWS

Poultry soups and stews are a mainstay in many parts of the world. They are healthful and economical, and appeal to the health conscious. Here you will find a wide selection of the old standbys, as well as contemporary and ethnic-inspired soups and stews for family and friends.

# CHICKEN, HAM, AND VEGETABLE CHOWDER

**SERVES 6**

Chowders were originally made with seafood, but now they include other meats as well. They are thick and chunky and usually contain potatoes and other vegetables. Serve this hearty chowder for a light supper with Three-Cheese Bread (page 47).

In a large Dutch oven over medium heat, warm oil. Add onion and bell pepper and sauté until tender, about 5 minutes. Stir in ham and chicken and cook for 5 minutes. Add potatoes and stock. Bring to a boil. Reduce heat to medium-low and simmer, covered, 10 minutes. Add zucchini, corn, thyme, salt, and pepper and cook, covered, until vegetables are tender and chicken turns white, about 10 minutes longer.

In a cup or small bowl, blend flour and milk. Add to soup and stir until thickened, about 2 minutes. Ladle into bowls and sprinkle with parsley.

1 tablespoon vegetable oil

1 cup chopped yellow onion

1/2 red bell pepper, seeded and chopped

1 cup cooked cubed ham

2 boned, skinned chicken breast halves (about 1 pound), cut into bite-sized pieces

2 large russet potatoes (about 1 1/2 pounds), peeled and cubed

4 cups chicken stock or broth

1 zucchini, unpeeled, quartered lengthwise and sliced

1 cup corn kernels, fresh or frozen

1/2 teaspoon dried thyme

1 teaspoon salt

Freshly ground pepper to taste

3 tablespoons all-purpose flour

1 cup milk

Chopped parsley for topping

**Crisp bacon adds a salty flavor to this chicken chowder. Creamed corn makes it extra creamy. Serve with Basic Crostini (page 59).**

3 slices thick bacon, diced

1 cup chopped yellow onion

2 leeks, white and light green parts only, sliced

1 clove garlic, minced

4 cups chicken stock or broth

2 large russet potatoes (about 1½ pounds), peeled and chopped

2 boned, skinned chicken breast halves (about 1 pound), cut into bite-sized pieces

3 tablespoons chopped parsley

1 teaspoon dried thyme

½ teaspoon salt

Freshly ground pepper to taste

1 can (15 ounces) creamed corn

In a large Dutch oven over medium heat, cook bacon until crisp, about 5 minutes. With a slotted spoon, remove bacon to a plate, leaving 2 tablespoons drippings in pan. Add onion, leeks, and garlic and sauté until tender, about 5 minutes. Add stock and potatoes. Bring to a boil. Reduce heat to medium-low and simmer, covered, 10 minutes. Add chicken, reserved bacon, parsley, thyme, salt, and pepper and bring to a boil. Reduce heat to medium-low and simmer, covered, until chicken turns white and potatoes are tender, about 10 minutes longer. Add creamed corn and simmer, uncovered, until flavors are blended, 5 to 10 minutes longer.

**SERVES 4**

# CHICKEN AND VEGETABLE CHOWDER

**SERVES 4 TO 6**

**Puréed vegetables and rice are the thickening agents in this delicious soup. It is made without cream but is still rich tasting. This will be a family favorite.**

In a large soup pot over high heat, bring vegetables, garlic, rice, and 3 cups of the stock to a boil. Reduce heat to medium-low and simmer, covered, until vegetables and rice are tender, about 20 minutes.

Transfer in batches to a food processor or blender, and blend the soup until slightly chunky. Return to pot. Stir in remaining 1 cup stock, buttermilk, chicken, cheese, salt, thyme, and pepper. Simmer, uncovered, until cheese melts and flavors are blended, about 10 minutes.

1 cup chopped yellow onion

1 medium russet potato (about ½ pound), peeled and cubed

1 carrot, chopped

1 stalk celery, chopped

1 turnip, peeled and chopped

1 clove garlic, sliced

¼ cup uncooked long-grain white rice

4 cups chicken stock or broth

1 cup buttermilk or milk

2 cups cubed cooked chicken breast

1 cup grated Cheddar cheese

¾ teaspoon salt

½ teaspoon dried thyme

Freshly ground pepper to taste

**This makes a big pot of chunky, colorful soup filled with tasty ingredients. It's perfect for a crisp fall day. Serve with Herbed Buttermilk Sticks (page 51).**

3 slices bacon, diced

1 cup chopped yellow onion

$^1/_2$ green bell pepper, chopped

2 cloves garlic, minced

3 cups chicken stock or broth

$1^1/_2$ cups unpeeled cubed red potatoes (about 2 medium)

$1^1/_2$ cups corn kernels, fresh or frozen

3 tablespoons all-purpose flour

3 cups milk

2 cups cubed cooked chicken breast

1 cup seeded, peeled, chopped tomato

$^1/_2$ cup grated Cheddar cheese

$^3/_4$ teaspoon salt

Freshly ground pepper to taste

In a large Dutch oven over medium heat, cook bacon until crisp. Transfer bacon to a plate, leaving 1 tablespoon drippings in Dutch oven. Add onion, bell pepper, and garlic and sauté until tender, about 5 minutes. Add stock and potatoes and bring to a boil. Reduce heat to medium-low and simmer, covered, until potatoes are tender, about 20 minutes. Stir in corn.

In a bowl, blend flour and milk. Stir into soup. Increase heat to medium-high and stir until thickened, about 5 minutes. Reduce heat to medium-low and add chicken, reserved bacon, tomato, cheese, salt, and pepper. Simmer, uncovered, until flavors are blended and cheese is melted, about 15 minutes longer.

**SERVES 6**

# CHEDDAR CHICKEN CORN CHOWDER

# CHICKEN-MUSHROOM SOUP

**SERVES 4**

**Mushrooms and chicken pieces in a rich cream base make an elegant combination to serve for any occasion.**

In a large soup pot over medium heat, melt butter. Add onion and sauté for 3 minutes. Add mushrooms and lemon juice and sauté until vegetables are tender, about 5 minutes longer. Add flour and stir until bubbly. Add stock and soy sauce and bring to a boil over high heat, stirring constantly until thickened, about 2 minutes.

Transfer in batches to food processor or blender and purée. Return soup to pan and add half-and-half, sherry, thyme, salt, pepper, and chicken. Reduce heat to low and simmer until flavors are blended, about 5 minutes. Ladle into bowls and swirl about 1 tablespoon sour cream into each bowl. Serve immediately.

3 to 4 tablespoons butter or margarine

1 cup chopped yellow onion

1 pound white mushrooms, sliced

1 tablespoon fresh lemon juice

$\frac{1}{4}$ cup all-purpose flour

3 cups chicken stock or broth

1 teaspoon soy sauce

$1\frac{1}{4}$ cups half-and-half

$\frac{1}{4}$ cup dry sherry or dry white wine

$\frac{1}{2}$ teaspoon dried thyme

$\frac{3}{4}$ teaspoon salt

Freshly ground pepper to taste

1 cup diced cooked chicken

Sour cream for topping

**This creamy soup is far superior to the canned variety. For best flavor, make it with homemade stock. Serve with Flaky Cheese Biscuits (page 55).**

3 tablespoons butter or margarine

$1/4$ cup finely chopped yellow onion

$3/4$ teaspoon salt

$1/8$ teaspoon white pepper

$1/4$ cup all-purpose flour

3 cups rich chicken stock or broth

1 cup half-and-half or milk

$1^1/2$ cups shredded or diced cooked chicken

2 ounces ($1/2$ jar) chopped pimientos, drained

In a soup pot over medium heat, melt butter. Add onion and sauté until tender, about 5 minutes. Add salt and white pepper. Add flour and blend until bubbly. Slowly whisk in stock. Increase heat to medium-high and bring to a boil, whisking constantly until thickened, about 5 minutes. Add half-and-half, chicken, and pimientos. Reduce heat to low and simmer, uncovered, until flavors are blended, 5 to 10 minutes.

SERVES 4

# RICH CREAM OF CHICKEN SOUP WITH VEGETABLES

**SERVES 4**

**This creamy, rich soup has a superb flavor and is a special treat—just don't count the calories.**

In a soup pot over medium heat, melt butter. Add onion, celery, and carrot and sauté for 2 minutes. Add mushrooms and sauté until vegetables are soft, about 5 minutes longer. Add flour and stir until bubbly. Add stock, thyme, salt, and pepper and stir until slightly thickened and smooth, about 5 minutes. Reduce heat to medium-low. Add half-and-half and chicken and simmer, uncovered, until flavors are blended, about 5 minutes longer.

2 tablespoons butter or margarine

$^1/_2$ cup chopped onion

$^1/_2$ cup chopped celery

1 carrot, chopped

4 ounces mushrooms, sliced

3 tablespoons all-purpose flour

3 cups rich chicken stock or broth (preferably homemade)

$^1/_4$ teaspoon dried thyme

1 teaspoon salt

Freshly ground pepper to taste

$^3/_4$ cup half-and-half

1$^1/_2$ cups diced cooked chicken

**Chicken slowly simmered with vegetables makes a flavorful stock for this popular soup.**

1 chicken (3 to 3½ pounds), quartered

12 cups water

1 tablespoon peppercorns

2 stalks celery, sliced

1 carrot, cut into 1-inch slices

1 yellow onion, quartered

2 cloves garlic, cut up

½ teaspoon dried basil

1 bay leaf

½ cup uncooked long-grain white rice

¼ cup chopped parsley

Salt and freshly ground pepper to taste

In a large soup pot over high heat, combine all ingredients except rice, parsley, salt, and pepper. Bring to a boil and skim off foam. Reduce heat to medium-low and simmer, covered, until chicken is no longer pink in the center, about 1 hour. Remove chicken to a plate to cool. Strain stock into a bowl and discard solids.

Remove chicken from bones, cut into bite-sized pieces, and set aside. Discard skin and bones. Using a fat separator, remove fat from stock and discard. (If time allows, cool stock in the refrigerator all day or overnight and then remove the layer of fat that forms on top.)

Return stock to pot and bring to a boil. Add rice and cook, covered, until tender, about 20 minutes. Return chicken to pot, add parsley, and simmer until heated through, about 10 minutes longer. Season with salt and pepper.

SERVES 6

# "CHICKEN SOUP FOR THE SOUL" (CHICKEN NOODLE SOUP)

**SERVES 6**

**Freshly made stock is the key to this warming soup. It's just what the doctor ordered!**

In a large soup pot, combine chicken, water, vegetables, and garlic. Bring to a boil. Skim off foam. Add parsley, basil, thyme, salt, peppercorns, bay leaf, and wine, if using. Reduce heat to medium-low, and simmer, covered, until chicken is very tender, 1 to 1½ hours. Remove chicken to a plate to cool. Drain stock into a bowl and discard solids.

Using a fat separator, degrease stock and return to the pan, or, if time allows, refrigerate overnight and remove fat that forms on top. Remove skin and bones from chicken and discard. Cut chicken into bite-sized pieces and add 2 to 3 cups chicken to stock (use the remainder for other purposes). Add noodles and bring to a boil. Reduce heat to medium-low and cook, uncovered, until noodles are tender, about 10 minutes. Taste for seasoning.

1 chicken (3 to 3½ pounds), quartered

10 cups water

1 yellow onion, quartered

3 carrots, each cut into 4 pieces

2 stalks celery, including some tops, cut up

2 cloves garlic, halved

3 sprigs parsley

3 or 4 fresh basil leaves, or ½ teaspoon dried basil

1 teaspoon dried thyme

1 teaspoon salt

1 teaspoon peppercorns

1 bay leaf

¼ cup dry white wine (optional)

4 ounces (2 cups) egg noodles

**A Southern soup with a little Creole influence. Serve over rice. Careful browning of the oil and flour adds flavor and color.**

¹/₄ cup vegetable oil

¹/₄ cup all-purpose flour

4 cups chicken stock or broth

1 can (14¹/₂ ounces) crushed tomatoes in thick purée

¹/₂ teaspoon salt

Freshly ground pepper to taste

¹/₂ teaspoon dried thyme

¹/₂ teaspoon Tabasco sauce

1 package (10 ounces) frozen okra, thawed, rinsed, and halved

2 cups cubed cooked chicken

In a heavy soup pot over medium-high heat, warm oil. Blend in flour and stir constantly until golden brown, 5 to 7 minutes. Add stock, tomatoes, salt, pepper, thyme, Tabasco sauce, okra, and chicken. Reduce heat to medium-low and simmer, uncovered, until flavors are blended, 15 to 20 minutes. Serve in bowls.

**100**

# MEXICAN CHICKEN, CORN, AND BEAN TORTILLA SOUP

**SERVES 6 TO 8**

**This hearty, thick soup loaded with chicken, corn, and beans serves as a main course. The toppings make it fun for a company dinner.**

In a large soup pot over medium-high heat, combine stock, chicken, onion, garlic, bell pepper, zucchini, chili powder, cumin, oregano, salt, and pepper. Cover and cook for 10 minutes. Reduce heat to medium-low. Add corn, black beans, and salsa and simmer, covered, until flavors are blended, stirring occasionally, about 30 minutes. Stir in cilantro and simmer, uncovered, 5 minutes. Ladle into bowls, top with a few crisp tortilla strips, and pass additional toppings separately.

5 to 6 cups chicken stock or broth

3 boned, skinned chicken breast halves (about 1½ pounds), cut into bite-sized pieces

1 yellow onion, chopped

1 clove garlic, minced

1 small red bell pepper, seeded and chopped

1 medium zucchini, quartered lengthwise and sliced

1 teaspoon chili powder

1 teaspoon dried ground cumin

1 teaspoon dried oregano

½ teaspoon salt

Freshly ground pepper to taste

2 cups corn kernels, fresh or frozen

1 can (15 ounces) black beans, drained and rinsed

1 cup Fresh Tomato Salsa (page 42) or purchased medium-hot salsa

⅓ cup chopped fresh cilantro or parsley

### TOPPINGS

10 corn tortillas, cut into strips and crisped (see page 26), or tortilla chips

Sour cream

Grated Monterey Jack cheese

Chopped green onions

Lime wedges

This famous Indian soup was originally developed by cooks who served in English homes during the colonization of India in the 18th century. It is based on chicken and vegetables cooked in a rich stock seasoned with curry. Sautéing the curry for a short period eliminates the raw taste and sweetens the spice. This version includes garbanzo beans and shredded coconut. For a heartier soup, serve it over a mound of cooked white rice.

1 tablespoon vegetable oil

$\frac{1}{2}$ tablespoon butter or margarine

1 cup chopped carrot

$\frac{1}{2}$ cup chopped onion

1 cup chopped celery

1 clove garlic, minced

$\frac{3}{4}$ cup chopped green bell pepper

$\frac{1}{2}$ cup chopped, peeled turnip

1 Granny Smith apple, unpeeled, chopped

1 teaspoon curry powder

$\frac{1}{4}$ teaspoon ground coriander

$\frac{1}{4}$ teaspoon ground cloves

$\frac{1}{4}$ teaspoon ground ginger

1 teaspoon salt

Freshly ground pepper to taste

6 cups chicken stock or broth

2 tablespoons cornstarch

$\frac{1}{3}$ cup cold water

2 cups cubed cooked chicken

1 can (15 ounces) garbanzo beans, drained and rinsed

Shredded coconut for topping

In a large soup pot over medium heat, warm oil and butter. Add carrot and sauté for 2 minutes. Add remaining vegetables and apple and sauté until tender, about 10 minutes longer. Add curry powder, coriander, cloves, ginger, salt, and pepper and stir for 1 minute. Add stock and bring to a boil.

In a small bowl or cup, mix cornstarch and water. Add to soup and stir until thickened, about 2 minutes. Add chicken. Purée beans with 1 cup stock from soup in a food processor. Add to soup pot and mix well. Reduce heat to medium-low and simmer, uncovered, until flavors are blended, about 10 minutes. Ladle into bowls and sprinkle with coconut.

# THAI GINGER CHICKEN SOUP

**SERVES 4**

**Tender slices of chicken breast and ginger are simmered in coconut milk with green onions and spices. This recipe can easily be doubled.**

In a soup pot over medium heat, bring coconut milk and water to a boil. Reduce heat to medium-low. Add chicken and cook, uncovered, 3 minutes. Stir in ginger, fish sauce, lime juice, and zest and cook, uncovered, 3 minutes. Stir in green onions and cilantro and mix well. Ladle into bowls and garnish with slivered chiles and cilantro sprigs.

3 cups canned unsweetened coconut milk

2 cups water

2 boned, skinned chicken breast halves (about 1 pound), cut into $^1/_2$-inch strips

1-inch section fresh ginger, peeled and grated

1 to 3 tablespoons Asian fish sauce (nam pla)

$^1/_4$ cup fresh lime juice

1 tablespoon grated lime zest

2 tablespoons sliced green onions, including some tender green tops

1 tablespoon chopped cilantro

2 red chile peppers, seeded and slivered for garnish

Fresh cilantro sprigs for garnish

**This zesty soup with chicken and chiles highlights the flavors of Mexico. Serve for a Sunday night supper with a variety of toppings and a basket of warm, soft tortillas.**

1 cup finely chopped yellow onion

3 cloves garlic, minced

8 cups chicken stock or broth

1 can (28 ounces) diced tomatoes with juice

1 can (4 ounces) chopped green chiles, drained

2 tablespoons chopped parsley or cilantro

1 teaspoon ground cumin

1 teaspoon sugar

$\frac{1}{2}$ teaspoon chili powder

$\frac{1}{2}$ teaspoon salt

Freshly ground pepper to taste

Juice of 2 limes

3 cups cubed cooked chicken breast

**TOPPINGS**

Grated Monterey Jack cheese or Cheddar cheese

Broken corn chips

Sliced avocado

Sour cream

In a large soup pot over high heat, combine all ingredients except chicken and toppings and bring to a boil. Reduce heat to medium-low and simmer, uncovered, about 20 minutes. Add chicken and cook until flavors are blended, about 10 minutes longer. Ladle into bowls and pass the toppings separately.

104

# TURKEY SOUP WITH ROOT VEGETABLES

**SERVES 6**

**Root vegetables are the classic winter vegetable because they are easily stored and keep for a long time. Serve this soup when the weather turns frosty.**

In a large soup pot over high heat, combine all ingredients except turkey and parsley. Bring to a boil. Reduce heat to medium-low and simmer, covered, until vegetables are tender-crisp, 15 to 20 minutes. Add turkey and simmer, uncovered, until flavors are blended, about 10 minutes longer. Ladle into bowls and sprinkle with chopped parsley.

5 to 6 cups turkey or chicken stock or broth

1 medium sweet potato (about 3/4 pound), peeled and chopped

1 medium turnip, peeled and chopped

1 medium parsnip, peeled and chopped

2 carrots, chopped

1 small yellow onion, chopped

1 tablespoon fresh thyme, or 1 teaspoon dried thyme

1 teaspoon salt

Freshly ground pepper to taste

2 cups cubed cooked turkey

Chopped parsley for topping

105

**If you think turkey soup is tasteless and boring, try this one jazzed up with chiles. Use the turkey carcass to make the stock (page 34).**

1 tablespoon olive oil

1 cup chopped yellow onion

1 clove garlic, minced

1 teaspoon chili powder

1 teaspoon salt

Freshly ground pepper to taste

1 teaspoon ground cumin

1 teaspoon dried oregano

1 can (4 ounces) diced green chiles, drained

4 cups turkey or chicken stock or broth

1 can (14½ ounces) crushed tomatoes in thick purée

2 cups cubed cooked turkey

2 cups corn kernels, fresh or frozen

¼ cup chopped cilantro or parsley

**TOPPINGS**

Grated Monterey Jack cheese

Broken tortilla chips

In a soup pot over medium heat, warm oil. Add onion and garlic and sauté until tender, about 5 minutes. Add chili powder, salt, pepper, cumin, oregano, and chiles and mix well. Add stock and tomatoes and bring to a boil. Reduce heat to medium-low and simmer, uncovered, about 10 minutes. Add turkey, corn, and cilantro and simmer until heated through and flavors are blended, about 15 minutes longer. Ladle into bowls and pass the toppings separately.

SERVES 6

# TURKEY SOUP WITH GREEN CHILES

# TURKEY, HAM, AND VEGETABLE CHOWDER

**SERVES 6**

**Turkey is combined with ham, vegetables, and herbs in this hearty chowder.**

In a large soup pot over medium-high heat, combine 2 cups of the stock, and all the remaining ingredients except the turkey and ham, and bring to a boil. Reduce heat to medium-low and simmer, covered, until vegetables are tender, 15 to 20 minutes. Transfer half of mixture to food processor and purée. Return mixture to pot, add remaining 2 cups stock, turkey, and ham and simmer, uncovered, until flavors are blended, about 15 minutes.

4 cups turkey or chicken stock or broth

1 cup chopped yellow onion

1 clove garlic, minced

2 stalks celery, chopped

2 carrots, chopped

3 medium russet potatoes (about 1½ pounds), peeled and diced

1 zucchini, unpeeled, quartered lengthwise and sliced

½ teaspoon dried basil

½ teaspoon dried marjoram

½ teaspoon salt

Freshly ground pepper to taste

1 cup cubed cooked turkey

1 cup cubed cooked ham

**Cheese tortellini is found in the refrigerated or frozen section of most supermarkets. It makes a great addition to this easy-to-make soup.**

8 cups turkey or chicken stock or broth

1/2 cup chopped red bell pepper

2 zucchini, unpeeled, quartered lengthwise and sliced

1 package (9 ounces) uncooked cheese-filled tortellini

2 to 3 cups cubed cooked turkey

1/4 cup chopped parsley

Salt and freshly ground pepper to taste

In a soup pot over high heat, bring stock to a boil. Add vegetables and tortellini. Reduce heat to medium-low and simmer, uncovered, until vegetables and tortellini are tender, about 7 minutes. Add turkey, parsley, salt, and pepper and simmer until flavors are blended, 5 to 10 minutes longer.

**108**

# TURKEY, VEGETABLE, AND RICE SOUP

**SERVES 6**

**Enjoy the good turkey flavors another day with this post-holiday soup that makes good use of leftovers.**

In a large soup pot over medium heat, warm oil. Add onion, celery, carrot, and bell pepper and sauté for 3 minutes. Add mushrooms and garlic and sauté until vegetables are tender, about 5 minutes longer. Stir in rice. Add stock, salt, poultry seasoning, marjoram, and pepper. Bring to a boil. Reduce heat to medium-low and simmer, covered, until rice is tender, about 20 minutes. Add turkey and simmer, uncovered, until flavors are blended, about 10 minutes longer.

2 tablespoons vegetable oil

1 cup chopped yellow onion

1 cup chopped celery

1 carrot, chopped

½ red bell pepper, seeded and chopped

8 ounces mushrooms, sliced

1 clove garlic, minced

½ cup uncooked long-grain white rice

8 cups turkey or chicken stock or broth

1 teaspoon salt

½ teaspoon poultry seasoning

¼ teaspoon dried marjoram

Freshly ground pepper to taste

2 cups cubed cooked turkey

109

# CREAMY MEXICAN TURKEY SOUP

**Mexican flavors are combined with vegetables and turkey in this flavorful soup. If you prefer less heat, reduce the amount of chili powder.**

1 carrot, chopped

1 stalk celery, chopped

1 cup chopped yellow onion

2 cloves garlic, chopped

2 cups turkey or chicken stock or broth

1 can (4 ounces) diced green chiles, drained

2 cups milk

$\frac{1}{4}$ cup all-purpose flour

1 teaspoon salt

1 teaspoon chili powder

$\frac{1}{4}$ teaspoon ground cumin

2 cups cubed cooked turkey

$\frac{3}{4}$ cup corn kernels, fresh or frozen

3 tablespoons chopped fresh cilantro
  or parsley

1 cup grated Monterey Jack cheese

In a large soup pot over high heat, combine vegetables, garlic, and stock and bring to a boil. Reduce heat to medium-low and simmer, covered, until vegetables are tender, 15 minutes. Add chiles.

In a bowl, whisk together milk, flour, salt, chili powder, and cumin. Increase heat to high and whisk milk mixture into soup. Stir until bubbly and thickened, about 5 minutes. Reduce heat to low. Add turkey, corn, cilantro, and cheese and stir until cheese is melted and soup is hot, 5 to 10 minutes.

**SERVES 6**

# ONE BIG POT OF CHICKEN AND VEGETABLE STEW

**SERVES 6**

**As this delicious chicken stew simmers away, you will enjoy the tempting aroma that fills the air. Your family will want seconds, but leftovers are good, too.**

In a large Dutch oven over medium-high heat, warm oil. Brown chicken in batches, about 5 minutes on each side. Transfer chicken to a plate as it browns. Pour off excess grease. Return chicken to Dutch oven. Add stock, marjoram, thyme, paprika, salt, pepper, carrots, turnip, onion, and garlic. Reduce heat to low and simmer, covered, 20 minutes, stirring once. Add potatoes and mushrooms and stir. Continue to simmer, covered, 40 minutes longer. Stir in peas and cook, uncovered, until vegetables are tender and chicken is no longer pink in the center, about 10 minutes longer.

In a small bowl, mix flour with water. Bring stew to a boil and add flour mixture. Cook, stirring constantly, until slightly thickened, about 2 minutes.

Serve in bowls and sprinkle with parsley.

1 tablespoon vegetable oil

1 large chicken (4 to 4½ pounds), cut up (meaty parts only)

1¾ cups chicken stock or broth

¼ teaspoon dried marjoram

¼ teaspoon dried thyme

½ teaspoon paprika

1 teaspoon salt

Freshly ground pepper to taste

2 carrots, cut diagonally in 1-inch slices

1 turnip, peeled and quartered

1 small yellow onion, quartered

3 whole cloves garlic

2 medium new potatoes, peeled and quartered

6 ounces medium mushrooms

1 cup peas, fresh or frozen

3 tablespoons all-purpose flour

½ cup water

Chopped parsley for topping

**The contrasting colors of red, green, and yellow bell peppers make a colorful centerpiece. Include crusty bread for a satisfying meal.**

2 tablespoons vegetable oil

8 chicken drumsticks

1 yellow onion, chopped

2 cloves garlic, minced

1 large green bell pepper, seeded and cut into strips

1 large red bell pepper, seeded and cut into strips

1 large yellow bell pepper, seeded and cut into strips

8 ounces medium mushrooms, thickly sliced

1 can (14$\frac{1}{2}$ ounces) diced tomatoes, with juice

1 teaspoon dried oregano

$\frac{1}{2}$ teaspoon salt

Freshly ground pepper to taste

Chopped parsley for topping

In a Dutch oven over medium heat, warm 1 tablespoon of the oil. Add chicken and brown on all sides, about 10 minutes. Remove to a plate. Add remaining 1 tablespoon oil. Add onion, garlic, bell peppers, and mushrooms and sauté until slightly soft, about 3 minutes. Stir in tomatoes, oregano, salt, and pepper. Reduce heat to low, return chicken to pan, and simmer, covered, until chicken is no longer pink in the center and vegetables are tender, 40 to 50 minutes. Sprinkle with parsley.

**112**

# CHICKEN THIGHS AND VEGETABLE STEW ON POLENTA

**SERVES 4 TO 6**

**This Italian dish was a favorite at one of our tasting parties. We served it with polenta for a complete entrée along with olive bread, a tossed green salad, and spumoni ice cream.**

On a piece of waxed paper, combine flour, salt, and pepper. Roll chicken in mixture to coat evenly. Reserve any remaining flour mixture.

In a large Dutch oven over medium-high heat, warm oil. Add chicken and brown for about 5 minutes on each side. Transfer browned chicken to a plate. Reduce heat to medium. Add onion, garlic, celery, and carrot and sauté until tender, about 5 minutes. Return chicken to Dutch oven. Add stock, tomatoes, wine, basil, and parsley. Bring to a boil. Reduce heat to medium-low and simmer, covered, 30 minutes. Stir in reserved flour. Add zucchini and simmer, uncovered, until chicken is no longer pink in the center, about 30 minutes longer. Spoon over polenta.

¼ cup all-purpose flour

1 teaspoon salt

¼ teaspoon freshly ground pepper

6 chicken thighs (about 2¼ pounds), fat and skin removed (see page 25)

1½ tablespoons olive oil

½ cup chopped yellow onion

1 clove garlic, minced

2 stalks celery, chopped

1 carrot, chopped

1 cup chicken stock or broth

1 can (14½ ounces) whole tomatoes, coarsely chopped, with juice

¼ cup dry white wine

¾ teaspoon dried basil

¼ cup chopped parsley

1 zucchini, unpeeled, quartered lengthwise and cut into ½-inch slices

Basic Polenta (recipe follows)

# BASIC POLENTA

**This Italian staple is basically a porridge made of corn-meal. It can be served soft or can be chilled until set, sliced, and then fried, broiled, or grilled.**

1 cup yellow cornmeal
3½ cups cold water
¼ teaspoon salt
¼ cup freshly grated Parmesan cheese
1 tablespoon butter or margarine

In a bowl, mix cornmeal with 1 cup of the water. In a saucepan over high heat, combine remaining 2½ cups water and salt and bring to a boil. Slowly pour cornmeal mixture into boiling water, stirring constantly. Reduce heat to low and simmer, uncovered, stirring constantly until thick and smooth, about 3 to 5 minutes. Remove from heat. Stir in Parmesan cheese and butter. Immediately spoon onto plates or bowls and serve with stew.

# CHICKEN, TOMATO, ZUCCHINI, AND ORZO STEW

**SERVES 4**

**If you need a quick dinner, this is it. Tender bites of chicken breast simmer together with vegetables and orzo in this one-step stew. It goes together fast and is easy to make.**

In a large soup pot over medium heat, combine tomatoes, stock, garlic, basil, thyme, marjoram, salt, and pepper. Bring to a boil. Add chicken, wine, orzo, and zucchini. Reduce heat to medium-low and simmer, covered, until chicken is no longer pink in the center and orzo is tender, 20 to 25 minutes.

2 cans (14½ ounces each) diced tomatoes, with juice

1½ cups chicken stock or broth

2 cloves garlic, minced

1 teaspoon dried basil

½ teaspoon dried thyme

½ teaspoon dried marjoram

1 teaspoon salt

Freshly ground pepper to taste

2 boned, skinned chicken breast halves (about 1 pound), cut into bite-sized pieces

¼ cup dry white wine

1 cup uncooked orzo

2 medium zucchini, trimmed and cut into ½-inch slices

**This Creole specialty is a mainstay of New Orleans cuisine. As with all popular dishes, there are many variations. It often includes other meats and shellfish along with vegetables, but it always features okra. Serve in bowls over hot, fluffy rice.**

1 tablespoon vegetable oil

1 yellow onion, chopped

1 green bell pepper, seeded and cut into bite-sized pieces

2 cloves garlic, minced

2 stalks celery, chopped

$1\frac{1}{2}$ tablespoons all-purpose flour

2 cups chicken stock or broth

1 can ($14\frac{1}{2}$ ounces) diced tomatoes, with juice

$\frac{1}{4}$ teaspoon dried thyme, crumbled

1 teaspoon Worcestershire sauce

1 bay leaf

$\frac{1}{2}$ teaspoon salt

$\frac{1}{8}$ teaspoon cayenne pepper

4 boned, skinned chicken breast halves (about 2 pounds), cut into bite-sized pieces

1 cup frozen okra, thawed, rinsed, and halved (see Note)

3 tablespoons chopped parsley

In a Dutch oven over medium heat, warm oil. Add onion, bell pepper, garlic, and celery (see Note). Sauté until tender, about 5 minutes. Sprinkle with flour and cook, stirring, for 2 minutes. Add stock, tomatoes, thyme, Worcestershire sauce, bay leaf, salt, and cayenne. Stir until slightly thickened, about 2 minutes. Add chicken. Reduce heat to medium-low and cook, covered, until chicken is no longer pink in the center, about 30 minutes, stirring occasionally. Add okra and parsley and cook, uncovered, until heated through, about 10 minutes longer. Remove bay leaf and discard. Serve in large bowls.

**NOTE:** *If you prefer to use fresh okra, trim it and cook it with the other vegetables.*

115

# CHICKEN AND BUTTERMILK-THYME DUMPLINGS

**SERVES 4 TO 6**

**For old-fashioned goodness and flavor, here is an easy way to make this classic dish. You can make it ahead and then cook the dumplings in it just before serving.**

In a large soup pot over high heat, bring stock, chicken, vegetables, thyme, salt, pepper, and bay leaf to a boil. Reduce heat to medium-low and simmer, covered, until chicken is no longer pink in the center, about 45 minutes. Remove bay leaf and discard.

Meanwhile, make dumpling batter and set aside.

Increase heat to medium-high. Blend flour and water in a small bowl or cup and stir into stew until thickened, 1 to 2 minutes.

To cook dumplings, drop batter by heaping teaspoonfuls on top of hot stew. Reduce heat to medium and cook, uncovered, 10 minutes. Cover and cook until a tester comes out clean when inserted into a dumpling, about 10 minutes longer. Serve immediately.

5 cups chicken stock or broth

4 chicken thighs (about 1½ pounds), fat and skin removed (see page 25)

4 chicken drumsticks (about 1½ pounds), fat and skin removed

1 cup chopped yellow onion

½ cup sliced celery

2 cups baby carrots

½ teaspoon dried thyme

¾ teaspoon salt

Freshly ground pepper to taste

1 bay leaf

Buttermilk-Thyme Dumplings (recipe follows)

¼ cup all-purpose flour

¼ cup water

# BUTTERMILK-THYME DUMPLINGS

2 cups all-purpose flour

1 tablespoon baking powder

½ teaspoon salt

¼ teaspoon dried thyme

1 cup buttermilk

Combine all ingredients in a bowl and stir until just blended.

# CHICKEN IN SPICY TOMATO SAUCE ON PASTA

**SERVES 4**

**This is a fusion of Greek and Italian flavors. The chicken is cooked in a fragrant, spicy sauce and served over pasta. Serve with Parmesan Crostini (page 62).**

In a large Dutch oven over medium-high heat, warm oil. Add chicken and brown 5 minutes on each side. Remove to a platter. In a small bowl, mix flour, spices, sugar, salt, and pepper.

Add onion and celery to Dutch oven and sauté until tender, about 5 minutes. Add spice mixture and stir until fragrant, about 1 minute. Stir in tomatoes, stock, vinegar, and tomato paste. Return chicken to Dutch oven. Reduce heat to medium-low and simmer, partially covered, until chicken is tender, about 45 minutes.

Remove lid and simmer, uncovered, until sauce is slightly thickened, about 30 minutes longer.

Meanwhile, in a large pot of boiling water, cook pasta until tender, 10 to 12 minutes. Drain well and place on platter. Arrange chicken on top and pour sauce over. Sprinkle generously with Parmesan cheese.

3 tablespoons olive oil

1 chicken (3 to 3½ pounds), cut into serving pieces (use meaty pieces)

1 tablespoon all-purpose flour

1 teaspoon ground cumin

1 teaspoon paprika

½ teaspoon ground allspice

½ teaspoon ground cinnamon

¼ teaspoon ground cloves

⅛ teaspoon cayenne pepper

1 teaspoon sugar

1 teaspoon salt

Freshly ground pepper to taste

1 cup chopped red onion

2 stalks celery, sliced

1 can (28 ounces) whole tomatoes, coarsely chopped, with juice

½ cup chicken stock or broth

2 tablespoons red wine vinegar

2 tablespoons tomato paste

10 ounces uncooked vermicelli pasta

Freshly grated Parmesan cheese for topping

**Whoever heard of a peanut butter, jelly, and chicken stew? Well, here it is, and it's delicious. The jelly adds just a touch of sweetness, and the peanut butter lends a nutty taste and extra crunch. Serve with white bread.**

2 tablespoons vegetable oil

1 chicken (3 to 3½ pounds), cut up

1 large yellow onion, quartered

1 red bell pepper, seeded and cut into ½-inch strips

8 ounces large mushrooms, quartered

2 cups chicken stock or broth

1 tablespoon tomato paste

1 tablespoon berry jelly or jam

½ cup chunky peanut butter

½ teaspoon salt

2 tablespoons chopped parsley

Chopped peanuts for topping (optional)

In a large Dutch oven over medium-high heat, warm oil. Add chicken and brown in batches, about 5 minutes on each side. Remove chicken to a plate as it browns. Add onion, bell pepper, and mushrooms and sauté for 2 minutes. Return chicken to Dutch oven.

In a small bowl, whisk together stock, tomato paste, jelly, peanut butter, salt, and parsley and pour over chicken. Reduce heat to medium-low and simmer, covered, until chicken is no longer pink in the center, about 1 hour. To serve, sprinkle a few chopped peanuts on top, if desired.

**118**

# CAJUN STEW, NEW ORLEANS STYLE

**SERVES 4**

**Andouille sausage is a smoked, spicy sausage of French origin often used in Cajun cooking. Cajun seasoning is a blend of seasonings available in supermarkets, or you can make your own using the recipe given here. This combination of chicken and sausage makes a great stew. Serve over hot, fluffy rice.**

In a large Dutch oven over medium-high heat, warm oil. Add chicken and brown for about 5 minutes on each side. Remove to a plate. Add sausage and brown for 3 to 4 minutes. Remove to plate holding chicken. Reduce heat to medium. Add onion, garlic, and bell pepper and sauté until tender, about 5 minutes. Add flour and stir until bubbly. Add stock and stir until slightly thickened, 1 to 2 minutes. Return chicken and sausage to pan. Add Cajun seasoning and salt. Reduce heat to medium-low and simmer, covered, until chicken is no longer pink in center, about 45 minutes. Serve in large bowls.

1 to 2 tablespoons vegetable oil

4 chicken thighs (about 1$\frac{1}{2}$ pounds)

6 ounces andouille sausage (2 sausages), cut into $\frac{1}{2}$-inch slices

1 large yellow onion, chopped

2 cloves garlic, minced

1 green bell pepper, seeded and chopped

2 tablespoons all-purpose flour

2 cups chicken stock or broth

1 to 2 teaspoons Cajun seasoning, depending on taste (recipe follows)

1 teaspoon salt

119

# CAJUN SEASONING

1 teaspoon garlic powder

1 teaspoon dried basil

1 teaspoon dried thyme

1/4 teaspoon dried oregano

1 teaspoon paprika

1/2 teaspoon celery salt

1/2 teaspoon ground white pepper

1/2 teaspoon finely ground black pepper

1/2 teaspoon onion powder

1/4 teaspoon ground cayenne pepper

In a small bowl, mix all ingredients. Store in a tightly covered jar.

# CHICKEN STEW WITH ARTICHOKES AND MUSHROOMS

**SERVES 4**

**A good mix and match of chicken with vegetables. Fresh rosemary is added at the end for extra flavor.**

On a piece of waxed paper, combine flour, salt, and pepper. Roll chicken in mixture to coat. Reserve any remaining flour mixture. In a large Dutch oven over medium-high heat, warm oil. Add chicken and brown for 5 minutes on each side.

Add onions, potatoes, and stock. Bring to a boil. Reduce heat to medium-low and simmer, covered, 45 minutes. Add mushrooms, artichokes, and rosemary and simmer, covered, 15 minutes. Add peas and cook, uncovered, until vegetables are tender and chicken is no longer pink in the center, about 5 minutes longer.

To thicken sauce, blend remaining flour mixture with ¼ cup water and stir into stew until thickened, 1 to 2 minutes.

¼ cup all-purpose flour

¾ teaspoon salt

Freshly ground pepper to taste

6 chicken thighs (about 2¼ pounds), fat and skin removed (see page 25)

1 tablespoon vegetable oil

8 small boiling onions, peeled (see page 24)

1 pound medium red new potatoes, unpeeled, cut into quarters

1½ cups chicken stock or broth

8 ounces medium mushrooms, halved

1 can (14 ounces) quartered artichoke hearts, drained

1 tablespoon snipped fresh rosemary or 1 teaspoon dried rosemary

1 cup peas, fresh or frozen

**This Asian-inspired stew consists of chicken, snow peas, bean sprouts, and water chestnuts. Marinating the chicken in a beer sauce gives it a sensational flavor. Serve with rice to absorb the flavorful sauce.**

1 chicken (3 to 3½ pounds), cut into serving pieces

1 can (12 ounces) beer, allowed to go flat

6 green onions, including some tender green tops, sliced

2 cloves garlic, chopped

½ cup soy sauce

1 tablespoon vegetable oil

1 tablespoon fresh lemon juice

1 packed tablespoon brown sugar

1 tablespoon hoisin sauce

1 tablespoon grated fresh ginger, or 1 teaspoon ground ginger

8 ounces snow peas, ends trimmed

1 can (5 ounces) sliced water chestnuts, drained

2 tablespoons cornstarch

3 tablespoons water

2 cups bean sprouts, rinsed

In a large nonreactive soup pot, combine all ingredients except peas, water chestnuts, cornstarch, water, and sprouts. Cover and marinate in the refrigerator for several hours, turning once. Place the pot containing chicken and marinade over high heat and bring to a boil. Reduce heat to medium-low and simmer, covered, basting several times, until chicken is tender and no longer pink in the center, about 1 hour. Add peas and water chestnuts and simmer, uncovered, 10 to 15 minutes longer.

In a small bowl, blend cornstarch and water. Stir into stew and cook until liquid is thickened and clear, about 2 minutes. Stir in sprouts. Remove chicken to a platter. Pour sauce over chicken and serve.

**NOTE:** *This marinated chicken is also good cooked on the grill.*

# COQ AU VIN

**SERVES 6 TO 8**

**In French, *coq au vin* means chicken cooked in wine. White or red wine can be used, but red is more traditional. The chicken stews in a flavorful sauce along with bacon, carrots, onions, mushrooms, and herbs. This recipe takes time to prepare, but once it is made, you have an elegant dish to serve company.**

In a Dutch oven over medium-high heat, cook bacon until crisp, about 5 minutes. With a slotted spoon, remove bacon to a large plate. Leave 2 tablespoons bacon drippings in Dutch oven. Reduce heat to medium. Brown chicken in batches in bacon drippings, about 5 minutes on each side. Transfer chicken to the plate holding the bacon as it browns. (If there are not enough bacon drippings, add a little oil or butter).

Preheat oven to 350°F. Over medium heat, add flour to Dutch oven and stir until bubbly. Add thyme, marjoram, salt, pepper, bay leaf, wine, stock, and tomato paste. Stir until thickened, about 2 minutes. Add mushrooms, carrots, and onions. Return bacon and chicken and any accumulated juices to Dutch oven.

Bake, covered, until chicken is no longer pink in the center and vegetables are tender, about 1 hour and 15 minutes. Remove bay leaf and discard. Sprinkle with parsley before serving.

4 thick slices bacon, diced

3 pounds meaty chicken parts, excess fat and skin removed (see page 25)

3 tablespoons all-purpose flour

1/2 teaspoon dried thyme

1/2 teaspoon dried marjoram

1/2 teaspoon salt

Freshly ground pepper to taste

1 bay leaf

1 cup dry red wine

1 cup chicken stock or broth

1 tablespoon tomato paste

8 ounces medium mushrooms

1 1/2 cups baby carrots

1 cup small boiling onions, peeled (see page 24), or 1 cup frozen small onions

3 tablespoons chopped fresh parsley for topping

**Dating back to 1828 in Brunswick County, Virginia, this stew was originally made with squirrel and onion. Today, it is made with rabbit or chicken, along with vegetables that simmer in a flavorful tomato sauce.**

3 slices thick bacon, diced

1 cup chopped yellow onion

1 chicken (3 to 3½ pounds), cut into serving pieces

2 cups chicken stock or broth

2 cups water

2 cups peeled, diced potatoes

3 carrots, cut diagonally into 1-inch slices

2 stalks celery, chopped

1 teaspoon salt

1 can (14½ ounces) whole tomatoes, coarsely chopped, with juice

1 can (8 ounces) tomato sauce

1 cup cubed ham

1 package (10 ounces) frozen okra, thawed, rinsed, and halved

1 package (10 ounces) frozen baby lima beans, rinsed

1 cup corn kernels, fresh or frozen

1 teaspoon Worcestershire sauce

2 or 3 drops Tabasco sauce

3 tablespoons all-purpose flour

⅓ cup water

In a large Dutch oven over medium heat, cook bacon and onion until bacon is crisp and onion is tender, 5 to 6 minutes. With a slotted spoon, remove bacon and onion to a plate, leaving drippings in Dutch oven. Add chicken and brown in batches, about 5 minutes on each side. Add stock, water, potatoes, carrots, celery, salt, and reserved bacon and onion. Bring to a boil. Reduce heat to medium-low and simmer, covered, about 45 minutes. Skim off fat. Add tomatoes, tomato sauce, ham, okra, lima beans, corn, Worcestershire sauce, and Tabasco sauce. Bring to a boil. Reduce heat and simmer, covered, until vegetables are tender and chicken is no longer pink in the center, 15 to 20 minutes longer.

In a small bowl or cup, blend flour and water. Increase heat to medium-high and stir into stew until slightly thickened, 1 to 2 minutes. Taste for seasonings.

# GREEK CHICKEN STEW WITH RICE

**SERVES 4 TO 6**

**Add variety to your menu with this Greek-style chicken stew with olives, topped with feta cheese. Serve with warm pita bread.**

In a large Dutch oven over medium-high heat, warm oil. Add chicken and brown, about 5 minutes on each side. Transfer browned chicken to a plate. Reduce heat to medium. Add more oil if needed. Add onion and garlic and sauté until tender, about 5 minutes. Stir in rice. Return chicken to pan. Add stock, lemon juice, oregano, salt, and pepper. Reduce heat to medium-low and cook, covered, until chicken is no longer pink in the center, rice is tender, and liquid is absorbed, about 1 hour and 15 minutes. Stir in olives. Place on a platter with chicken on top of rice, and sprinkle with feta cheese.

1 tablespoon olive oil

1 chicken (3 to 3½ pounds), cut into serving pieces

1 small yellow onion, chopped

3 cloves garlic, minced

1 cup long-grain brown rice

1¾ cups chicken stock or broth

¼ cup fresh lemon juice

1 teaspoon dried oregano

½ teaspoon salt

Freshly ground pepper to taste

½ cup pitted kalamata olives or ripe black olives

¼ cup crumbled feta cheese for topping

**This Italian specialty is prepared "hunter style," with chicken baked in a tomato sauce seasoned with onions and herbs. Serve over plain spaghetti or noodles and offer a simple tossed green salad.**

¼ cup all-purpose flour

½ teaspoon salt, plus more to taste

⅛ teaspoon freshly ground pepper, plus more to taste

3½ to 4 pounds meaty chicken parts (legs, thighs, breasts)

2 tablespoons olive oil, plus more if needed

1 cup chopped yellow onion

8 ounces mushrooms, sliced

1 can (16 ounces) plum tomatoes, coarsely chopped, with juice

1 can (16 ounces) tomato sauce

2 cloves garlic, minced

¼ cup dry white wine

¼ cup chopped parsley

½ teaspoon dried basil

¼ teaspoon dried marjoram

¼ teaspoon dried thyme

¼ teaspoon dried oregano

Freshly grated Parmesan cheese for topping

Preheat oven to 350°F. On a large piece of waxed paper, mix together flour, ½ teaspoon salt, and ⅛ teaspoon pepper. Roll chicken pieces in mixture to coat evenly. Reserve any remaining flour mixture.

In a large Dutch oven over medium-high heat, warm 2 tablespoons oil. Add chicken and brown, about 5 minutes on each side. Transfer browned chicken to a plate. Reduce heat to medium. Add onion and sauté for 3 minutes, adding more oil, if needed. Add mushrooms and cook until mushrooms are just beginning to give off their juices, 2 to 3 minutes longer. Transfer to plate holding chicken.

To Dutch oven, add tomatoes and their juice, tomato sauce, garlic, wine, parsley, herbs, salt and pepper to taste, and any remaining flour mixture. Stir a few minutes to blend. Return chicken and vegetables to Dutch oven.

Bake, covered, until chicken is tender and no longer showing pink in the center, about 1 hour. Serve sprinkled with Parmesan cheese.

# COUNTRY CAPTAIN

**SERVES 6**

This spicy, fragrant stew dates back to early colonial times. It is said that a British sea captain brought the recipe back from India via England and that it was served by a famous hostess from Georgia to Franklin Roosevelt. It is traditionally served on rice and sprinkled with almonds.

In a large Dutch oven over medium heat, warm 1 tablespoon oil. Add onion, bell pepper, mushrooms, and garlic and sauté until tender, about 5 minutes. Add chicken and sauté for 2 minutes. Add more oil, if needed. Add spices and cook until chicken turns white, stirring often. Add stock, tomatoes, salt, pepper, and raisins. Bring to a boil. Reduce heat to medium-low. Simmer, covered, until flavors are blended, about 20 minutes. Serve in bowls and sprinkle with almonds.

1 to 2 tablespoons vegetable oil

1 large yellow onion, chopped

1 green bell pepper, seeded and chopped

8 ounces mushrooms, sliced

2 cloves garlic, minced

4 boned, skinned chicken breast halves (about 2 pounds), cut into 1-inch pieces

1 tablespoon curry powder

1 teaspoon dried ginger

$\frac{1}{2}$ teaspoon ground cinnamon

$\frac{1}{4}$ teaspoon ground cloves

$\frac{1}{4}$ teaspoon ground nutmeg, or freshly grated nutmeg

$2\frac{1}{2}$ cups chicken stock or broth

1 can ($14\frac{1}{2}$ ounces) diced tomatoes, with juice

$\frac{3}{4}$ teaspoon salt

Freshly ground pepper to taste

$\frac{1}{2}$ cup raisins or dried currants

$\frac{1}{3}$ cup toasted sliced almonds (see page 26) for topping

172

# MEDITERRANEAN CHICKEN STEW

**The aromatic flavor of fennel and the addition of kalamata olives give this stew a Mediterranean accent. Serve with a loaf of peasant bread and a tossed Greek salad.**

1 to 2 tablespoons olive oil

3 pounds mixed chicken thighs and drumsticks

³/₄ teaspoon salt, plus more to taste

Freshly ground pepper to taste

1 large bulb fennel, green foliage removed, thinly sliced (save some foliage for garnish)

1 cup chopped yellow onion

1 red bell pepper, seeded and sliced into strips

8 ounces mushrooms, halved

2 cloves garlic, minced

1 can (14¹/₂ ounces) diced tomatoes, with juice

¹/₂ cup chicken stock or broth

2 tablespoons lemon juice

¹/₂ teaspoon dried oregano

2 tablespoons all-purpose flour

¹/₄ cup water

¹/₄ cup pitted kalamata olives

Fennel foliage for garnish

In a Dutch oven over medium heat, warm 1 tablespoon oil. Brown chicken, about 5 minutes on each side. Season with salt and pepper to taste while cooking. Transfer to a plate.

Add fennel, onion, bell pepper, mushrooms, and garlic, and sauté until slightly tender, about 5 minutes. Add more oil if needed. Add tomatoes, stock, lemon juice, oregano, ³/₄ teaspoon salt, and pepper to taste. Return chicken to Dutch oven. Reduce heat to medium-low and simmer, covered, until chicken is no longer pink in the center and vegetables are tender, about 40 minutes. In a bowl, blend flour and water and stir into stew. Add olives and cook, uncovered, 10 minutes longer. Garnish each serving with a small piece of fennel foliage.

SERVES 4

# CHICKEN OR TURKEY MEATBALL STEW WITH PASTA

**SERVES 4 TO 6**

**These meatballs are baked in the oven, eliminating browning and extra fat, and then simmered in a basil-scented vegetable sauce with pasta added. You can make the meatballs in advance.**

Preheat oven to 400°F. In a bowl, mix ground chicken, bread crumbs, shallots, Parmesan cheese, poultry seasoning, basil, salt, and pepper. Cover and refrigerate for 30 minutes. Form mixture into 1½-inch balls, flouring hands to prevent sticking. Place on a baking sheet and bake until lightly browned and firm, 15 minutes. Meanwhile, prepare Tomato-Vegetable Sauce with Basil.

Add meatballs and cooked ziti to tomato-vegetable sauce. Simmer, uncovered, until flavors are blended, about 10 minutes. Sprinkle with Parmesan cheese before serving.

1½ pounds ground chicken or ground turkey

1 cup fresh sourdough bread crumbs (1 slice)

¼ cup fine dry bread crumbs

2 shallots, finely chopped

2 tablespoons grated Parmesan cheese

¼ teaspoon poultry seasoning

2 tablespoons chopped fresh basil, or ½ teaspoon dried basil

½ teaspoon salt

Freshly ground pepper to taste

Flour, for coating hands while making meatballs

Tomato-Vegetable Sauce with Basil (recipe follows)

4 ounces (1½ cups) ziti, cooked as directed on package

Freshly grated Parmesan cheese for topping

# TOMATO-VEGETABLE SAUCE WITH BASIL

1 tablespoon vegetable oil

$\frac{1}{2}$ green bell pepper, chopped

$\frac{1}{2}$ red bell pepper, chopped

1 medium onion, chopped

1 clove garlic, chopped

1 can (28 ounces) crushed tomatoes in thick purée

3 basil leaves, chopped, or $\frac{1}{2}$ teaspoon dried basil

$\frac{1}{2}$ teaspoon sugar

$\frac{1}{2}$ teaspoon salt

Freshly ground pepper to taste

In a large Dutch oven over medium heat, warm oil. Add bell peppers, onion, and garlic and sauté until tender, about 5 minutes. Add tomatoes, basil, sugar, salt, and pepper. Reduce heat to medium-low and simmer, uncovered, about 10 minutes, stirring occasionally.

# ITALIAN CHICKEN AND SQUASH STEW WITH ROTELLE

**SERVES 4**

**Chicken and vegetables simmer in a flavorful sauce with pasta added for a complete meal. Serve with focaccia and a tossed green salad with Italian dressing.**

In a soup pot over high heat, combine tomatoes, stock, garlic, sugar, basil, oregano, salt, and pepper. Bring to a boil. Reduce heat to medium-low and simmer, covered, 5 minutes.

Add chicken, squashes, and mushrooms. Bring to a boil. Reduce heat to medium-low and simmer, covered, until vegetables are tender-crisp and chicken is no longer pink in the center, about 10 minutes. Add pasta and parsley and cook, uncovered, until pasta is tender, about 10 minutes longer. In a bowl or cup, blend flour with water. Stir into stew until thickened, about 2 minutes. Sprinkle with Parmesan cheese before serving.

1 can (14$\frac{1}{2}$ ounces) Italian-style tomatoes with juice, slightly puréed

2 cups chicken stock or broth

2 cloves garlic, minced

$\frac{1}{2}$ teaspoon sugar

$\frac{1}{2}$ teaspoon dried basil

$\frac{1}{4}$ teaspoon dried oregano

$\frac{1}{2}$ teaspoon salt

Freshly ground pepper to taste

3 boned, skinned chicken breast halves (about 1$\frac{1}{2}$ pounds), cut into 1-inch pieces

1 small crookneck squash, unpeeled, cut into 1-inch slices

1 small zucchini, unpeeled, cut into 1-inch slices

1 cup sliced mushrooms

2 ounces (about 1 cup) uncooked rotelle pasta

$\frac{1}{4}$ cup chopped parsley

2 tablespoons all-purpose flour

$\frac{1}{4}$ cup water

Parmesan cheese for topping

# CARIBBEAN TURKEY STEW

Here is a highly distinctive stew with the flavors of the Caribbean. Serve with rice for a delicious and substantial meal.

2 turkey thighs (about 1¼ pounds)

1 cup orange juice

½ cup chicken stock or broth

1 teaspoon cider vinegar

¼ teaspoon ground allspice

¼ teaspoon ground ginger

Dash of ground nutmeg

½ teaspoon salt

Freshly ground pepper to taste

1 sweet potato (about 1 pound), peeled and cubed

1 small yellow onion, cut into ½-inch wedges

½ green bell pepper, cut into 1-inch pieces

Cooked white rice

In a large soup pot over high heat, bring turkey, orange juice, stock, vinegar, allspice, ginger, nutmeg, salt, and pepper to a boil. Reduce heat to medium-low and simmer, covered, about 35 minutes. Add sweet potato, onion, and bell pepper, and cook, covered, until turkey is no longer pink in the center, about 20 minutes longer. Transfer turkey to a plate and cool. Remove meat from bones and set aside. Discard bones and skin.

Return turkey to pot and simmer, uncovered, until heated through and flavors are blended, about 10 minutes longer. Serve over rice.

SERVES 4

# CHICKEN CACCIATORE SOUP

**SERVES 4**

**131**

**All the good flavors of this popular Italian dish made into a hearty soup. Serve with Classic Garlic Bread (page 49).**

In a large soup pot over medium heat, warm oil. Add onion, bell pepper, and garlic and sauté 2 minutes. Add mushrooms and chicken and sauté until chicken turns white and vegetables are tender, about 5 minutes longer. Add stock, basil, oregano, salt, pepper, and rotini. Raise heat to high and bring to a boil, then reduce heat to medium-low and cook, uncovered, until rotini is tender, about 7 minutes. Add tomato sauce, wine, and parsley and cook, uncovered, until flavors are blended, about 10 minutes longer. To thicken, mix flour and water in a bowl and stir into soup. Bring to a boil and stir until thickened, 1 to 2 minutes. Ladle into bowls, sprinkle with Parmesan cheese, and serve immediately.

2 tablespoons vegetable oil

1 cup chopped yellow onion

1/2 cup chopped green bell pepper

2 cloves garlic, minced

4 ounces medium mushrooms, sliced

2 boned and skinned chicken breast halves, cut into bite-sized pieces

4 cups chicken stock or broth

1/4 teaspoon dried basil

1/4 teaspoon dried oregano

1 teaspoon salt

Freshly ground pepper to taste

1 cup uncooked rotini

1 can (8 ounces) tomato sauce

1/4 cup dry white wine

1/4 cup chopped parsley

2 tablespoons all-purpose flour

1/4 cup water

Freshly grated Parmesan cheese for topping

# SEAFOOD

## SOUPS & STEWS

Seafood soups and stews add variety and health benefits to the menu. Coastal areas have the advantage of easy access to a large supply and selection, but with today's air transportation, seafood is regularly available in most parts of the country.

Adding seafood to soups and stews provides more flavor at less cost, because smaller amounts of fish or shellfish are required.
Included in this chapter are the traditional chowders, tasty seafood and vegetable soups, seafood stews, and other popular combinations.

# SHRIMP AND SCALLOP CHOWDER

**SERVES 6**

**When it comes to seafood soup, this is one of the best. You can add or substitute other seafood in this basic recipe. Sprinkle each serving with sliced chives. Serve with Parmesan Crostini (page 62).**

In a large soup pot over medium heat, melt butter. Add onion and celery and sauté until tender, about 5 minutes. Add potatoes, stock, clam juice, wine, tomato paste, tomatoes, thyme, paprika, salt, and pepper. Reduce heat to medium-low and simmer, covered, until potatoes are tender, 20 to 25 minutes.

In a bowl, whisk flour and milk together until blended. Add to chowder and cook over medium heat until thickened, stirring constantly, about 3 minutes. Add shrimp, scallops, and parsley and mix well. Cook, covered, until seafood is done and flavors are blended, 5 to 10 minutes longer. Ladle into bowls and sprinkle with chives.

**NOTE:** *Bay shrimp and bay scallops are the small ones.*

1 tablespoon butter or margarine

1 cup chopped yellow onion

1 large stalk celery, chopped

2 medium new potatoes, unpeeled, cubed

1 cup chicken stock or broth

1 bottle (8 ounces) clam juice

½ cup dry white wine

1 tablespoon tomato paste

1 can (14½ ounces) whole tomatoes, coarsely chopped, with juice

½ teaspoon dried thyme

1 teaspoon paprika

½ teaspoon salt

Freshly ground pepper to taste

¼ cup all-purpose flour

1 cup milk

⅓ pound bay shrimp (see Note)

⅓ pound bay scallops (see Note)

½ cup chopped parsley

Sliced chives for topping

**Make this big pot of seafood soup the centerpiece for a party, with guests helping themselves. Provide large, wide bowls and several ladles. Serve with tangy coleslaw and Three-Cheese Bread (page 47).**

3 tablespoons butter or margarine

2 yellow onions, chopped

1 green bell pepper, seeded and chopped

4 stalks celery, chopped

2 cloves garlic, minced

2 large russet potatoes (about 1$^{1}/_{2}$ pounds), peeled and cubed

8 cups chicken stock or broth

1 teaspoon salt

$^{1}/_{4}$ teaspoon freshly ground pepper

$^{1}/_{2}$ teaspoon dried thyme

2 bay leaves

$^{1}/_{2}$ cup all-purpose flour

1 cup cold water

2 cans (6$^{1}/_{2}$ ounces each) minced clams, with juice

2 cups corn kernels, fresh or frozen

1 pound halibut, cut into bite-sized pieces

1 pint small oysters, drained and halved

$^{3}/_{4}$ pound medium shrimp, shelled and deveined

1 cup half-and-half or milk

$^{1}/_{2}$ cup chopped parsley

In a large Dutch oven over medium heat, melt butter. Add onions, bell pepper, celery, and garlic and sauté for about 5 minutes. Add potatoes, stock, salt, pepper, thyme, and bay leaves. Bring to a boil. Reduce heat to medium-low and simmer, covered, until potatoes and vegetables are tender, about 15 minutes.

In a small bowl or cup, blend flour with water. Add to soup, stirring until bubbly and thickened, about 2 minutes. Add clams and their juice and corn and mix well. Increase heat to medium. Add seafood and cook, uncovered, until fish flakes and shrimp turn pink, about 10 minutes longer. Stir in half-and-half and parsley and heat to serving temperature over low heat. Remove bay leaves and discard.

# CLAM CHOWDER

**SERVES 6 TO 8**

**Don't wait until Friday to make this popular soup; it's good any day of the week. Too many clam chowders are thick and floury. This one is just right. Add more clams if you like.**

In a soup pot over medium heat, combine potatoes, celery, carrots, onion, water, and reserved clam juice. Bring to a boil. Reduce heat to low and simmer, covered, until vegetables are very soft, about 15 minutes. Sprinkle with flour and stir until blended. Add drained clams, milk, salt, pepper, and bacon. Simmer, uncovered, 10 minutes.

Ladle into bowls and top each with butter, if desired. Sprinkle with paprika.

6 medium uncooked new potatoes, unpeeled, cubed

1 stalk celery, sliced

2 carrots, chopped

1 cup chopped yellow onion

1 cup water

2 cans (6½ ounces each) chopped clams (drain juice and reserve)

1 tablespoon all-purpose flour

2½ to 3 cups milk or half-and-half

1 teaspoon salt

Freshly ground pepper to taste

4 slices bacon, cooked and crumbled

**TOPPINGS**

4 tablespoons butter (optional)

Paprika

184

**The difference between Manhattan clam chowder and New England clam chowder is that the Manhattan version includes tomatoes and omits the cream. New England clam chowder is thick and creamy.**

4 thick slices bacon, diced

1 medium yellow onion, chopped

2 stalks celery, chopped

2 large russet potatoes (about 1½ pounds), peeled and cubed (about 3 cups)

1 can (28 ounces) whole tomatoes, coarsely chopped, with juice

3 cups water

2 cans (6½ ounces each) minced clams with juice (drain and reserve juice)

½ teaspoon dried thyme

1¼ teaspoons salt

2 drops Tabasco sauce

Freshly ground pepper to taste

Chopped parsley for topping

In a large soup pot over medium heat, cook bacon until crisp, 5 to 6 minutes. Add onion, celery, and potatoes and mix well. Cook for 1 minute. Add tomatoes, water, reserved clam juice, thyme, salt, Tabasco sauce, and pepper. Reduce heat to medium-low and simmer, covered, until vegetables are tender, 15 to 20 minutes. Add clams and simmer, uncovered, until flavors are blended, about 10 minutes longer. Ladle into bowls and sprinkle with parsley.

# PACIFIC FRESH CHOWDER

**SERVES 6**

**This chowder is a tasty combination of vegetables, scallops, shrimp, and seasonings. It's perfect for an impromptu get-together; just add a salad and some crusty bread for a complete meal.**

In a soup pot over medium heat, combine celery, onion, potatoes, and water. Cover and cook over medium heat until vegetables are slightly tender, about 10 minutes. Add seafood, cover, and cook 10 minutes longer.

In a small bowl, stir together flour and clam juice. Add to fish mixture and stir until slightly thickened, 1 to 2 minutes. Add half-and-half, butter, salt, and pepper. Heat to serving temperature over low heat; do not boil.

Ladle into bowls and garnish with parsley and paprika. Serve immediately.

2 stalks celery, sliced

1 yellow onion, chopped

2 medium russet potatoes (about 1 pound), peeled and cubed

1½ cups water

½ pound snapper or any white fish fillets, cut into bite-sized pieces

¼ pound large scallops, cut in half vertically

¼ pound small cooked shrimp

¼ cup all-purpose flour

1 bottle (8 ounces) clam juice

1½ cups half-and-half or milk

2 tablespoons butter or margarine

1 teaspoon salt

¼ teaspoon freshly ground pepper

Chopped parsley for garnish

Paprika for garnish

**This chowder makes a great traditional soup to serve for Christmas Eve. Vary the seafood depending on taste and availability. Serve with broiled crostini topped with cheese and chopped olives.**

2 to 3 tablespoons butter or margarine

1/2 cup chopped yellow onion

3/4 cup chopped celery

1 carrot, grated

3 medium russet potatoes (about 1 1/2 pounds), peeled and cubed

2 cups chicken stock or broth

1 teaspoon salt

1/4 teaspoon freshly ground pepper

1/4 teaspoon dried thyme

1 bay leaf

1/4 cup all-purpose flour

1/2 cup cold water

1 cup milk or half-and-half

1 can (6 1/2 ounces) chopped clams, including juice

3/4 pound white fish fillets, cut into bite-sized pieces

1/2 pound small scallops

1/4 pound small cooked shrimp

1/4 cup chopped parsley for topping

In a large soup pot over medium heat, melt butter. Add onion, celery, and carrot and sauté until vegetables are slightly tender, 8 to 10 minutes.

Add potatoes, stock, salt, pepper, thyme, and bay leaf and bring to a boil over high heat. Reduce heat to medium-low or low and cook, covered, until vegetables are tender, about 15 minutes. Remove bay leaf and discard.

In a small bowl or cup, blend flour and water. Add to soup and stir until thickened, 1 to 2 minutes. Add milk and clams and mix well.

Add seafood and simmer, covered, until seafood is done and flavors are blended, about 10 minutes longer. Ladle into bowls and sprinkle with parsley. Serve immediately.

**137**

# SALMON-VEGETABLE-CHEESE CHOWDER

**SERVES 4 TO 6**

**Use fresh cooked salmon, if available, to make this recipe special; but good-quality canned salmon can also be used.**

In a large soup pot over high heat, bring vegetables, garlic, rice, and 3 cups of the stock to a boil. Reduce heat to medium-low and simmer, covered, until vegetables and rice are tender, about 20 minutes.

Transfer to a food processor and blend in batches until slightly chunky. Return to soup pot. Stir in remaining 1 cup stock, half-and-half, salmon, cheese, salt, thyme, and pepper. Simmer, uncovered, until cheese melts and flavors are blended, about 10 minutes.

**NOTE:** *If using canned salmon, remove dark skin and flesh.*

1 cup chopped yellow onion

2 medium russet potatoes (about 1 pound), peeled and cubed

1 carrot, chopped

1 stalk celery, chopped

1 clove garlic, sliced

1/4 cup uncooked long-grain white rice

4 cups chicken stock or broth

1 cup half-and-half or milk

1 cup flaked cooked salmon (see Note)

1 cup Monterery Jack cheese

3/4 teaspoon salt

1/2 teaspoon dried thyme

Freshly ground pepper to taste

**I served this chowder to my son when he was home for a visit, and he said it was the best he'd ever had. He ate it all. The small taste I had was indeed superb. Serve with Pesto Biscuits (page 56).**

2 tablespoons butter or margarine

1 tablespoon vegetable oil

1 cup chopped yellow onion

2 cloves garlic, minced

$\frac{1}{2}$ cup diced celery

$\frac{1}{3}$ cup all-purpose flour

6 cups fish or chicken stock or broth

2 russet potatoes (about 1 pound),
   peeled and diced

1 teaspoon dried tarragon

1 teaspoon dried thyme

$\frac{1}{2}$ teaspoon dried dill weed

1 teaspoon paprika

8 ounces smoked salmon, skin removed
   and flaked

1 tablespoon lemon juice

2 drops Tabasco sauce

1 teaspoon salt

Freshly ground pepper to taste

$\frac{1}{4}$ cup dry white wine

1 cup half-and-half

In a large Dutch oven over medium heat, melt butter with oil. Add onion, garlic, and celery and sauté until vegetables are tender, about 5 minutes.

Add flour and stir until bubbly. Add stock and stir until slightly thickened. Add potatoes, tarragon, thyme, dill, and paprika, cover, and simmer until potatoes are tender, about 15 minutes. Add salmon, lemon juice, Tabasco sauce, salt, pepper, and wine. Simmer, uncovered, 10 minutes. Add half-and-half and simmer over low heat until heated through, about 5 minutes.

SERVES 6 TO 8

# SEAFOOD AND VEGETABLE SOUP

**SERVES 6**

**140**

**Sitting down to a bowl of this thick seafood soup with a tossed green salad is pure pleasure. Serve with crusty Italian bread.**

In a large Dutch oven over medium heat, sauté bacon until partially cooked, about 3 minutes. Add onion, leeks, bell pepper, and garlic and sauté until vegetables are tender and bacon is crisp, about 5 minutes longer. Add potatoes, stock, tomatoes, tomato sauce, fennel seed, salt, and pepper and bring to a boil. Reduce heat to medium-low and simmer, covered, until potatoes are tender, about 20 minutes. Add seafood and wine and simmer, uncovered, until fish is cooked, 6 to 10 minutes longer. Ladle into large bowls and sprinkle with parsley.

6 slices bacon, diced

1 cup chopped yellow onion

2 leeks, white and light green parts only, chopped

$\frac{1}{2}$ red bell pepper, seeded and chopped

2 cloves garlic, minced

2 cups cubed, peeled russet potatoes (about 1 pound)

3 cups chicken stock or broth

2 cans (14$\frac{1}{2}$ ounces each) diced tomatoes, with juice

1 can (8 ounces) tomato sauce

1 teaspoon fennel seed, crushed

1 teaspoon salt

Freshly ground pepper to taste

1 pound halibut, cut into bite-sized pieces

1 pound small bay scallops, or large scallops cut into bite-sized pieces

$\frac{1}{2}$ cup dry white wine

Chopped fresh parsley for topping

**Fresh oysters are available year-round from oyster farms, but bay oysters are at their best in the cool months of fall and winter. They are often paired with spinach, as in this creamy soup.**

3 tablespoons butter or margarine

1 stalk celery, sliced

1 cup chopped yellow onion

3 tablespoons all-purpose flour

$3\frac{1}{2}$ cups milk, or part milk and part half-and-half

1 cup chicken stock or broth

1 cup rinsed, chopped fresh oysters

1 cup chopped, cooked fresh spinach, or 5 ounces frozen chopped spinach (half of a 10-ounce package), thawed and squeezed dry

1 teaspoon salt

$\frac{1}{4}$ teaspoon dried thyme

Dash of ground nutmeg

$\frac{1}{8}$ teaspoon ground white pepper

Few grinds of nutmeg for topping (optional)

In a large soup pot over medium-low heat, melt butter. Add celery and onion and sauté until vegetables are tender, about 5 minutes. Add flour and stir until bubbly. Add milk and stock, bring to a boil, and stir until slightly thickened, 1 to 2 minutes. Add oysters along with juices accumulated from chopping, spinach, salt, thyme, nutmeg, and pepper. Reduce heat to medium-low, and simmer, stirring occasionally, until flavors are blended, about 15 minutes. Ladle into bowls and sprinkle with fresh nutmeg, if desired.

141

# HALIBUT AND SHRIMP SOUP WITH FETA CHEESE

**SERVES 6**

**Feta adds a tangy flavor to this seafood soup with succulent shrimp and mild, firm halibut. Serve with Pita Bread Wedges (page 65).**

In a large saucepan over medium heat, warm oil. Add onion and garlic and sauté until tender, about 5 minutes. Add tomatoes, wine, stock, sugar, oregano, salt, pepper, and parsley. Bring to a boil. Reduce heat to medium-low and simmer, covered, until vegetables are tender, about 10 minutes longer. Add halibut and simmer, covered, until fish almost flakes, about 5 minutes. Stir in shrimp and simmer, covered, until shrimp turn pink, 4 to 5 minutes. Just before serving, stir in cheese.

1 tablespoon vegetable oil

1½ cups chopped yellow onion

2 cloves garlic, chopped

1 can (28 ounces) tomatoes, coarsely chopped, with juice

½ cup dry white wine

1¼ cup chicken stock or broth

1 teaspoon sugar

¾ teaspoon dried oregano

1 teaspoon salt

Freshly ground pepper to taste

¼ cup chopped parsley

¾ pound halibut, cut into large bite-sized pieces

½ pound large shrimp, shelled and deveined

1 cup (8 ounces) crumbled feta cheese

142

# 143

**Halibut is a low-fat, white, firm, and mild-flavored fish. Here, it is paired with complementary peppers in a rich-tasting soup.**

1 tablespoon vegetable oil

2 large red bell peppers, seeded and chopped (about 2 cups)

1 cup chopped yellow onion

1 stalk celery, chopped

1 clove garlic, minced

1 large russet potato (about ¾ pound), peeled and chopped

4 cups chicken stock or broth

1 teaspoon dried thyme

⅛ teaspoon crushed red pepper flakes

½ teaspoon paprika

½ teaspoon salt

Freshly ground pepper to taste

1 pound halibut, cut into 1-inch pieces

½ cup small bay shrimp

¼ cup chopped parsley for topping

In a large Dutch oven over medium heat, warm oil. Add peppers, onion, celery, and garlic and sauté until tender, about 5 minutes.

Add potato and 1 cup of the stock and simmer, covered, until vegetables are tender, about 20 minutes. Transfer to a food processor or blender in batches and purée vegetables. Return to Dutch oven. Add remaining 3 cups stock, thyme, red pepper flakes, paprika, salt, pepper, fish, and shrimp. Bring to a boil. Reduce heat to medium-low and simmer, uncovered, until fish flakes, about 5 minutes. Ladle into bowls and sprinkle with parsley.

**SERVES 4**

# HALIBUT AND RED BELL PEPPER SOUP

# QUICK CRAB BISQUE

**SERVES 4 TO 6**

**Make this delightful soup when fresh crab is in season. Serve for a luncheon with a fresh fruit salad.**

In a soup pot over medium heat, melt butter. Add onion and sauté until tender, about 5 minutes. Add flour and stir until bubbly. Gradually add chicken stock and tomato paste. Whisk until smooth.

Add half-and-half, salt, pepper, wine (if using), and crab. Bring to a boil, then reduce heat to low. Simmer, uncovered, 5 minutes.

Serve hot with a sprinkle of parsley on top.

2 tablespoons butter or margarine

2 tablespoons minced yellow onion

2$\frac{1}{2}$ tablespoons all-purpose flour

2 cups chicken stock or broth

$\frac{1}{4}$ cup tomato paste

2 cups half-and-half

$\frac{1}{2}$ teaspoon salt

Dash of white pepper

2 tablespoons dry white wine (optional)

$\frac{3}{4}$ pound crab meat, flaked and picked over

1 tablespoon chopped parsley

**A bisque is a thick, rich, puréed soup with seafood. This appealing, rosy-pink soup with fresh shrimp makes an elegant first course. You can substitute lobster for the shrimp.**

1½ pounds large shrimp, shelled and deveined

1½ cups water

3 cups peeled (see page 23), seeded, and coarsely chopped fresh tomatoes

2 cups chicken stock or broth

½ cup chopped yellow onion

2 stalks celery, chopped

2 carrots, chopped

3 sprigs parsley

½ teaspoon dried thyme

1 teaspoon salt

Dash of ground white pepper

3 tablespoons uncooked long-grain white rice

1 bay leaf

1 cup half-and-half

1 cup milk

½ cup dry white wine

Chopped chives or chopped parsley for topping

In a saucepan over high heat, cook shrimp in water until they turn pink, 2 to 3 minutes. Drain and discard water. Cut shrimp into small bite-sized pieces and set aside.

In a soup pot, combine all remaining ingredients except half-and-half, milk, wine, and chives. Bring to a boil. Reduce heat to medium-low and simmer, covered, until vegetables are tender, about 30 minutes. Remove bay leaf and parsley sprigs and discard.

Transfer to food processor or blender in batches and purée. Return to pan and add half-and-half, milk, wine, and cooked shrimp. Simmer, uncovered, until flavors are blended, 10 to 15 minutes longer. Ladle into bowls and sprinkle with chives or parsley.

145

# SHRIMP AND WILD RICE SOUP

**SERVES 4**

**A taste of the sea and a taste of the land are teamed together in this rich, creamy soup.**

In a large soup pot over medium heat, melt butter with oil. Add vegetables and sauté until tender, 6 to 7 minutes. Stir in wild rice. Add stock and bring to a boil. Reduce heat to medium-low and simmer, covered, until rice is tender, about 1 hour. Add half-and-half, wine, if desired, salt, pepper, and shrimp. Simmer, uncovered, until flavors are blended and soup is slightly thickened, 10 to 15 minutes.

1 tablespoon butter or margarine

1 tablespoon vegetable oil

$\frac{1}{2}$ cup chopped yellow onion

$\frac{1}{2}$ cup chopped carrot

$\frac{1}{2}$ cup chopped celery

4 ounces ($\frac{1}{2}$ cup) wild rice, thoroughly rinsed

4 cups chicken stock or broth

1 cup half-and-half

$\frac{1}{4}$ cup dry white wine (optional)

$\frac{1}{2}$ teaspoon salt

Freshly ground pepper to taste

6 ounces small bay shrimp

**Bring this interesting combination of mixed fish to the table in a decorative tureen for an impressive presentation. The topping of mango cubes adds a touch of sweetness.**

1 tablespoon butter or margarine

1 cup chopped yellow onion

2 cloves garlic, minced

2 cups fish stock or clam juice (see Note)

2 cups chicken stock or broth

1/2 cup dry white wine

3/4 teaspoon salt

1/8 teaspoon ground white pepper

1/2 teaspoon dried marjoram

1 bay leaf

1 carrot, sliced

1/2 red bell pepper, chopped

2 fresh tomatoes, peeled (see page 23), seeded, chopped, and drained

3 tablespoons chopped parsley

1 1/2 pounds assorted white fish fillets (halibut, swordfish, sea bass, snapper, or cod), cut into bite-sized pieces (use whatever fish is fresh and available)

2 tablespoons cornstarch

2 tablespoons cold water

1 small mango, peeled and cubed for topping

In a large soup pot over medium heat, melt butter. Add onion and garlic and sauté until tender, about 5 minutes. Add fish stock, chicken stock, wine, salt, white pepper, marjoram, bay leaf, carrot, and bell pepper. Bring to a boil. Reduce heat to medium-low and simmer, covered, until vegetables are tender, about 30 minutes. Add tomatoes, parsley, and fish. Increase heat to medium and simmer, uncovered, until fish flakes, about 10 minutes, stirring once.

In a bowl, blend cornstarch with water. Stir into stew and cook until thickened, 1 to 2 minutes. Remove bay leaf and discard. Reduce heat and simmer until ready to serve. Serve topped with mango cubes.

**NOTE:** *For a milder fish flavor, use all chicken stock (4 cups total).*

# PEPPERY SOUP WITH SHRIMP BALLS

**SERVES 6**

**Just like magic, these ugly, gray shrimp balls turn a beautiful pink as they float in the hot stock. This one-dish Chinese meal is best served when freshly made.**

Prepare shrimp balls. In a large soup pot over high heat, bring stock, soy sauce, and sherry to a boil. Drop shrimp balls into stock and cook for 1 minute. Add vegetables, salt, and pepper. Reduce heat to medium-low and simmer, uncovered, until balls turn pink and vegetables are tender, about 5 minutes. Simmer 10 minutes longer. Ladle immediately into bowls and sprinkle with sliced green onion tops.

Shrimp Balls (recipe follows)

6 cups chicken stock or broth

2 tablespoons soy sauce

2 tablespoons dry sherry

1 cup snow peas or sugar snap peas

4 cups sliced bok choy

1 cup packed sliced spinach

6 green onions, including some tender green tops, sliced

Salt and freshly ground pepper to taste

Sliced green onion tops for topping

## SHRIMP BALLS

½ pound large fresh shrimp, deveined and cut up

⅓ cup sliced water chestnuts, drained and cut up

1 clove garlic, cut up

1 green onion, cut up

1 teaspoon peeled, chopped fresh ginger, or ½ teaspoon dried ginger

1 tablespoon dry sherry

3 tablespoons cornstarch

¼ teaspoon salt

1 egg white

Place all ingredients in food processor and blend. Mixture will be sticky. Shape into 1-inch balls. (Oil palm of hand and use a teaspoon to form balls. They will not be uniform). Place on a plate lined with waxed paper and set aside.

# SHELLFISH SOUP

**SERVES 8**

**Make the herb stock ahead, and then combine it with the shellfish at serving time. Serve with Classic Garlic Bread (page 49) and a dry white wine.**

In a large soup pot over medium heat, warm oil. Add vegetables and garlic and sauté until tender, about 10 minutes. Add stock, clam juice, wine, salt, pepper, basil, thyme, saffron (if using), bay leaves, orange zest, and parsley. Reduce heat to low. Simmer, uncovered, 15 to 20 minutes. (Recipe can be prepared ahead to this point and refrigerated. Do not add seafood until ready to serve.)

Just before serving, return herb stock to a boil. Add seafood and cook, uncovered, until clams open and shrimp turn pink, 5 to 10 minutes. Remove bay leaves and parsley sprigs and discard.

2 tablespoons vegetable oil

1 yellow onion, chopped

1 carrot, chopped

1 leek, white and light green parts only, chopped

1 stalk celery, chopped

2 cloves garlic, minced

5 cups chicken stock or broth

1 bottle (8 ounces) clam juice

1 cup dry white wine

$\frac{1}{2}$ teaspoon salt

Freshly ground pepper to taste

$\frac{1}{2}$ teaspoon dried basil

$\frac{1}{2}$ teaspoon dried thyme

Pinch of saffron (optional)

2 bay leaves

1 teaspoon grated orange zest

2 sprigs parsley

18 to 20 baby clams

$\frac{1}{2}$ pound medium shrimp, shelled and deveined

1 pint small oysters, drained and halved

149

**Some snappy ingredients add flavor to this seafood soup. Serve with warm tortillas.**

1 tablespoon vegetable oil

1 cup chopped yellow onion

1 stalk celery, chopped

1 clove garlic, minced

$^3/_4$ cup diced ham

$^1/_2$ cup uncooked long-grain white rice

6 cups chicken stock or broth

1 can ($6^1/_2$ ounces) minced clams, with juice

1 can (4 ounces) diced green chiles, drained

$^1/_2$ teaspoon salt

Freshly ground pepper to taste

1 teaspoon paprika

$^1/_2$ pound snapper or other white fish, cut into bite-sized pieces

$^1/_2$ pound small bay shrimp

$^1/_4$ cup chopped parsley

In a large soup pot over medium heat, warm oil. Add onion, celery, garlic, and ham and sauté until vegetables are tender, about 5 minutes. Stir in rice. Add stock, clams, chiles, salt, pepper, and paprika. Bring to a boil. Reduce heat to medium-low and cook, covered, until rice is tender, about 20 minutes. Add fish and cook 10 minutes. Add shrimp and parsley and cook until warmed through, 5 to 10 minutes longer.

# SAN FRANCISCO CIOPPINO

**SERVES 6**

There is a difference of opinion as to the origin of this classic seafood stew made with a variety of fish and shellfish in a tomato base. Some say it was brought to San Francisco by Italian immigrants; others give the credit to Italian fishermen who made the stew with the "catch of the day." Any assortment of seafood can be used.

In a large Dutch oven over medium heat, warm oil. Add onion, garlic, and bell pepper and sauté until tender, about 5 minutes. Add tomatoes, tomato sauce, stock, wine, salt, thyme, basil, oregano, pepper, and bay leaf. Simmer, uncovered, to blend flavors, about 15 minutes. Add fish, scallops, and shrimp and simmer for 10 minutes; do not boil. Add clams and simmer until clams open (discard any that do not open), about 5 minutes.

Remove bay leaf and discard. Stir parsley into stew and serve in large bowls.

2 tablespoons vegetable oil

1 large yellow onion, chopped

2 cloves garlic, minced

1 green bell pepper, seeded and chopped

1 can (28 ounces) plum tomatoes, coarsely chopped, with juice

1 can (16 ounces) tomato sauce

1 cup chicken stock or broth

1 cup dry white wine

1 teaspoon salt

½ teaspoon dried thyme

¼ teaspoon dried basil

¼ teaspoon dried oregano

¼ teaspoon freshly ground pepper

1 bay leaf

1½ pounds white fish fillets such as snapper, flounder, halibut, or ling cod, cut into ½-inch chunks

½ pound sea scallops, halved

½ pound large shrimp, peeled and deveined

16 to 20 steamer clams in the shell, well scrubbed

¼ cup chopped fresh parsley

**This version of the famous Italian fisherman's stew includes sausage for a spicy twist.**

1½ tablespoons olive oil

1 cup chopped yellow onion

2 cloves garlic, minced

1 cup dry white wine

1 can (28 ounces) Italian-style tomatoes with basil, coarsely chopped, with juice

1 cup fish or chicken stock or broth

1 teaspoon salt

½ teaspoon freshly ground pepper

¼ teaspoon dried thyme

¼ teaspoon dried oregano

½ teaspoon sugar

½ pound kielbasa sausage, cut into ½-inch slices

½ pound sea scallops, halved

½ pound large shrimp (about 12), shelled and deveined

1 cup minced parsley

In a large Dutch oven over medium heat, warm oil. Add onion and garlic and sauté until tender, about 5 minutes. Add wine and boil for 1 minute. Add remaining ingredients except seafood and parsely. Reduce heat to medium-low and simmer, uncovered, 20 minutes. Add scallops, shrimp, and parsley and simmer, uncovered, until shrimp turn pink and scallops are firm, about 5 minutes longer.

152

# PACIFIC COAST FISHERMAN'S STEW

**SERVES 6**

**During summer fishing season off the West Coast, fishermen will catch halibut, snapper, cod, and other bottom fish along with scallops and shrimp. This stew of mixed seafood simmered in a zesty tomato stock was a favorite among our tasters. Serve in large bowls along with a leafy salad and sliced baguette.**

In a large soup pot over medium heat, warm oil. Add onion and garlic and sauté until tender, about 5 minutes. Add remaining ingredients except fish, shellfish, and parsley. Reduce heat to medium-low and simmer, uncovered, about 20 minutes. Add fish and shellfish and simmer, covered, until fish is cooked, shrimp turn pink, and clams open (discard any that do not open), about 15 minutes. Remove bay leaf and discard. Ladle into large bowls and sprinkle with parsley.

1 tablespoon olive oil

1 large yellow onion, chopped

2 cloves garlic, minced

2 cans (14$\frac{1}{2}$ ounces each) crushed tomatoes in thick purée

1 cup dry white wine

1 bottle (8 ounces) clam juice

2 tablespoons tomato paste

2 cups chicken stock or broth

1 cup water

1 tablespoon fresh lemon juice

1 teaspoon dried thyme

1 bay leaf

1 teaspoon salt

$\frac{1}{8}$ teaspoon cayenne pepper

1 pound white fish fillets (halibut, cod, or snapper), cut into bite-sized pieces

$\frac{1}{2}$ pound sea scallops, halved

1 pound large shrimp, shelled and deveined

20 clams in the shell

$\frac{1}{4}$ cup chopped parsley for topping

154

**This is more like a soup, but it is traditionally called a stew. Fresh, plump oysters are the prominent ingredient. Serve with oyster crackers.**

2 tablespoons butter or margarine

2 jars (12 ounces each) small oysters, with juice

½ cup half-and-half

2 cups milk

1 teaspoon Worcestershire sauce

½ teaspoon salt

½ teaspoon celery salt

⅛ teaspoon ground white pepper

Paprika for topping

In a large soup pot over medium heat, melt butter. Add oysters and their juice and cook until edges start to curl, about 5 minutes. Add half-and-half, milk, Worcestershire sauce, salt, celery salt, and white pepper. Heat, but do not boil. Ladle into bowls and sprinkle with paprika.

# NORTHWEST OYSTER STEW

**SERVES 2**

**155**

**For oyster lovers, a bowl of this creamy stew is genuine pleasure. This version includes vegetables for a more stewlike texture. For a richer stew, use half-and-half instead of milk.**

In a soup pot over medium heat, melt butter. Add celery, onion, and garlic and sauté until vegetables are tender, about 5 minutes. Add flour and stir until bubbly. Gradually add milk and reserved oyster liquid and stir until slightly thickened, 1 to 2 minutes. Add potatoes, salt, pepper, Worcestershire sauce, and Tabasco sauce and bring to a boil. Reduce heat to low and simmer until potatoes are tender, about 15 minutes. Add oysters and spinach and simmer until edges of oysters begin to curl and spinach wilts, 6 to 7 minutes. Ladle into bowls and sprinkle with parsley.

$\frac{1}{4}$ cup butter or margarine

2 cups thinly sliced celery

1 yellow onion, chopped

2 cloves garlic, minced

$\frac{1}{4}$ cup all-purpose flour

5 cups whole milk or half-and-half

2 jars (12 ounces each) small oysters, drained, liquid reserved

2 large russet potatoes (about 1$\frac{1}{2}$ pounds), peeled and cubed

1$\frac{1}{2}$ teaspoons salt

Freshly ground pepper to taste

2 teaspoons Worcestershire sauce

3 or 4 drops Tabasco sauce

2 cups packed torn spinach leaves

Chopped parsley for topping

**In this French stew, the vegetables and herbs bake in their own juices, with fish added just before serving. Olive oil provides additional flavor.**

¹/₂ cup chopped parsley

¹/₄ cup chopped fresh basil, or 1 teaspoon dried basil

1 tablespoon chopped fresh oregano, or 1 teaspoon dried oregano

1 tablespoon chopped fresh thyme, or 1 teaspoon dried thyme

2 teaspoons salt

¹/₄ teaspoon freshly ground pepper

1 large yellow onion, sliced

2 cloves garlic, minced

2 large zucchini, unpeeled, cut into ³/₄-inch slices

1 small eggplant, unpeeled, cut into ³/₄-inch cubes

1 red bell pepper, seeded and cut into strips

1 green bell pepper, seeded and cut into strips

2 tomatoes, seeded and quartered

8 ounces whole mushrooms

3 tablespoons olive oil

1³/₄ pounds white fish fillets (red snapper, halibut, or cod), cut into bite-sized pieces

Preheat oven to 400°F. In a small bowl, combine herbs, salt, and pepper.

In a large, lightly sprayed or oiled Dutch oven, layer vegetables and herb mixture. Drizzle olive oil over the top. Do not stir. Bake, covered, about 1 hour and 15 minutes. Add fish and cook, uncovered, until fish flakes, about 10 minutes longer.

**NOTE:** *You can cook the vegetables ahead of time, then reheat them and add the fish at serving time.*

# SNAPPER STEW WITH ZUCCHINI, RED BELL PEPPER, AND CAPERS

**SERVES 4**

**Snapper is a firm fish that works well for a stew because it does not fall apart when cooked. Red bell pepper adds color, and capers provide a salty accent.**

In a large soup pot over medium heat, warm oil. Add onion and sauté until tender, about 5 minutes. Sprinkle flour over onion and stir to coat. Pour in wine and mix well. Whisk in chicken stock, fish stock, thyme, salt, pepper, and bell pepper. Bring to a boil. Add zucchini and capers. Reduce heat to medium-low and simmer, covered, 5 minutes. Add fish and cook, uncovered, until fish flakes and vegetables are tender, about 10 minutes.

1 tablespoon vegetable oil

1 large yellow onion, sliced

1 tablespoon all-purpose flour

½ cup dry white wine

1 cup chicken stock or broth

1 cup fish stock or bottled clam juice

½ teaspoon dried thyme

½ teaspoon salt

Freshly ground pepper to taste

1 red bell pepper, seeded, cut into ½-inch strips, and then halved

1 zucchini, unpeeled, halved lengthwise, then halved horizontally and cut into ½-inch strips

2 teaspoons capers, rinsed and drained

1 pound snapper fillets, cut into bite-sized pieces

157

**This combination of tempting shrimp in a bed of spinach and rice has a lot of flavor and eye appeal.**

1 tablespoon butter or margarine

1 cup chopped yellow onion

$\frac{1}{2}$ cup uncooked long-grain white rice

2 cups chicken stock or broth

1 tablespoon lemon juice

$\frac{1}{4}$ teaspoon dried thyme

$\frac{1}{2}$ teaspoon salt

Freshly ground pepper to taste

1 package (10 ounces) frozen spinach, thawed and squeezed dry

1 cup water

$\frac{1}{8}$ teaspoon crushed red pepper flakes

$\frac{3}{4}$ pound medium shrimp, peeled and deveined

In a large Dutch oven over medium heat, melt butter. Add onion and sauté until tender, about 5 minutes. Stir in rice and mix well. Add stock, lemon juice, thyme, salt, and pepper and bring to a boil. Reduce heat to low and simmer, covered, until rice is tender, about 20 minutes. Add spinach and mix well.

Meanwhile, just before serving, in a saucepan over high heat, bring water and red pepper flakes to a boil. Add shrimp and cook until shrimp turn pink, about 3 minutes. Drain. To serve, place spinach-rice mixture on a platter and arrange shrimp on top.

**SERVES 4**

# SHRIMP, RICE, AND SPINACH STEW

# SEAFOOD STEW WITH CLAMS AND MUSSELS

**SERVES 6**

**This stew contains an array of seafood—mussels, clams, halibut, and shrimp—something for everyone. Serve with a creamy coleslaw.**

In a medium bowl, toss halibut, shrimp, and garlic with 2 tablespoons of the oil. Set aside for 10 minutes.

In a large Dutch oven over medium heat, warm the remaining 2 tablespoons oil. Add onion and bell pepper and sauté until tender, about 5 minutes. Stir in flour and tomato paste and blend. Add clam juice and stir until thickened, about 1 minute. Add tomatoes, salt, oregano, basil, Tabasco sauce, and pepper. Reduce heat to medium-low and simmer, uncovered, 5 minutes. Add halibut and shrimp mixture.

In another medium pan over high heat, combine mussels, clams, and wine. Bring to a boil and cook until shells open, about 2 minutes. Discard any that do not open.

Stir clams and mussels, along with their cooking liquid, into stew. Add parsley. Cook until flavors are blended, about 10 minutes. Serve in large bowls.

1¼ pounds halibut, cut into bite-sized pieces

24 medium shrimp, shelled and deveined

3 cloves garlic, minced

4 tablespoons olive oil

1 cup chopped yellow onion

1 green bell pepper, cut into ¼-inch strips

3 tablespoons all-purpose flour

1 tablespoon tomato paste

2 bottles (8 ounces each) clam juice

1 can (14½ ounces) whole tomatoes with juice, slightly puréed

1 teaspoon salt

½ teaspoon dried oregano

½ teaspoon dried basil

2 or 3 drops Tabasco sauce

Freshly ground pepper to taste

18 mussels in the shell, scrubbed and debearded

18 steamer clams in the shell, scrubbed

1 cup dry white wine

½ cup chopped parsley

There are as many versions of gumbo as there are cooks. Gumbo is a thick, stewlike dish that can have any of a number of ingredients, including meat, shellfish, fish, and poultry, along with vegetables and herbs and a thickening agent such as a roux, filé powder, or okra. It is traditionally served over rice. Cooking the roux until it is very browned gives the sauce a rich flavor and dark color. Serve this colorful dish for an impressive dinner party.

$\frac{1}{4}$ cup vegetable oil

$\frac{1}{4}$ cup all-purpose flour

2 stalks celery, coarsely chopped

1 cup chopped yellow onion

1 medium green bell pepper, coarsely chopped

1 bay leaf

1 teaspoon salt

1 teaspoon dried oregano

$\frac{1}{4}$ teaspoon cayenne pepper

1 bottle (8 ounces) clam juice

4 cups chicken stock or broth

1 can (15$\frac{1}{2}$ ounces) whole tomatoes, coarsely chopped, with juice

2 cups cubed cooked ham

2 cups frozen sliced okra

1 pound large shrimp, shelled and deveined

8 ounces crabmeat, flaked and picked over

Cooked white rice

Chopped parsley for topping

In a large Dutch oven over high heat, heat oil until very hot. Add flour and cook until dark brown but not burned, stirring constantly, 6 to 8 minutes. Add celery, onion, bell pepper, bay leaf, salt, oregano, and cayenne (it will look dirty). Reduce heat to medium. Sauté until vegetables are tender, about 5 minutes. Add clam juice, stock, tomatoes, and ham. Cook for 10 minutes. Add okra and reduce heat to medium-low. Simmer, uncovered, 10 minutes. (Gumbo can be made ahead up to this point and then reheated and the shrimp and crabmeat added just before serving.)

Add shrimp and crabmeat and simmer, uncovered, until shrimp turn pink, about 5 minutes. Remove bay leaf and discard.

Place a small amount of rice in each bowl and ladle some of the gumbo over. Sprinkle with parsley.

160

# NEW ORLEANS SHRIMP CREOLE

### SERVES 4 TO 6

**Creole cooking reflects the combination of French, Spanish, and African cuisines. This dish includes shrimp and vegetables simmered in a thick tomato sauce. Serve over hot rice. A good dish to serve for a Mardi Gras party.**

In a large skillet over medium-high heat, fry bacon until crisp, about 6 minutes. With a slotted spoon, remove bacon to a plate, leaving 2 tablespoons bacon drippings in skillet.

Reduce heat to medium. Add onions, bell pepper, celery, and garlic and sauté until tender, about 6 to 7 minutes. Add tomatoes, tomato paste, stock, vinegar, mustard, Tabasco sauce, salt, and pepper. Return bacon to pan. Simmer over medium-low heat, uncovered, for 20 minutes, stirring occasionally. Add wine and shrimp and cook until shrimp turn pink, about 5 minutes.

8 slices bacon, diced

½ cup chopped yellow onion

½ cup chopped green onion, including some tender green tops

1½ cups chopped green bell pepper

1 cup chopped celery

1 garlic clove, minced

2 cans (14½ ounces each) whole tomatoes, coarsely chopped, with juice

3 tablespoons tomato paste

½ cup chicken stock or broth

¼ cup red wine vinegar

½ teaspoon dry mustard

4 drops Tabasco sauce, or to taste

1 teaspoon salt

Freshly ground pepper to taste

½ cup dry red wine

1 pound large raw shrimp, peeled and deveined

# VEGETABLE

## SOUPS & STEWS

Vegetable soups and stews are popular with vegetarians and non-vegetarians alike. These creative recipes make vegetables exciting to eat. Vegetable soups can be made all year-round because many types of vegetables are always available, but garden vegetables provide the best flavor. Vegetable soups also play an important role in dieting.

# BORSCHT

**SERVES 4 TO 6**

**There are many versions of this Russian and Polish beet soup. This one includes fresh beets along with other vegetables. It can be served hot or cold, but always with a dollop of sour cream on top.**

In a large soup pot, combine stock, cabbage, onion, celery, carrot, and garlic. Bring to a boil. Reduce heat to medium-low and simmer, covered, 15 minutes. Add beets, sugar, paprika, salt, pepper, and dill weed and simmer, covered, until all vegetables are tender, 20 to 25 minutes longer. Add vinegar and mix well. Serve in bowls with a dollop of sour cream.

**NOTE:** *You can use cooked beets, but the flavor won't be as intense. If using cooked beets, reduce the final cooking period to 10 minutes.*

5 cups chicken stock or broth

2 cups shredded cabbage

1 cup chopped yellow onion

2 stalks celery, chopped

1 carrot, chopped

1 clove garlic, minced

1½ cups peeled, chopped raw beets (see Note)

2 teaspoons sugar

1 teaspoon paprika

¼ teaspoon salt

Freshly ground pepper to taste

1 teaspoon dried dill weed

1 tablespoon red wine vinegar

Sour cream for topping

**Here is a shortcut version of this famous soup. This recipe calls for canned beans and pickled beets for convenience and easy preparation—but with the same great flavor.**

$^{1}/_{2}$ head (about 1$^{1}/_{2}$ pounds) cabbage,
　core removed, shredded

1 carrot, chopped

$^{1}/_{2}$ cup chopped yellow onion

1$^{1}/_{2}$ cups vegetable or chicken stock
　or broth

1 can (15 ounces) Great Northern beans,
　drained and rinsed

1 can (14$^{1}/_{2}$ ounces) diced tomatoes
　with juice, slightly puréed

1 can (8 ounces) tomato sauce

1 can (14$^{1}/_{2}$ ounces) pickled beets, coarsely
　chopped, with juice

$^{1}/_{2}$ teaspoon salt

Freshly ground pepper to taste

Sour cream for topping

In a large soup pot over medium heat, combine all ingredients except sour cream. Bring to a boil. Reduce heat to medium-low and simmer, covered, until vegetables are tender, about 30 minutes. Add more stock if soup is too thick. Serve in bowls with a dollop of sour cream.

# QUICK BORSCHT

**SERVES 4**

**Another borscht? I had to include this one because it is entirely different and can be made in minutes. A good soup to serve unexpected guests. Serve hot or cold for a first course or a luncheon.**

Place beets, their juice, and onion in food processor and purée. Add remaining ingredients except sour cream and fresh dill and blend until smooth. Serve in bowls with a dollop of sour cream and a sprinkle of dill, if desired. Garnish with a dill sprig.

1 can (15 ounces) whole pickled beets, with red wine vinegar, cut up, with juice

1/4 cup chopped yellow onion

1 can (11 1/2 ounces) tomato juice

1 tablespoon red wine vinegar

1 teaspoon dried dill weed (optional)

1 teaspoon salt

1 teaspoon sugar

Sour cream for topping

Chopped fresh dill for topping (optional)

Fresh dill sprigs for garnish

**Corn is a traditional ingredient in Mexican cooking and is the basis of this soup. This is a fun party soup served with different toppings. It is even good without the chicken.**

8 cups corn kernels, fresh or frozen (if frozen, use 2 packages, 10 ounces each, thawed and rinsed)

$^{1}/_{2}$ cup chopped yellow onion

1 clove garlic, sliced

$2^{1}/_{2}$ to 3 cups chicken stock or broth

3 tablespoons butter or margarine

1 teaspoon ground cumin

$^{3}/_{4}$ teaspoon salt

$^{1}/_{4}$ teaspoon white pepper

2 cups buttermilk

1 can (4 ounces) diced green chiles, drained

2 or 3 drops Tabasco sauce

2 cups cubed cooked chicken

1 tomato, peeled (see page 23), seeded, and chopped

1 tablespoon chopped cilantro or parsley

**TOPPINGS**

6 corn tortillas, crisped (see page 26), and broken up

Salsa

Sour cream

Sliced green onions

Chopped olives

Grated Monterey Jack cheese

In a food processor, combine corn, onion, garlic, and 1 cup of the stock and process in batches until smooth.

In a large soup pot over medium heat, melt butter. Add corn mixture, cumin, salt, and white pepper. Simmer, covered, 5 minutes. Add buttermilk and $1^{1}/_{2}$ cups more stock and bring to a boil. Add chiles, Tabasco sauce, chicken, tomato, and cilantro. Reduce heat to medium-low and simmer, uncovered, for 30 minutes. Add remaining $^{1}/_{2}$ cup stock if soup is too thick.

Serve in bowls topped with a few broken tortilla pieces. Pass the additional toppings separately.

**SERVES 8** MEXICAN CORN SOUP (SOPA DE MAIZ)

# BROCCOLI, MUSHROOM, AND PEANUT BUTTER SOUP

**SERVES 6**

**If you are a peanut butter fan, you'll love this soup. It's easy to make and fun to serve.**

In a large soup pot over medium-high heat, combine stock and pepper. Bring to a boil. Add barley, reduce heat to low, and simmer, covered, until barley is tender, about 50 minutes.

Using a wire whisk, blend in peanut butter. Add broccoli, mushrooms, and lemon juice and simmer, covered, over medium-low heat until vegetables are tender, about 15 minutes. Add salt and simmer, uncovered, 5 to 10 minutes.

8 cups chicken stock or broth

Freshly ground pepper to taste

⅓ cup pearl barley, thoroughly rinsed

1 cup chunky-style peanut butter

2 cups chopped fresh broccoli florets, or 1 package (10 ounces) frozen chopped broccoli, thawed and drained

½ pound fresh mushrooms, chopped

1 tablespoon fresh lemon juice

Salt to taste

**The combination of whole corn and creamed corn adds extra corn flavor to this easy-to-make chowder.**

2 large russet potatoes (about
 1½ pounds), peeled and cubed

½ cup chopped yellow onion

1 cup chicken stock or broth

1 cup corn kernels, fresh or frozen

1 can (15 ounces) creamed corn

1 cup milk

¾ teaspoon salt

Freshly ground pepper to taste

In a soup pot over high heat, bring potatoes, onion, and stock to a boil. Reduce heat to medium-low and simmer, covered, until potatoes are tender, about 12 minutes. Add corn kernels. Transfer half of the mixture to a food processor and purée. Return mixture to pot. Add creamed corn, milk, salt, and pepper and mix well. Simmer until flavors are blended, about 10 minutes.

# ITALIAN ROASTED GARLIC SOUP

**SERVES 6**

**This is a soup for garlic lovers! Roasted garlic has a milder, sweeter flavor than raw garlic and is less intimidating. Serve for an introductory first course to wake up the taste buds.**

Preheat oven to 350°F. Peel off some of the papery outer skins, but do not peel the garlic cloves. Leave the garlic heads intact. Slice ¼ inch off the top of each garlic head. Place heads, cut-side up, in a lightly sprayed or oiled baking dish. Drizzle ½ teaspoon oil over each head. Bake, uncovered, until golden, about 1 hour. Cool slightly. Press the whole head with your hand all at once to release the garlic pulp. Place pulp in a bowl and set aside.

In a large soup pot over medium heat, warm the remaining oil. Add onion and celery and sauté until tender, about 5 minutes. Add reserved garlic pulp, stock, beans, basil, salt, pepper, and bay leaf. Bring to a boil. Reduce heat to medium-low and simmer, uncovered, 15 minutes. Remove bay leaf and discard. In a food processor or blender, purée soup in batches. Return to pot and stir in half-and-half. Simmer until flavors are blended, about 5 minutes. Ladle into bowls and sprinkle with Parmesan cheese and parsley.

4 whole heads garlic

1½ tablespoons olive oil

1 cup chopped yellow onion

2 stalks celery, chopped

3½ cups chicken stock or broth

1 can (15 ounces) cannellini beans or white beans, drained and rinsed

½ teaspoon dried basil

¾ teaspoon salt

Freshly ground pepper to taste

1 bay leaf

½ cup half-and-half or milk

Freshly grated Parmesan cheese for topping

Chopped parsley for topping

168

**The addition of sherry complements the mild mushroom flavor. Rice thickens this soup, adding body and texture.**

2 tablespoons butter or margarine

1 cup chopped yellow onion

2 cloves garlic, minced

1 pound medium mushrooms, sliced and halved

$1/4$ cup uncooked long-grain white rice

$1/2$ teaspoon dried thyme

6 cups chicken stock or broth

$1/4$ cup dry sherry or dry white wine

$1/2$ teaspoon salt

Freshly ground pepper to taste

$1/4$ cup chopped parsley for topping

In a large soup pot over medium heat, melt butter. Add onion, garlic, and mushrooms and sauté until vegetables are tender, 5 to 6 minutes. Add rice and thyme and stir for 1 minute. Add stock, sherry, salt, and pepper and bring to a boil. Reduce heat to medium-low and simmer, covered, until rice is tender, about 20 minutes. Ladle into bowls and sprinkle with parsley.

# MUSHROOM, BARLEY, AND SPINACH SOUP

**SERVES 4**

**Barley is a hardy grain, adding substance and a chewy consistency to this colorful and tasty soup.**

In a large soup pot over medium heat, melt butter with oil. Add mushrooms, onion, bell pepper, and carrots. Sauté until tender, about 7 minutes. Add stock, barley, and vinegar. Bring to a boil. Reduce heat to medium-low and simmer, covered, until barley is tender, about 35 minutes. Add spinach, salt, and pepper and simmer, uncovered, 10 minutes longer.

1 tablespoon butter or margarine

1 tablespoon vegetable oil

1 pound medium mushrooms, sliced

1 cup chopped yellow onion

½ cup chopped red bell pepper

2 carrots, chopped

6 cups chicken stock or broth

⅓ cup pearl barley, rinsed thoroughly

1 tablespoon red wine vinegar

5 ounces frozen chopped spinach (half of a 10-ounce package), thawed and squeezed dry

1 teaspoon salt

Freshly ground pepper to taste

**This rich soup combines dried and fresh wild mushrooms for an earthy, pungent flavor. Shiitake mushrooms are native to Japan, but they are now also grown in the United States. They have a strong, woodsy flavor. The stems are tough and should be discarded or used for flavoring in other dishes. Porcini mushrooms have a smooth, meaty texture and are often called "little treasures."**

3 to 4 cups chicken stock or broth

1 ounce dried porcini mushrooms, rinsed

¼ cup butter or margarine

½ cup chopped yellow onion

½ red bell pepper, seeded and chopped

1 stalk celery, chopped

2 cloves garlic, minced

6 ounces fresh shiitake mushrooms, stems removed and caps sliced

½ teaspoon salt

Freshly ground pepper to taste

2 tablespoons all-purpose flour

1 cup half-and-half

2 drops Tabasco sauce

1 tablespoon soy sauce, or more to taste

3 tablespoons sliced green onions, including some tender green tops, for topping

In a large saucepan over medium-high heat, bring stock to a boil. Add porcini mushrooms and remove from heat. Cover and let stand for 20 minutes. Strain liquid into a bowl, discarding any sediment left in pan, and chop porcini. Set soaking liquid and porcini aside.

In a soup pot over medium heat, melt butter. Add onion, bell pepper, celery, and garlic and sauté for 7 or 8 minutes. Add porcini and shiitake mushrooms and sauté until mushrooms are tender, 3 to 4 minutes.

Add salt, pepper, and flour and blend. Gradually stir in porcini soaking liquid and half-and-half. Increase heat to medium-high and stir until slightly thickened, 1 to 2 minutes. Reduce heat to low. Add Tabasco sauce and soy sauce and simmer, uncovered, until flavors are blended, about 10 minutes. Ladle into bowls and sprinkle with green onions.

**171**

# EGG FLOWER SOUP WITH PEA PODS

**SERVES 4**

**This is a classic Chinese soup of clear stock, snow peas, and mushrooms, with a beaten egg added just before serving.**

In a large soup pot over high heat, bring stock to a boil. Add peas and mushrooms. Reduce heat to medium-low and simmer, uncovered, until vegetables are tender, about 10 minutes. Add water chestnuts. Bring soup to a boil. Add egg and stir until strands form, 30 seconds to 1 minute. Season with salt and pepper. Ladle into bowls and serve immediately, topped with green onions.

6 cups chicken stock or broth

1 cup snow peas or sugar snap peas

1 cup sliced mushrooms

1 can (8 ounces) sliced water chestnuts, drained

1 egg, beaten

Salt and freshly ground pepper to taste

Chopped green onions, including some tender green tops, for topping

172

This favorite soup is easy to make, but you must be patient: the onions need to simmer in butter for a long time to bring out their sweet, natural flavor. Topped with cheese croutons, it's even better. Serve as a first course for a prime rib dinner.

¹/₄ cup butter (no substitute)

4 medium yellow onions (about 2 pounds), sliced

2 cloves garlic, minced

¹/₂ teaspoon sugar

6 cups rich beef stock or broth (preferably homemade)

1 teaspoon Worcestershire sauce

¹/₄ cup dry red wine

¹/₄ teaspoon dried thyme

¹/₂ to ³/₄ teaspoon salt

Freshly ground pepper to taste

1 bay leaf

**CROUTONS**

6 slices French bread

1 cup grated packed Gruyère cheese

In a heavy soup pot or Dutch oven over medium heat, melt butter. Add onions and garlic and mix well. Reduce heat to medium-low and simmer, covered, 15 minutes. Stir in sugar and cook, uncovered, until onions are tender and lightly colored, about 30 minutes longer, stirring occasionally.

Add remaining ingredients except bread and cheese and cook until flavors are blended, about 20 minutes longer. Remove bay leaf and discard.

Meanwhile, to make croutons: preheat broiler and place bread on a baking sheet. Broil bread on one side until browned, about 2 minutes. Turn bread over, cover with cheese, and broil until bubbling, about 1 minute. Cut into large pieces.

Ladle soup into bowls and float croutons on top.

# POTATO SOUP WITH BACON AND GORGONZOLA CHEESE

**SERVES 4**

**Keep the ingredients for this soup in the pantry and you'll always have a supper in reserve. The bacon and cheese add extra flavor.**

In a large soup pot over medium heat, cook bacon until crisp. Remove with a slotted spoon to a plate, leaving 2 tablespoons bacon drippings in pan. Add onion and celery to pan and sauté until vegetables are slightly tender, about 6 minutes. Add potatoes and stock and bring to a boil. Reduce temperature to medium-low and simmer, covered, until vegetables are tender, about 20 minutes. Transfer 1 cup of the vegetables to a food processor or blender and process until smooth. Return to pan and add milk and parsley. Season with salt and pepper and reheat over medium heat for about 5 minutes. Ladle into bowls and sprinkle with bacon and cheese, if desired.

4 slices bacon, diced

1 cup chopped yellow onion

2 stalks celery, sliced

2 large russet potatoes (about 1½ pounds), peeled and cubed

1 cup chicken or vegetable stock or broth

2 cups milk

¼ cup chopped parsley

¾ teaspoon salt

Freshly ground pepper to taste

4 ounces crumbled Gorgonzola or blue cheese for topping (optional)

**This is a good soup to serve on Christmas Eve. It's easy to make, and everyone has fun adding different toppings. For variety, try adding clams or corn.**

4 large russet potatoes (about 2½ pounds), peeled and cubed

1 small yellow onion, chopped

1½ cups chicken stock or broth

2 cups milk

3 ounces cream cheese, cut into small pieces

2 tablespoons freshly grated Parmesan cheese

¼ cup chopped parsley

1 teaspoon dried dill weed

½ teaspoon celery salt

1 teaspoon salt

⅛ teaspoon ground white pepper

**TOPPINGS**

Chopped hard-cooked eggs

Chopped green onions, including some tender green tops

Chopped fresh tomatoes, seeded and drained

Diced cucumbers

Cooked, crumbled bacon bits

Chopped peanuts

Small shrimp

In a large soup pot over high heat, combine potatoes, onion, and stock. Bring to a boil. Reduce heat to medium-low and simmer, covered, until tender, about 15 minutes. Transfer half of the mixture to food processor and purée. Return to the pot. Add remaining ingredients except toppings and stir until cheese melts, 5 to 10 minutes. Add more milk if too thick. Ladle into bowls and pass the toppings separately.

**VARIATIONS:** *Add 2 cans minced clams (6½ ounces each), with juice, or 1½ cups corn kernels, fresh or frozen, at the end of the cooking time and warm until heated through.*

175

# ROASTED RED PEPPER, WHITE BEAN, AND PASTA SOUP

**SERVES 4**

**This creative vegetarian soup is filling and flavorful. It is even better when reheated the next day. Serve with Herbed Toasts (page 63) and some fresh seasonal fruit.**

In a soup pot over medium heat, warm oil. Add onion and garlic and sauté until tender, about 5 minutes. Add stock, thyme, salt, and pepper and bring to a boil. Reduce heat to medium. Add pasta, beans, and bell pepper and cook, uncovered, until pasta is tender and flavors are blended, 10 to 15 minutes longer.

1 tablespoon vegetable oil

1/2 cup chopped yellow onion

1 clove garlic, minced

3 1/2 cups vegetable stock or broth

1/4 teaspoon dried thyme, finely crumbled

1/2 teaspoon salt

Freshly ground pepper to taste

1/2 cup bow tie pasta or other small dried pasta

1 can (15 ounces) white beans, rinsed and drained

1 red bell pepper, roasted (see page 23) and coarsely chopped, or 1 jar (7 ounces) roasted red bell peppers, drained and chopped

176

**A perfect soup to serve with assorted grilled sausages, German potato salad, rye bread, and a glass of beer.**

1 tablespoon butter or margarine

1 cup chopped red onion

2 cups sauerkraut, drained and rinsed

5 cups beef stock or broth

1 cup beer, allowed to go flat

$\frac{1}{2}$ teaspoon dried thyme

1 teaspoon caraway seeds

1 bay leaf

$\frac{1}{2}$ teaspoon salt

Freshly ground pepper to taste

In a large Dutch oven over medium heat, melt butter. Add onion and sauté until tender, about 5 minutes. Stir in sauerkraut and mix well. Add remaining ingredients. Bring to a boil. Reduce heat to medium-low and simmer, covered, until flavors are blended, about 20 minutes. Remove bay leaf and discard. Serve in bowls.

**I was served this fantastic soup at an equally fantastic reunion. It is a medley of vegetables simmered in a flavorful stock for a long time and seasoned with a white sauce added at the end. Use the food processor for quick chopping.**

In a large Dutch oven over medium-high heat, cook bacon until crisp. Drain off drippings, leaving 1 tablespoon in Dutch oven. Add onion, cabbage, celery, carrot, potato, zucchini, and garlic and sauté until tender, about 5 minutes.

Add remaining ingredients except white sauce and vinegar. Bring to a boil. Reduce heat to medium-low and simmer, covered, until vegetables are very tender, about 1½ hours, stirring occasionally.

Meanwhile, make white sauce. After soup has cooked for 1½ hours, whisk in sauce and vinegar. Cook until flavors are blended, about 10 minutes longer.

½ pound bacon, diced

1 cup chopped yellow onion

1 cup chopped cabbage

1 cup chopped celery

1 cup chopped carrot

1 large russet potato (about ¾ pound), peeled and chopped

1 zucchini, sliced lengthwise and then cut into ¼-inch slices

2 cloves garlic, minced

¼ teaspoon dried chervil

½ teaspoon salt

Freshly ground pepper to taste

1 can (28 ounces) whole tomatoes, coarsely chopped, with juice

4 cups beef stock or broth

¼ cup uncooked barley, thoroughly rinsed

2 tablespoons brown or white long-grain rice

Seasoned White Sauce (recipe follows)

1 tablespoon cider vinegar

## SEASONED WHITE SAUCE

2 tablespoons butter or margarine

2 teaspoons all-purpose flour

1 cup milk

1 teaspoon Worcestershire sauce

1/2 teaspoon dried thyme

1/4 teaspoon garlic powder

1/2 teaspoon salt

In a saucepan over medium heat, melt butter. Add flour and stir until bubbly. Whisk in remaining ingredients and stir until thickened, 1 to 2 minutes. Sauce will become thick if it stands; do not thin.

# DUTCH FARMER'S SOUP

**SERVES 6**

**A traditional meatless vegetable soup from Holland, with large cheese croutons floating on top.**

In a large Dutch oven over medium heat, melt butter. Add vegetables and sauté until tender, about 10 minutes. Add stock, salt, and pepper. Bring to a boil. Reduce heat to medium-low and simmer, covered, until vegetables are tender, 20 to 25 minutes.

Ladle into soup bowls and place a crouton on top of each. Serve immediately.

2 tablespoons butter or margarine

2 large russet potatoes (about 1½ pounds), peeled and diced

1 yellow onion, chopped

3 stalks celery, chopped

3 carrots, chopped

¾ pound (about 3 cups) cauliflower florets, cut into bite-sized pieces

6 cups vegetable stock

½ teaspoon salt

Freshly ground pepper to taste

Gouda Cheese Croutons (recipe follows)

179

# GOUDA CHEESE CROUTONS

6 slices French bread

8 ounces Gouda cheese, wax rind removed and sliced to fit bread (see Note)

Preheat broiler. Place bread on baking sheet and broil 6 inches from heat for about 2 minutes. Turn, top bread with cheese, and broil until cheese is melted, 1 to 2 minutes.

**NOTE:** *You can substitute another type of cheese if you prefer.*

# MINESTRONE WITH PESTO

**SERVES 8 TO 10**

There are many versions of this classic Italian soup. This one, without tomatoes and with pesto added, is from northern Italy. It involves a lot of chopping but is easy to make. Serve with French Bread with Garlic Spread (page 50).

In a large soup pot over high heat, combine carrots, leeks, celery, onion, garlic, stock, oregano, salt, and pepper. Bring to a boil. Reduce heat to medium-low and simmer, covered, 15 minutes.

Add beans, macaroni, zucchini, and bell pepper. Bring to a boil again. Reduce heat and simmer, uncovered, until vegetables and macaroni are tender, 10 minutes longer. Stir in pesto and peas and cook, uncovered, until flavors are blended, about 10 minutes. Ladle into bowls and sprinkle with Parmesan cheese.

3 carrots, sliced

2 leeks, white and light green parts only, sliced

2 stalks celery, sliced

½ cup chopped yellow onion

2 cloves garlic, minced

10 cups chicken stock or broth

½ teaspoon dried oregano

1 teaspoon salt

Freshly ground pepper to taste

2 cans (15 ounces each) cannellini beans, drained and rinsed

1 cup uncooked elbow macaroni

1 large zucchini, quartered lengthwise and sliced into ½-inch-thick slices

1 red bell pepper, cut into ½-inch chunks (about 2 cups)

½ cup Basil Pesto (page 41)

5 ounces frozen peas (half of a 10-ounce package), thawed and rinsed

Freshly grated Parmesan cheese for topping

Greek seasonings flavor this savory soup that is a takeoff on an Italian minestrone. Rice is used instead of the usual pasta, and feta cheese is sprinkled on top. I served this for a simple summer supper on our deck overlooking the Willamette Valley along with cheese bread and a fresh peach cobbler. It was delightful.

$\frac{1}{2}$ cup chopped red onion

$\frac{1}{2}$ small eggplant, unpeeled, cut into bite-sized pieces

2 carrots, coarsely chopped

2 stalks celery, coarsely chopped

3 cloves garlic, minced

6 cups chicken stock or broth

$\frac{1}{2}$ cup uncooked long-grain white rice

1 can (28 ounces) tomatoes, coarsely chopped, with juice

1 can (15 ounces) small white beans, drained and rinsed

1 zucchini, quartered lengthwise and cut into $\frac{1}{2}$-inch slices

$\frac{1}{2}$ teaspoon dried dill weed

$\frac{1}{2}$ teaspoon dried oregano

$\frac{1}{2}$ teaspoon salt

Freshly ground pepper to taste

3 cups sliced fresh spinach (about 3 ounces)

$\frac{1}{2}$ cup crumbled feta cheese for topping

In a large soup pot over high heat, combine onion, eggplant, carrots, celery, garlic, stock, rice, and tomatoes. Bring to a boil. Reduce heat to medium-low and simmer, covered, until vegetables and rice are tender, about 25 minutes.

Increase heat to medium and add beans, zucchini, dill, oregano, salt, and pepper. Simmer, covered, for 10 minutes, stirring once. Stir in spinach and simmer, uncovered, until spinach is wilted and all vegetables are tender, about 5 minutes longer (see Note). Ladle into bowls and sprinkle with feta.

**NOTE:** *If not serving immediately, add the spinach just before serving to retain the bright color and prevent overcooking.*

181

# VEGETARIAN MINESTRONE

## SERVES 8

**Thick with vegetables, this hearty soup is nourishing and tasty but low in calories and fat. Sprinkle generously with freshly grated Parmesan cheese. It's even better the next day.**

In a large soup pot over high heat, combine drained beans, tomatoes, tomato juice, stock, water, onion, carrots, celery, parsley, salt, basil, thyme, oregano, and pepper. Bring to a boil, reduce heat to medium-low, and simmer, covered, 1 hour and 15 minutes. Add cabbage, zucchini, and macaroni and cook, covered, until macaroni and vegetables are tender, about 20 minutes longer.

For a thicker soup, remove about 1 cup of the vegetables and purée in a food processor or blender. Return to soup pot and simmer, uncovered, until blended. Ladle into bowls and top with Parmesan cheese and Garlic Crumbs.

1 cup dried Great Northern beans, presoaked (see page 29)

1 can (14$\frac{1}{2}$ ounces) whole tomatoes, coarsely chopped, with juice

3 cups tomato juice

2 cups vegetable stock or broth, or water

2 cups water

1 small yellow onion, chopped

3 carrots, sliced

2 stalks celery, sliced

$\frac{1}{4}$ cup chopped parsley

1$\frac{1}{2}$ teaspoons salt

1 teaspoon dried basil

$\frac{1}{2}$ teaspoon dried thyme

$\frac{1}{2}$ teaspoon dried oregano

Freshly ground pepper to taste

2 cups chopped cabbage

1 medium zucchini, unpeeled, quartered lengthwise and sliced

$\frac{3}{4}$ cup uncooked macaroni or other small pasta

Freshly grated Parmesan cheese for topping

Garlic Crumbs (page 58) for topping

# ORIGINAL BLT SOUP

**SERVES 6**

Here's a fun soup that was inspired by the famous BLT sandwich. It includes all of the favorite ingredients, even shredded lettuce on top. Serve with white bread spread lightly with mayonnaise.

6 slices bacon, diced

1 cup chopped yellow onion

2 cloves garlic, minced

8 medium tomatoes (about 3 pounds), peeled (see page 23), seeded, and chopped

6 cups chicken stock or broth

¼ cup chopped fresh basil leaves, or 1 teaspoon dried basil

¾ teaspoon salt

Freshly ground pepper to taste

¼ teaspoon sugar

1 tablespoon tomato paste

1 cup finely shredded lettuce for topping

In a Dutch oven over medium-high heat, cook bacon until crisp, 6 to 7 minutes. Transfer to a plate, leaving 1 tablespoon bacon drippings in Dutch oven. Reduce heat to medium. Add onion and garlic and sauté until tender, about 5 minutes. Add remaining ingredients except lettuce and bring to a boil. Reduce heat to medium-low and simmer, uncovered, until vegetables are tender, about 20 minutes. Transfer in batches to a food processor or blender and purée. Return to Dutch oven and reheat. Ladle into bowls and top with bacon and lettuce.

# TOMATO FLORENTINE SOUP

**SERVES 6**

**The addition of spinach gives a contrasting color and taste to this rich tomato-based soup. The pasta adds variety and substance.**

In a large soup pot over medium heat, warm oil. Add onion and garlic and sauté until tender, about 5 minutes. Stir in oregano, basil, thyme, salt, and pepper and then the wine. Add chicken stock, beef stock, and tomatoes. Bring to a boil. Add macaroni. Reduce heat to medium and cook, uncovered, until macaroni is tender, about 10 minutes. Add spinach and cook until wilted, stirring occasionally, about 5 minutes longer. Stir in vinegar. Ladle into bowls and sprinkle with Parmesan cheese.

1 tablespoon olive oil

1 cup chopped yellow onion

4 cloves garlic, minced

1 teaspoon dried oregano

1 teaspoon dried basil

½ teaspoon dried thyme

½ teaspoon salt

Freshly ground pepper to taste

⅓ cup dry red wine

2 cups chicken stock or broth

2 cups beef stock or broth

1 can (28 ounces) crushed tomatoes in thick purée

½ cup uncooked elbow macaroni

1 package (6 ounces) fresh baby spinach, rinsed, stems removed if desired

1 tablespoon balsamic vinegar

Freshly grated Parmesan cheese for topping

**This soup is a good way to beat the winter doldrums when fresh tomatoes are not in season. Serve with Pesto Biscuits (page 56).**

1 tablespoon vegetable oil

1 yellow onion, chopped

4 cloves garlic, chopped

¼ cup dry red wine

7 cups chicken stock or broth

2 cans (14½ ounces each) diced Italian-
  style tomatoes, with juice

1 can (6 ounces) tomato paste

1 package (10 ounces) frozen chopped
  spinach, thawed and squeezed dry

1 teaspoon dried oregano

1 teaspoon dried basil

Salt and freshly ground pepper to taste

In a large soup pot over medium heat, warm oil. Add onion and garlic and sauté until tender, about 5 minutes. Add wine and stir for 1 minute. Add remaining ingredients and simmer, uncovered, 30 minutes.

# ROASTED TOMATO AND ONION SOUP WITH FRESH HERBS

**SERVES 4 TO 6**

**Roasting the tomatoes and onions brings out a slight smoky flavor in this sophisticated soup with garlic croutons floating on top.**

Preheat oven to 400°F. Place tomatoes cut-side up in a lightly sprayed 9-by-13-inch glass baking dish. Add onions and sprinkle tomatoes and onions with salt and pepper. In a small bowl, mix oil, garlic, and herbs. Spoon over tomatoes and onions. Roast until tomatoes are soft and lightly browned, 45 to 50 minutes. Scrape tomatoes, onions, and juices into food processor and purée until smooth.

Transfer puréed mixture to a soup pot over medium heat. Add remaining ingredients except croutons and simmer, uncovered, 10 to 15 minutes. Add more salt if needed. Ladle into bowls and top each with a few croutons.

10 to 12 (about 1½ pounds) plum (Roma) tomatoes, halved lengthwise

2 yellow onions, quartered

Salt and freshly ground pepper to taste

¼ cup olive oil

2 cloves garlic, minced

2 tablespoons finely chopped fresh basil, or 1 teaspoon dried basil

1 tablespoon finely chopped fresh rosemary, or 1 teaspoon dried rosemary

1 tablespoon finely chopped fresh thyme, or 1 teaspoon dried thyme

4 cups chicken stock or broth

¼ cup dry red wine

2 tablespoons tomato paste

½ cup half-and-half

2 tablespoons Parmesan cheese

Baked Garlic Croutons (page 57) for topping

186

# GARDEN-FRESH TOMATO-BASIL SOUP

**Fresh tomatoes and basil complement each other in this summertime soup. Make it when fresh tomatoes and herbs are in season.**

3 tablespoons butter or margarine

$^1/_2$ cup chopped yellow onion

2 cloves garlic, minced

3 tablespoons all-purpose flour

2 cups chicken stock or broth

3 pounds medium tomatoes (9 or 10), peeled (see page 23), seeded, and chopped

3 sprigs parsley, chopped

1 teaspoon sugar

$^1/_2$ teaspoon salt

1 tablespoon chopped fresh thyme, or $^1/_2$ teaspoon dried thyme

$^1/_4$ cup chopped fresh basil, or 1 teaspoon dried basil

$^1/_4$ teaspoon paprika

1 bay leaf

2 or 3 drops Tabasco sauce

Freshly ground pepper to taste

Light sour cream or plain nonfat yogurt for topping (optional)

Chiffonade of fresh basil leaves (see page 25) for topping

In a soup pot over medium heat, melt butter. Add onion and garlic and sauté until tender, about 5 minutes. Stir in flour and blend until bubbly. Add stock and stir until slightly thickened, 1 to 2 minutes. Add remaining ingredients, except toppings. Reduce heat to medium-low and simmer, covered, for 30 minutes. Remove bay leaf and discard.

Transfer in batches to a food processor or blender and purée. Return to pot to reheat. Ladle into bowls and top with a dollop of sour cream, if desired, and a few strips of basil.

**SERVES 4**

# ITALIAN COUNTRY VEGETABLE SOUP

**SERVES 6**

**This thick soup, loaded with vegetables and packed with flavor, is perfect to serve guests for a casual supper. Include Fresh Herb Garlic Bread (page 48) and a mixed green salad with Italian dressing.**

In a large Dutch oven over medium heat, warm oil. Add prosciutto, onion, carrot, celery, and garlic. Sauté until tender, about 5 minutes. Add parsley, cabbage, salt, pepper, basil, and oregano and cook for 1 minute. Add stock, tomato paste, and Parmesan cheese and mix well. Add drained beans. Bring to a boil. Reduce heat to medium-low and simmer, covered, until beans are tender, about 1 hour and fifteen minutes. Add more liquid if soup seems too thick.

Remove lid, add chard, and simmer, uncovered, until chard is tender, about 10 minutes, stirring several times. Ladle into bowls and sprinkle with Garlic Crumbs.

1 tablespoon olive oil

2 ounces prosciutto, chopped

1 cup chopped yellow onion

1 carrot, chopped

1 stalk celery, chopped

1 large clove garlic, chopped

¼ cup chopped parsley

2 cups shredded cabbage

1 teaspoon salt

¼ teaspoon freshly ground pepper

³⁄₄ teaspoon dried basil

½ teaspoon dried oregano

4 cups chicken stock or broth

1 tablespoon tomato paste

2 tablespoons freshly grated Parmesan cheese

1 cup Great Northern beans, presoaked (see page 29)

2 cups sliced red chard, stems removed, or sliced fresh spinach leaves

Garlic Crumbs (page 58) for topping

**Top this hearty main-course soup with lots of grated Parmesan cheese. Serve with Basic Crostini (page 59) and a glass of wine. You might think you are in Italy!**

1 tablespoon olive oil

1 cup chopped yellow onion

1 cup chopped red bell pepper

2 large cloves garlic, chopped

$\frac{1}{2}$ teaspoon dried basil

$\frac{1}{2}$ teaspoon dried oregano

$\frac{1}{8}$ teaspoon crushed red pepper flakes

1 teaspoon salt

$5\frac{1}{2}$ cups chicken stock or broth

1 carrot, chopped

1 package (9 ounces) fresh cheese ravioli

2 small zucchini (about $\frac{1}{2}$ pound), chopped

Freshly grated Parmesan cheese for topping

In a large soup pot or Dutch oven over medium heat, warm oil. Add onion, bell pepper, garlic, basil, oregano, red pepper flakes, and salt and sauté until vegetables are tender, 5 to 6 minutes. Add stock and carrot. Reduce heat to medium-low and simmer, covered, 10 minutes. Increase heat and bring soup to a boil. Add ravioli and zucchini and cook, uncovered, until ravioli is tender, 6 to 7 minutes. Ladle into bowls and sprinkle with Parmesan cheese.

# MEXICAN VEGETABLE SOUP

**SERVES 4 TO 6**

**This soup is convenient to make because you will have most of the ingredients on hand. Serve with an avocado and jicama salad and warm tortillas for a well-rounded meal.**

In a large soup pot over medium heat, warm oil. Sauté onion, bell pepper, and garlic until tender, about 5 minutes. Add remaining ingredients except toppings and simmer, covered, until vegetables are tender, about 30 minutes. Ladle into bowls and top with a dollop of sour cream and a few crushed tortilla chips.

1 tablespoon vegetable oil

½ cup chopped yellow onion

½ cup chopped red bell pepper

2 cloves garlic, minced

2 cups chicken or vegetable stock or broth

1 tomato, peeled (see page 23), seeded, and chopped

1 can (14½ ounces) whole tomatoes, coarsely chopped, with juice

2 medium russet potatoes (about 1 pound), peeled and cubed

1 cup fresh or frozen corn kernels

3 tablespoons canned diced green chiles, drained

½ teaspoon salt, or more to taste

½ teaspoon ground cumin

¼ teaspoon dried oregano

Freshly ground pepper to taste

Light sour cream for topping

Crushed tortilla chips for topping

180

**This soup of mixed vegetables is healthful and soothing. It is a good soup to take to a sick friend. Include some Flaky Cheese Biscuits (page 55) as well.**

2 tablespoons butter or margarine

1 yellow onion, chopped

1 clove garlic, minced

1 medium russet potato (about ½ pound), peeled and cubed

1 medium sweet potato (about ½ pound), peeled and cubed

2 carrots, sliced

1 stalk celery, chopped

2 sprigs parsley

1 can (14½ ounces) diced tomatoes, with juice

3 cups chicken stock or broth

1 teaspoon salt

½ teaspoon dried basil

¼ teaspoon dried marjoram

¼ teaspoon dried oregano

Freshly ground pepper to taste

¼ cup plain nonfat yogurt for topping

In a soup pot over medium heat, melt butter. Add onion and garlic and sauté until tender, about 5 minutes. Add potato, sweet potato, carrots, celery, parsley, tomatoes, 2 cups of the stock, salt, basil, marjoram, oregano, and pepper. Bring to a boil. Reduce heat to medium-low and simmer, covered, until vegetables are tender, 25 to 30 minutes. Transfer in batches to a food processor and process until mixture is chunky.

Return to pan, add remaining 1 cup stock, and reheat. Ladle into bowls and top with a dollop of yogurt.

SERVES 4

## HERBED VEGETABLE SOUP

# VEGETABLE CHILI WITH SOUR CREAM TOPPING

### SERVES 6

**This vegetarian chili has lots of fresh vegetables simmered in a rich sauce. The addition of cocoa gives it an authentic, unique flavor.**

In a Dutch oven over medium heat, warm oil. Add zucchini, celery, carrot, onion, and garlic and sauté until tender, about 6 minutes. Add remaining ingredients, except topping. Bring to a boil. Reduce heat to medium-low and simmer, uncovered, until flavors are blended, 45 minutes to 1 hour. Ladle into bowls and pass the topping separately.

1 tablespoon vegetable oil

1 zucchini, unpeeled, quartered lengthwise and sliced

1 stalk celery, chopped

1 carrot, chopped

1 cup chopped yellow onion

2 cloves garlic, minced

2 cans (14½ ounces each) kidney beans, drained and rinsed

1 can (14½ ounces) whole tomatoes, coarsely chopped, with juice

1 can (14½ ounces) tomatoes in thick purée

1 cup vegetable stock or broth or water

1 tablespoon chili powder

1 tablespoon unsweetened cocoa powder

½ teaspoon dried oregano

½ teaspoon ground cumin

2 drops Tabasco sauce

½ teaspoon salt

Freshly ground pepper to taste

Sour Cream Topping (recipe follows)

## SOUR CREAM TOPPING

½ cup light sour cream

½ cup firmly packed grated Cheddar cheese

4 green onions, including some tender green tops, finely chopped

In a small bowl, mix all ingredients together. Serve at room temperature.

# SUMMER VEGETABLE STEW WITH PENNE, FETA CHEESE, AND PINE NUTS

**SERVES 4**

**Bring the garden to the table with vine-ripened tomatoes, zucchini, and fresh herbs. Prepare the vegetables ahead and add the pasta, cheese, and nuts just before serving. This makes a good side dish for a grilled dinner.**

In a large soup pot over medium heat, warm oil. Add zucchini and onion and sauté for about 5 minutes. Add garlic, basil, oregano, salt, pepper, and stock. Reduce heat to medium-low and simmer, covered, stirring occasionally, until vegetables are slightly tender, about 5 minutes. Add tomatoes and parsley and cook, covered, 6 to 7 minutes longer. Do not overcook.

Meanwhile, cook penne in a large pot of boiling water until just tender, 7 to 10 minutes. Drain and add to stew. Simmer, uncovered, until flavors are blended, 5 to 10 minutes. Transfer to a serving dish and sprinkle with feta cheese and pine nuts.

2 tablespoons olive oil

2 large zucchini, unpeeled, cut into 1/2-inch slices

1 large yellow onion, sliced and separated into rings

4 cloves garlic, chopped

1/4 cup fresh basil, or 1 teaspoon dried basil

3/4 teaspoon dried oregano

1 teaspoon salt

Freshly ground pepper to taste

1/2 cup vegetable or chicken stock or broth

4 summer tomatoes (about 1 1/2 pounds) peeled (see page 23), seeded, and chopped

1/4 cup chopped parsley

4 ounces uncooked penne (about 1 1/2 cups)

1/3 cup crumbled feta cheese

1/4 cup pine nuts, toasted (see page 26)

193

**The secret to a good vegetable stew is to simmer the vegetables gently and not allow them to boil. Boiling causes the vegetables to be mushy and lose flavor. Serve this stew with Fresh Herb Garlic Bread (page 48).**

3 carrots, sliced

3 stalks celery, sliced

1 yellow onion, sliced

2 leeks, white and light green parts only, sliced

1 red bell pepper, seeded and cut into strips

2 cloves garlic, minced

2 cups shredded cabbage

1 large zucchini, cut into ½-inch slices

1 Roma tomato, sliced

½ cup chopped parsley

½ teaspoon dried oregano

1 teaspoon dried basil

1 teaspoon salt

Freshly ground pepper to taste

2 tablespoons olive oil

¼ cup chicken stock or broth or water

¼ cup dry white wine

Parmesan cheese for topping

Layer vegetables in the order listed in a large, lightly sprayed or oiled nonstick pot or Dutch oven. Sprinkle each layer with some of the parsley, oregano, basil, salt, pepper, and a few drops of olive oil. Mix stock and wine together and pour over stew. Do not stir.

Cover and simmer over low heat until vegetables are tender-crisp, about 30 minutes, or longer if you like them soft. Ladle into bowls and sprinkle with Parmesan cheese.

# UNION STREET RATATOUILLE (RA-TAH-TOO-EE)

**SERVES 8 TO 10**

**195**

A popular dish with a melodic name from the French region of Provence. Vegetables and herbs are layered and topped with olive oil, then slowly baked in the oven until very soft. It can be served hot or cold. This makes a large amount.

Preheat oven to 325°F. In a large Dutch oven, layer onions, eggplant, zucchini, bell peppers, and tomatoes. Sprinkle each layer with a little salt, pepper, herbs, and garlic. Drizzle oil over the top. Do not stir. Bake, covered, until vegetables are very tender, about 1 hour and 15 minutes. Baste with juices. Serve in bowls or as a side dish.

2 large yellow onions, sliced

1 medium eggplant, unpeeled, cut into ³/₄-inch cubes

3 large zucchini, cut into ¹/₂-inch slices

1 green bell pepper, seeded and cut into 1-inch pieces

1 red bell pepper, seeded and cut into 1-inch pieces

4 medium tomatoes, cut into wedges

2 teaspoons salt

Freshly ground pepper to taste

¹/₄ cup chopped basil leaves, or 2 teaspoons dried basil

2 teaspoons snipped fresh rosemary, or ¹/₂ teaspoon dried rosemary

¹/₂ cup chopped parsley

4 cloves garlic, minced

¹/₄ cup olive oil

# LEGUME

SOUPS & STEWS

Legumes (beans, lentils, peas, soybeans, and peanuts) are wonderful in soups. They add texture and flavor and, when combined with vegetables, produce soups full of nutrients. They are economical and convenient, and are often used as a meat substitute.

Spicy Black Bean Soup is just one of the favorites, along with Tuscan White Bean Soup with Tomatoes and a warming Lentil, Split Pea, and Ham Soup included in this chapter.

# SPICY BLACK BEAN SOUP

### SERVES 4 TO 6

**There are many versions of this soup, but this is one of the best to serve on a midwinter day. Purée it in the food processor until it's the consistency you prefer—chunky or smooth. Offer a choice of toppings in small bowls.**

In a large soup pot over medium heat, warm oil. Add vegetables and garlic and sauté until tender, about 5 minutes. Add drained beans to soup pot. Add stock, water, cumin, oregano, and coriander. Bring to a boil over high heat. Reduce heat to medium-low and cook, covered, until beans are tender, about 2 hours. Add salt and pepper and cook, uncovered, 10 minutes longer.

Transfer in batches to food processor and purée to desired consistency. Return soup to pan, add lime juice and cilantro, if desired, and reheat. Ladle into bowls and serve, passing toppings separately.

1 tablespoon vegetable oil

1 cup chopped yellow onion

1 cup chopped celery

1 large carrot, chopped

2 cloves garlic, minced

2 cups dried black beans, picked over, rinsed, and presoaked (see page 29)

4 cups chicken stock or broth

4 cups water

1 teaspoon ground cumin

1 teaspoon dried oregano

¼ teaspoon ground coriander

1 teaspoon salt

Freshly ground pepper to taste

2 tablespoons lime juice

¼ cup chopped cilantro or parsley (optional)

### TOPPINGS

Grated Monterey Jack cheese

Chopped tomatoes

Sour cream or plain nonfat yogurt

Tomatillo salsa

Lime wedges

**Canned beans are used in this soup for convenience and quick preparation, but with the same good flavor.**

1 tablespoon vegetable oil

1 cup chopped red onion

2 cloves garlic, minced

4 cans (15 ounces each) black beans, drained and rinsed

4 cups chicken stock or broth

1 cup crushed tomatoes with rich purée

1 teaspoon ground cumin

1 teaspoon dried thyme

$1/2$ teaspoon chili powder

1 teaspoon salt

Freshly ground pepper to taste

**TOPPINGS**

Chopped cilantro or parsley

Grated Monterey Jack cheese

Chopped tomatoes

Sour cream or plain nonfat yogurt

Tomatillo salsa

Lime wedges

In a large Dutch oven over medium heat, warm oil. Add onion and garlic and sauté until tender, about 5 minutes. Add remaining ingredients except toppings. Bring soup to a boil. Reduce heat to medium-low and simmer, uncovered, until flavors are blended, about 20 minutes. To thicken soup, purée half of the beans with some stock in a food processor. Return to Dutch oven and mix well. Ladle into bowls and sprinkle with cilantro. Pass the additional toppings separately.

197

# BLACK BEAN AND ROASTED TOMATO SOUP

**SERVES 4**

**Roasting the tomatoes and onion adds depth to this tempting soup. Serve it on a cool day with French Bread with Garlic Spread (page 50).**

Preheat oven to 350°F. In a roasting pan, combine tomatoes, onion, and garlic. Add oil and oregano and mix well. Roast vegetables until soft and lightly browned, about 50 minutes.

Pour ½ cup of the stock into the pan and stir to loosen bits. Transfer vegetables and stock to a food processor and blend. Add half the beans and blend again. Transfer to a soup pot over medium heat. Add remaining 1½ cups stock, remaining beans, chili powder, salt, and pepper. Simmer until flavors are blended, 10 to 15 minutes. Ladle into bowls and top with a dollop of sour cream and some green onions.

2 medium tomatoes (about 1 pound), peeled (see page 23), seeded, and cut into wedges

1 yellow onion, cut into wedges

2 large cloves garlic, chopped

1 tablespoon olive oil

¾ teaspoon dried oregano

2 cups chicken or vegetable stock or broth

2 cans (15 ounces each) black beans, drained and rinsed

½ teaspoon chili powder

½ teaspoon salt

Freshly ground pepper to taste

Sour cream for topping

Chopped green onions, including some tender green tops, for topping

188

**This old standby is still popular with all ages. The ham bone adds extra flavor, but it can be omitted, or you can use a pork bone instead. If you leave out the ham bone, taste for seasonings and add more salt.**

2 cups (1 pound) dried navy beans, sorted and presoaked (see page 29)

8 cups water

1 ham bone

1 bay leaf

1 medium yellow onion, chopped

3 stalks celery, sliced

2 cloves garlic, minced

1 teaspoon salt

Freshly ground pepper to taste

Put drained beans in a large soup pot. Add the water and bring to a boil. Add ham bone and bay leaf. Reduce heat to medium-low and simmer, covered, about 1 hour. Add onion, celery, and garlic and simmer, covered, until beans and vegetables are tender, stirring several times, about 1 hour longer.

Remove bone from soup, cut off meat, and return meat to soup. Remove bay leaf and discard. Mash some of the beans with the back of a spoon against the side of the pan until soup is desired consistency. It will thicken as it cooks. Season with salt and pepper. Simmer until ready to serve.

**SERVES 6**

# NAVY BEAN SOUP WITH HAM BONE

# TUSCAN WHITE BEAN SOUP WITH TOMATOES

**SERVES 6 TO 8**

**This timeless soup is from the Tuscan region of Italy. Classic Garlic Bread (page 49) is a must.**

In a large Dutch oven over medium heat, warm oil. Add onion, leek, carrot, and garlic and sauté until tender, about 5 minutes. Add herbs, tomatoes, drained beans, and stock.

Bring to a boil. Reduce heat to low and simmer, covered, 1 hour. Remove fresh herb sprigs, if using, and bay leaf and discard. Simmer, uncovered, until beans are tender, about 30 minutes longer. Add salt and pepper. Ladle into soup bowls and sprinkle with Parmesan cheese.

2 tablespoons olive oil

1 cup chopped yellow onion

1 leek, white and light green parts only, chopped

1 carrot, peeled and chopped

2 cloves garlic, chopped

1 sprig fresh rosemary, or $\frac{1}{4}$ teaspoon dried rosemary

1 sprig fresh thyme, or $\frac{1}{4}$ teaspoon dried thyme

1 bay leaf

1 can (14$\frac{1}{2}$ ounces) whole tomatoes, coarsely chopped, with juice

2 cups dried Great Northern beans, presoaked (see page 29)

6 cups chicken stock or broth

1$\frac{1}{2}$ teaspoons salt

Freshly ground pepper to taste

Freshly grated Parmesan cheese for topping

**Fresh sage adds a new dimension to this hearty soup. If you like, follow the Italian tradition of drizzling a little olive oil over the top just before serving. Serve with Parmesan Crostini (page 62).**

4 ounces pancetta or bacon (2 slices), chopped

2 stalks celery, chopped

1 carrot, chopped

½ cup chopped yellow onion

2 cloves garlic, minced

1 tablespoon olive oil

1½ cups Great Northern beans, presoaked (see page 29)

6 cups chicken stock or broth

4 large tomatoes (about 2 pounds), peeled (see page 23), seeded, and chopped

6 fresh sage leaves, chopped, or ½ teaspoon dried sage

½ teaspoon salt

Freshly ground pepper to taste

Olive oil for topping (optional)

Fresh sage leaves for garnish

In a large soup pot over medium heat, combine pancetta, vegetables, garlic, and olive oil. Sauté until pancetta is crisp and vegetables are tender, about 5 minutes. Add drained beans, stock, tomatoes, and sage. Bring to a boil. Reduce heat to medium-low and simmer, covered, until beans are tender, about 1½ hours. Transfer soup in batches to a food processor and purée until smooth. Return to pot and reheat. Season with salt and pepper. Ladle into bowls and drizzle a little olive oil on top, if desired. Garnish with sage leaves.

**201**

# BEAN AND BEER SOUP WITH HAM

**SERVES 4**

**Serve this hearty soup with cold beer and pretzels after a sporting event or for game watching on TV.**

In a large soup pot over medium heat, warm oil. Add vegetables and garlic and sauté until tender, about 5 minutes. Add remaining ingredients except toppings. Reduce heat to medium-low and simmer, uncovered, until flavors are blended, about 30 minutes.

For a thicker soup, transfer 2 cups vegetables to a food processor or blender and purée. Return to pan. Ladle into bowls and sprinkle with green onions, cheese, and crushed pretzels.

2 tablespoons vegetable oil

1 cup chopped yellow onion

2 carrots, chopped

2 stalks celery, chopped

2 cloves garlic, minced

6 cups chicken stock or broth

1 cup beer, allowed to go flat

1 teaspoon Worcestershire sauce

2 or 3 drops Tabasco sauce

$\frac{1}{2}$ teaspoon dried marjoram

1 teaspoon dried thyme

1 teaspoon salt

Freshly ground pepper to taste

2 cans (15 ounces) Great Northern beans or other white beans, drained and rinsed

2 cups cubed ham

$\frac{1}{4}$ cup chopped parsley

$\frac{1}{4}$ cup sliced green onions, including some tender green tops, for topping

1 cup grated Cheddar cheese for topping

Crushed pretzels for topping

202

# PASTA AND BEAN SOUP

**SERVES 6**

In this fragrant soup, pasta and beans are combined with a hint of rosemary. If you prefer, substitute fresh basil leaves for the rosemary.

2 slices thick bacon (about 3 ounces), diced

1 cup chopped onion

$^1/_2$ cup chopped red bell pepper

1 can (15 ounces) garbanzo beans, drained and rinsed

4 cups vegetable or chicken stock or broth

1 can (14$^1/_2$ ounces) crushed tomatoes in thick purée

1 teaspoon salt

Freshly ground pepper to taste

1 sprig fresh rosemary (2 inches), or 1 teaspoon dried rosemary

1 sprig parsley

3 ounces uncooked penne or other short pasta (about 1 cup)

Chopped fresh rosemary for topping

Freshly grated Parmesan cheese for topping

In a large Dutch oven over medium-high heat, cook bacon until crisp, about 5 minutes. Reduce heat to medium. Add onion and bell pepper and sauté until tender, about 5 minutes.

In a food processor, purée half of the beans with $^1/_2$ cup of the stock. Add puréed beans and whole beans to the Dutch oven. Add remaining 3$^1/_2$ cups stock, tomatoes, salt, pepper, rosemary, and parsley. Simmer, uncovered, 10 minutes. Increase heat to medium-high, add pasta, and cook until tender, about 10 minutes. Remove rosemary and parsley sprigs. Serve in bowls topped with some chopped rosemary and Parmesan cheese.

# MIXED BEAN SOUP

**SERVES 6 TO 8**

You can purchase packages of mixed beans containing ten different varieties. This makes a visually attractive soup with lots of color to serve for a Super Bowl party.

In a large soup pot over high heat, combine beans and water. Bring to a boil. Reduce heat to medium-low and simmer, partially covered, about 1 hour.

Add ham shanks, vegetables, garlic, and chili powder and simmer, covered, until beans and vegetables are tender, about 40 minutes. Remove ham shanks to a plate to cool.

Transfer 1 cup or more of the beans and vegetables and some of the stock to a food processor or blender and purée. Return to soup.

Remove meat from ham shanks and cut into bite-sized pieces. Add to soup. Add salt and pepper and stir in vinegar and Tabasco sauce. Simmer, uncovered, until flavors are blended, about 5 minutes.

1½ cups (10 to 12 ounces) mixed beans, presoaked (see page 29)

7 cups water

2 ham shanks (about 1 pound)

1 large yellow onion, chopped

2 stalks celery, chopped

2 carrots, chopped

2 cloves garlic, minced

1½ teaspoons chili powder, or more to taste

1½ teaspoons salt

Freshly ground pepper to taste

1 tablespoon red wine vinegar

2 or 3 drops Tabasco sauce

A warming and filling soup to take to a tailgate party on a chilly fall day. Transport it in several large thermoses to keep it hot. Serve with crudités and crostini with a beer cheese spread.

6 slices bacon, diced

2 cups chopped yellow onion

2 cloves garlic, minced

1 tablespoon chili powder

½ teaspoon ground allspice

⅛ teaspoon ground cloves

1 teaspoon salt

1 can (15 ounces) garbanzo beans, drained and rinsed

1 can (15 ounces) pinto beans, drained and rinsed

1 cup frozen lima beans, rinsed under hot water

1 can (28 ounces) tomatoes, coarsely chopped, with juice

3 cups beef stock or broth

2 tablespoons light molasses

1 teaspoon Worcestershire sauce

2 tablespoons brown sugar

1 teaspoon Tabasco sauce

1 tablespoon cider vinegar

In a Dutch oven over medium-high heat, cook bacon until crisp. Remove from Dutch oven, leaving 2 tablespoons bacon drippings. Add onion and garlic and sauté until tender, about 5 minutes. Stir in chili powder, allspice, cloves, and salt. Add bacon and remaining ingredients except vinegar.

Reduce heat to medium-low and simmer, covered, stirring occasionally, until flavors are blended, about 1 hour. Stir in vinegar and simmer for 5 minutes longer.

# LENTIL, SPLIT PEA, AND HAM SOUP

**SERVES 4 TO 6**

**Lentils and split peas do not have to be presoaked, but they need to be thoroughly rinsed and sorted for any rocks or debris. Combined with vegetables and ham, they make a substantial and wholesome soup. For a vegetarian version, use vegetable stock or water instead of the chicken stock, and omit the ham.**

In a large soup pot, combine all ingredients except vinegar, salt, pepper, and Parmesan cheese. Bring to a boil. Reduce heat to medium and simmer, covered, until lentils and peas are soft, about 1 hour. Remove ham bone, if using, cut off meat, and return meat to pot. Discard bone. Stir in vinegar, salt, and pepper and simmer 10 minutes longer. Remove bay leaf and discard. Ladle into bowls and sprinkle with Parmesan cheese.

4 cups chicken stock or broth

4 cups water

1 cup chopped yellow onion

1 carrot, chopped

1 leek, white and light green parts only, chopped

1 stalk celery, chopped

1 large clove garlic, chopped

½ cup brown lentils, rinsed and picked over

½ cup green split peas, rinsed and picked over

1 cup cubed ham, or 1 ham bone

1 cup chopped tomatoes, fresh or canned

¼ teaspoon dried thyme

1 bay leaf

1 tablespoon red wine vinegar

Salt and freshly ground pepper to taste

Freshly grated Parmesan cheese for topping

Lentils are a good source of vitamins and minerals and are often used as a meat substitute, especially in the Middle East. Here they are combined with brown rice and vegetables in a highly nutritious and easy-to-make soup.

1 cup dried brown lentils, rinsed and picked over

1/2 cup long-grain brown rice

3 cups chicken or vegetable stock or broth

4 cups water

2 teaspoons salt

1/2 teaspoon dried oregano

1/4 teaspoon dried thyme

Freshly ground pepper to taste

2 cloves garlic, minced

2 stalks celery, chopped

1 small yellow onion, chopped

2 carrots, sliced

1 can (14 1/2 ounces) whole tomatoes, coarsely chopped, with juice

1 tablespoon cider vinegar

Freshly grated Parmesan cheese for topping

Put lentils in a large soup pot. Add remaining ingredients except tomatoes, vinegar, and Parmesan cheese. Bring to a boil. Reduce heat to medium-low and simmer, covered, 45 minutes.

Add tomatoes and vinegar and simmer, uncovered, over low heat to blend flavors, 15 minutes longer. Ladle into bowls and sprinkle with cheese.

**SERVES 6 TO 8**

# LENTIL AND BROWN RICE SOUP

# GOOD OLD SPLIT-PEA SOUP

**SERVES 4 TO 6**

**Some of the old standbys that mother made are still the best. Ham adds flavor to this old-fashioned soup. You could also use a ham shank.**

In a large soup pot, combine all the ingredients except the salt and pepper. Bring to a boil. Reduce heat to medium-low and simmer, uncovered, until peas are tender, about 1 hour. Add salt and pepper. Remove bay leaf and discard. Mash some of the peas against the side of the pan with a spoon. Add more water if soup gets too thick.

4 cups water

2 cups chicken stock or broth

2 carrots, chopped

1/2 yellow onion, chopped

1 1/2 cups green split peas, rinsed and picked over

1/4 teaspoon dried thyme

1/4 teaspoon dried marjoram

1 bay leaf

1 cup diced ham

Salt and freshly ground pepper to taste

**Just throw it all in a pot and in about an hour you will have a healthy, hearty soup on the table.**

1 cup lentils, rinsed and picked over

1 cup split peas, rinsed and picked over

8 cups water

1 whole ham shank (about ³/₄ pound)

1 large yellow onion, chopped

2 cloves garlic, minced

2 carrots, chopped

2 stalks celery, chopped

2 bay leaves

1 teaspoon dried thyme

¹/₂ teaspoon dried oregano

1 teaspoon salt

Freshly ground pepper to taste

1 tablespoon balsamic vinegar

In a large soup pot over high heat, combine all ingredients except salt, pepper, and vinegar. Bring to a boil. Reduce heat to medium-low and simmer, covered, until lentils and peas are tender, about 1 hour, stirring occasionally.

Remove ham shank from soup and cool slightly. Cut meat into small pieces and return to soup. Season with salt and pepper and stir in vinegar. Remove bay leaves and discard.

**NOTE:** *To thicken soup, purée half the soup (before adding the ham meat) in the food processor. Return to the soup pot.*

209

# BLACK BEAN CHILI

## SERVES 6

**You won't miss the meat in this creative black bean-vegetable chili. The toppings add flavor and interest; garnish with a sprig of cilantro.**

In a soup pot over medium heat, warm oil. Add onion, celery, and garlic and sauté until tender, about 5 minutes. Add remaining ingredients except garnish and toppings. Reduce heat to medium-low and simmer, uncovered, until flavors are blended, about 40 minutes. Ladle into bowls, garnish with cilantro sprigs, and pass the toppings separately.

1 tablespoon olive oil

2 cups chopped yellow onion

1 cup finely chopped celery

4 cloves garlic, minced

3 cans (14$^{1}/_{2}$ ounces each) black beans, drained and rinsed

2 cans (14$^{1}/_{2}$ ounces each) diced tomatoes, with juice

1 can (4 ounces) diced green chiles, drained

1$^{1}/_{2}$ cups beef stock or broth

1 tablespoon chili powder

1 teaspoon dried oregano

1 teaspoon ground cumin

1 teaspoon salt

Freshly ground pepper to taste

3 tablespoons chopped cilantro or parsley

Cilantro sprigs for garnish

### TOPPINGS

Grated Monterey Jack cheese

Sour cream

Salsa

Chopped hard-cooked eggs

210

**This chili is served in a bowl lined with a tortilla. For a fun party, make several kinds of chili, such as Cabin Chili with Meat (page 79) and Black Bean Chili (opposite page), and let guests try them all. Include an assortment of toppings.**

1 pound dry navy beans or other white beans, sorted and presoaked (see page 29)

6 cups water or chicken stock or broth, or a combination

$\frac{1}{2}$ large yellow onion, chopped

4 cloves garlic, minced

1 teaspoon ground white pepper

1 teaspoon dried oregano

1 teaspoon ground cumin

1 can (4 ounces) diced green chiles, drained

3 to 4 cups shredded or diced cooked chicken or turkey breast

$\frac{1}{2}$ teaspoon salt

6 flour tortillas, warmed

**TOPPINGS**

Salsa

Sour cream

Chopped green onions

Chopped cilantro

Grated Monterey Jack cheese

Lime wedges

Tabasco sauce

In a large soup pot over high heat, combine drained beans, 5 cups of the water, onion, garlic, white pepper, oregano, and cumin and bring to a boil. Reduce heat to medium-low and simmer, covered, until beans are tender, $1\frac{1}{2}$ to 2 hours, stirring occasionally. Add chiles, chicken or turkey, and salt. Simmer, uncovered, 10 minutes longer. Add remaining 1 cup water if too thick. Line 6 large bowls with a tortilla and spoon in chili. Pass the toppings separately.

**SERVES 6**

# WHITE CHILI WITH CHICKEN OR TURKEY

# LENTIL, VEGETABLE SOUP WITH ANDOUILLE SAUSAGE

**SERVES 4 TO 6**

**Andouille sausage is a smoked, highly seasoned pork and beef sausage especially popular in the South. It adds a great spicy flavor to this soup.**

In a large soup pot over high heat, bring all ingredients except zucchini, sausage, and lemon wedges to a boil. Reduce heat to medium-low and simmer, covered, 45 minutes, stirring occasionally. Add zucchini and sausage and simmer, covered, until vegetables are tender and flavors are blended, about 15 to 20 minutes longer. Ladle into bowls and serve with a lemon wedge. Add a squeeze of lemon on top, if desired.

3 1/2 cups water

2 cups chicken broth

1 cup dried lentils, sorted and rinsed

1 cup chopped yellow onion

1 celery stalk, sliced

2 carrots, sliced

1 tablespoon chopped parsley

1 teaspoon salt

1 medium zucchini, cut in half lengthwise then sliced into 1/2-inch pieces

6 ounces andouille sausage, halved lengthwise and cut into 1/2-inch pieces

Lemon wedges for garnish (optional)

# CREAM SOUPS

Cream soups are usually smooth, not chunky. They are often served as a gracious first course for a dinner party or luncheon.

Cream soups are made in several ways:

- With a white sauce—milk or cream stirred into a butter-flour roux (béchamel).
- With a stock-based white sauce (velouté).
- With milk or cream added to puréed vegetables or other ingredients.

Almost any vegetable purée will make a delicious cream soup. Purées are made by processing vegetables in a food processor, blender, or food mill.

A blender will give cream soups the creamiest, smoothest consistency. Cool the soup slightly to guard against burns. Do not fill the blender more than one third full at a time. Always have the lid on the blender when operating.

Other ingredients used to thicken cream soups are potatoes, tapioca, grains, bread, a butter-flour mixture, or egg yolk.

Bisques are made by adding poultry, fish, or shellfish to cream soups.

Garnishes are important on cream soups to enhance visual appeal.

Cream soups should be served either very hot or very cold. They can be made ahead and reheated. To reheat, place the soup over medium heat, stirring constantly, or place it over a pan of boiling water (double boiler). Add more liquid if too thick. Take care because cream soups scorch easily. If the soup is too thick, add some milk or stock. Cream soups do not freeze as well as other soups.

**Asparagus is available most of the year, but the early crop of the season offers the best flavor. Serve this soup as a first course.**

1 tablespoon butter or margarine

1 cup chopped yellow onion

1 tablespoon all-purpose flour

4 cups chicken stock or broth

1 pound asparagus, tough ends removed and discarded, cut into 1-inch pieces (about 2 cups)

1 medium russet potato (about ½ pound), peeled and cubed

½ teaspoon dried thyme

½ teaspoon salt

⅛ teaspoon ground white pepper

Sour cream or plain yogurt for topping

In a soup pot over medium heat, melt butter. Add onion and sauté until tender, about 5 minutes. Stir in flour until bubbly. Add 2 cups of the stock and stir until blended, 1 to 2 minutes. Add asparagus, potato, thyme, salt, and white pepper. Bring to a boil. Reduce heat to medium-low and simmer, covered, until vegetables are tender, about 20 minutes. Transfer in batches to a food processor or blender and purée. Return to pot. Add remaining 2 cups stock and simmer, uncovered, until flavors are blended, about 5 minutes longer. Ladle into bowls and top with a dollop of sour cream or plain yogurt.

**NOTE:** *If desired, reserve a few chopped asparagus tips for a garnish.*

213

# CREAMY ASPARAGUS SOUP WITH SHRIMP

**SERVES 4**

It's hard to believe that this creamy, rich soup does not call for heavy cream. Low-fat buttermilk provides the creamy texture, and a sprinkling of bay shrimp on top adds interest and originality. Serve as a prelude to a formal dinner.

In a soup pot over medium heat, melt butter. Add leeks and celery and sauté until tender, about 5 minutes. Add potato and stock. Reduce heat to medium-low and simmer, covered, about 10 minutes. Add asparagus and simmer, covered, until potato and asparagus are tender, about 10 minutes longer.

Transfer to a blender or food processor in batches and purée. Return to pot and stir in salt, pepper, and buttermilk and reheat. For a creamier soup, purée again. Serve in bowls with a few shrimp sprinkled on top.

2 tablespoons butter or margarine

2 leeks, white and light green parts only, sliced

1/2 cup chopped celery

1 large russet potato (about 3/4 pound), peeled and cubed

3 cups chicken stock or broth

1 pound asparagus, tough ends removed and discarded, cut into 1-inch pieces

1/2 teaspoon salt

1/8 teaspoon ground white pepper

1 to 1 1/2 cups buttermilk

1/2 cup bay shrimp for topping

214

**Broccoli is available year-round, but it is especially popular in the winter, when many garden vegetables are not available. Part of the soup is puréed for a creamy texture, but bits of broccoli remain for added character.**

4 cups chopped broccoli florets

1 cup chopped yellow onion

2 stalks celery, sliced

1 clove garlic, minced

1 large russet potato (about $^3/_4$ pound), peeled and sliced

1 cup chicken stock or broth

$1^1/_2$ to $1^3/_4$ cups milk

$1^1/_2$ cups grated Cheddar cheese

$^1/_4$ teaspoon dried thyme

$^1/_2$ teaspoon salt

$^1/_4$ teaspoon ground white pepper

1 tablespoon minced parsley

In a saucepan over high heat, combine broccoli, onion, celery, garlic, potato, and stock. Bring to a boil. Reduce heat to medium-low and simmer, covered, until vegetables are tender, about 15 minutes.

Transfer three fourths of the mixture to a food processor or blender and purée. Return to pan and add remaining ingredients. Heat gently, stirring, until cheese melts and soup is hot. Serve in bowls.

# LOW-FAT BROCCOLI YOGURT SOUP

**SERVES 4**

**Low-fat milk and nonfat yogurt keep the calories down in this creamy soup with bright green flecks of brocolli. Serve with crusty French bread or sesame crackers.**

In a saucepan over high heat, combine broccoli, potato, celery, onion, and 1 cup of the stock and bring to a boil. Reduce heat to medium-low and simmer, covered, until vegetables are tender, about 20 minutes.

Transfer to a food processor or blender in batches and purée until smooth. Return purée to pan and add remaining 1 cup stock and the milk. Using a wire whisk, blend in yogurt. Stir in basil, salt, pepper, and butter, if using, and heat gently to serving temperature; do not boil.

Ladle into bowls and top each with a dollop of yogurt, if desired.

**NOTE:** *For extra crunch, reserve 2 tablespoons chopped raw broccoli florets to sprinkle on soup when served.*

3 cups chopped broccoli florets

1 large russet potato (about $^3/_4$ pound), peeled and sliced

2 stalks celery, sliced

1 cup chopped yellow onion

2 cups chicken stock or broth

$^1/_2$ to $^3/_4$ cup low-fat milk

$^1/_2$ cup plain nonfat yogurt

2 tablespoons chopped fresh basil, or $^3/_4$ teaspoon dried basil

$^1/_2$ teaspoon salt

Freshly ground pepper to taste

1 tablespoon butter or margarine (optional)

Plain nonfat yogurt for topping (optional)

**This is a good soup to make in the winter, incorporating two complementary vegetables.**

1½ cups chopped broccoli florets

1½ cups chopped cauliflower florets

2 large russet potatoes (about 1½ pounds), peeled and cubed

1 cup chopped yellow onion

1½ cups chicken stock or broth

2 cups milk

1 teaspoon dried thyme

1 teaspoon salt

Freshly ground pepper to taste

1 tablespoon butter or margarine (optional)

Freshly grated Parmesan cheese for topping

In a soup pot over high heat, combine vegetables and 1 cup of the stock and bring to a boil. Reduce heat to medium-low and simmer, uncovered, until tender, about 15 minutes. Add milk, remaining ½ cup stock, thyme, salt, pepper, and butter, if using, and simmer, uncovered, until ingredients are blended, about 10 minutes. Ladle into bowls and sprinkle with cheese.

# CARROT SOUP WITH BASIL PESTO

**SERVES 4**

**A contrasting swirl of green pesto and sour cream adds a colorful accent.**

In a large soup pot over medium heat, melt butter. Add onion and garlic and sauté for 2 minutes. Add carrots, potato, sugar, salt, thyme, paprika, and white pepper and sauté until vegetables are tender, about 5 minutes longer. Add 1 cup of the stock. Reduce heat to medium-low and simmer, covered, until vegetables are tender, about 20 minutes.

Transfer in batches to a food processor or blender and purée. Return to pot. Add remaining 2¼ cups stock. Ladle into bowls and top with a dollop each of pesto and sour cream. Swirl together slightly for an artistic touch.

1 tablespoon butter or margarine

1 cup chopped yellow onion

2 cloves garlic, minced

3 carrots, sliced (about 2 cups)

1 medium russet potato (about ½ pound), peeled and cubed

1 teaspoon sugar

½ teaspoon salt

¼ teaspoon dried thyme

½ teaspoon paprika

⅛ teaspoon ground white pepper

3¼ cups chicken stock or broth

2 tablespoons Basil Pesto (see page 41) for topping

2 tablespoons sour cream for topping

218

**CARROT SOUP WITH CURRY**

**SERVES 4**

This can be made at any time of the year, but fresh carrots from the garden will impart the best flavor. Serve as a first course or for lunch with Herbed Buttermilk Sticks (page 51).

4 cups sliced carrots (about 1½ pounds)

½ yellow onion, chopped

1 small turnip, peeled and chopped

1 medium russet potato (about ½ pound), peeled and quartered

1 cup water

3 cups chicken stock or broth

1 teaspoon salt

½ teaspoon dried thyme

¼ to ½ teaspoon curry powder, depending on taste

¼ teaspoon paprika

⅛ teaspoon ground white pepper

Light sour cream or plain nonfat yogurt, for topping

In a saucepan over medium-high heat, combine carrots, onion, turnip, potato, and water. Bring to a boil. Reduce heat to low and simmer, covered, until vegetables are tender, about 30 minutes.

Transfer vegetables and any remaining liquid in batches to a food processor or blender and purée. Return to pan and add remaining ingredients except sour cream. Simmer, uncovered, over low heat until flavors are blended, about 10 minutes longer, stirring occasionally.

Ladle into bowls and top with a dollop of sour cream.

# DILLED CREAMY CARROT AND SWEET POTATO SOUP

**SERVES 6**

**Here is a good wintertime soup that is quick to make and easy on the calories.**

In a large soup pot over medium-high heat, combine carrots, onion, sweet potato, garlic, and 2 cups of the stock. Bring to a boil. Reduce heat to medium-low and simmer, covered, until vegetables are tender, about 30 minutes.

Transfer to a blender or food processor and pureé in batches. Return to soup pot. Add remaining 1 cup stock, 1 teaspoon dill, salt, white pepper, and buttermilk and reheat. Ladle into bowls and sprinkle with more dill weed.

1 pound baby carrots

1 small yellow onion, cut into large pieces

1 small sweet potato (about ³/₄ pound), peeled and cubed

1 clove garlic, cut up

3 cups chicken stock or broth

1 teaspoon dried dill weed, plus more for topping

¹/₂ teaspoon salt

¹/₈ teaspoon ground white pepper

1 cup buttermilk or milk

**Serve this rich, festive soup for the first course of a holiday dinner along with Cheese Wafers (page 54).**

2 tablespoons butter or margarine

8 large stalks celery, peeled (use a vegetable peeler) and thinly sliced (about 5 cups)

1 cup chopped yellow onion

2 cloves garlic, sliced

1 large russet potato (³/₄ pound), peeled and cubed

2 cups chicken stock or broth

¹/₂ teaspoon salt

¹/₈ teaspoon ground white pepper

1 bay leaf

1 cup milk

1 cup half-and-half

Celery leaves for garnish

In a large soup pot over medium heat, melt butter. Add celery, onion, and garlic and sauté until vegetables are tender, about 10 minutes. Add potato, stock, salt, white pepper, and bay leaf. Bring to a boil. Reduce heat to medium-low and simmer, covered, stirring once, until vegetables are very tender, about 20 minutes. Remove bay leaf and discard. Transfer to food processor or blender in batches and purée. Return to pot. Stir in milk and half-and-half and reheat. Ladle into bowls and garnish with celery leaves.

# CREAM OF CAULIFLOWER AND CHEESE SOUP

**SERVES 4**

**Set the mood for a relaxing dinner party by serving this delightful creamy soup for the first course.**

In a soup pot over medium heat, melt butter. Add onion, garlic, and celery and sauté until tender, about 5 minutes. Add cauliflower, stock, salt, and white pepper and bring to a boil. Reduce heat to medium-low and simmer, covered, until cauliflower is tender, about 15 minutes.

Transfer to a food processor or blender in batches and purée. Return to pot and add half-and-half and cheese. Whisk until cheese is melted and soup is smooth, about 5 minutes. Ladle into bowls and sprinkle with parsley and chopped cauliflower, if desired.

1 tablespoon butter or margarine

1 cup chopped yellow onion

1 clove garlic, minced

1 stalk celery, chopped

4 to 5 cups chopped cauliflower (about 1¾ pounds)

2 cups chicken stock or broth

½ teaspoon salt

⅛ teaspoon ground white pepper

1 cup half-and-half

1 cup (about 4 ounces) grated Monterey Jack cheese

Chopped parsley for topping

2 tablespoons chopped raw cauliflower for topping (optional)

This delicious low-calorie soup is creamy without the addition of cream. Fennel gives it a slight, pleasant licorice flavor. Use some of the fennel foliage for a garnish.

6 cups cauliflower florets (about 2 pounds)

1 bulb fennel, top removed (reserve foliage) and bulb chopped

½ cup chopped yellow onion

1 clove garlic, cut up

2 medium russet potatoes (about 1 pound), peeled, quartered, and sliced

2 stalks celery, sliced

4 cups chicken stock or broth

¾ teaspoon salt

⅛ teaspoon ground white pepper

½ cup half-and-half or milk

1 tablespoon butter or margarine (optional)

2 tablespoons chopped fennel foliage for topping

In a soup pot over high heat, combine cauliflower, fennel, onion, garlic, potatoes, celery, and 2 cups of the stock. Bring to a boil. Reduce heat to medium-low and simmer, covered, until vegetables are tender, about 10 minutes.

Transfer to a food processor or blender in batches and process until chunky. Return to pot and add remaining 2 cups stock, salt, white pepper, and half-and-half and simmer, uncovered, until flavors are blended, about 10 minutes longer. Add butter, if desired. Ladle into bowls and sprinkle with fennel foliage.

SERVES 6

# CAULIFLOWER AND FENNEL SOUP

# CREAMY LEEK SOUP

## SERVES 4

**224**

**Guests will be impressed by this creamy, pale green soup. Don't tell them how easy it is to make!**

In a large Dutch oven over medium heat, melt butter. Add leeks, onion, celery, and garlic and sauté until tender, 6 to 7 minutes. Add stock, thyme, salt, and pepper. Bring to a boil. Reduce heat to medium-low and simmer, covered, until vegetables are very tender, about 10 minutes. Transfer to a blender or food processor in batches and purée. Return to Dutch oven.

In the blender or food processor, blend cream cheese and sour cream until smooth. Add to soup and stir until smooth. Ladle into bowls and sprinkle with parsley.

2 tablespoons butter or margarine

3 large leeks, white and light green parts only, sliced (about 1 cup)

1 cup chopped yellow onion

2 stalks celery, sliced (about 1 cup)

1 clove garlic, minced

3 cups chicken stock or broth

½ teaspoon dried thyme

½ teaspoon salt

Freshly ground pepper to taste

1 package (3 ounces) cream cheese, cubed

1 cup light sour cream

Chopped parsley for topping

**Here is a sophisticated soup to serve for a first course or luncheon. For a really rich soup, use whipping cream. The nuts add extra crunch.**

¼ cup butter or margarine

1 cup chopped yellow onion

1 leek, white and light green parts only, sliced

1 pound white mushrooms, finely chopped

1 clove garlic, minced

1 tablespoon fresh lemon juice

¼ cup all-purpose flour

3 cups chicken stock or broth

1½ cups half-and-half or whipping cream

¼ teaspoon dried thyme

⅛ teaspoon ground white pepper

¾ teaspoon salt

2 tablespoons dry sherry or dry white wine

¼ cup chopped pecans for topping

In a soup pot over medium heat, melt butter. Add onion and leek and sauté for 3 minutes. Add mushrooms, garlic, and lemon juice and sauté until vegetables are soft, about 5 minutes longer. Add flour and stir until bubbly. Add stock and stir until thickened, 1 to 2 minutes. Add remaining ingredients except pecans. Reduce heat to medium-low and simmer, uncovered, until flavors are blended, about 10 minutes. Ladle into bowls and sprinkle with chopped nuts.

**NOTE:** *For a thicker soup, purée half of it before adding half-and-half in a food processor or blender, return to pot and reheat.*

225

# CREAM OF PORTOBELLO MUSHROOM SOUP

### SERVES 4 TO 6

**Portobello mushrooms are mature cremini mushrooms. They have a strong, intense flavor. Cream and wine make this soup rich and elegant.**

In a large soup pot over medium heat, melt butter. Add mushrooms, leeks, and onion and sauté until tender, 5 to 6 minutes. Add stock, salt, and pepper and simmer, covered, until vegetables are soft, 10 to 15 minutes. Transfer to blender in batches and purée. Return to pot and add half-and-half and sherry and mix well. Simmer, uncovered, until flavors are blended, about 10 minutes. Ladle into bowls and sprinkle with chives.

2½ tablespoons butter or margarine

4 medium portobello mushrooms (about 1½ pounds), stems removed, loose gills scraped off, and chopped

2 leeks, white and light green parts only, sliced

1 cup chopped yellow onion

3 cups chicken stock or broth

½ teaspoon salt

Freshly ground pepper to taste

1½ cups half-and-half

¼ cup dry sherry or dry white wine

Chopped chives for topping

# FRESH MINT PEA SOUP

**SERVES 6**

**Mint and fresh peas have a special affinity in this bright, lively soup. Frozen peas can also be used, but the soup will not have the same fresh, garden taste. Serve with toasted baguette slices.**

2 tablespoons butter or margarine

2 leeks, white and light green parts only, sliced

4 cups fresh peas or 2 packages (10 ounces each) frozen peas, rinsed

2 or 3 fresh mint leaves, torn, plus more for garnish

4 cups chicken stock or broth

2 tablespoons dry white wine (optional)

1 cup plain nonfat yogurt

2 or 3 drops Tabasco sauce

½ teaspoon salt

⅛ teaspoon ground white pepper

In a large saucepan over medium heat, melt butter. Add leeks and sauté until tender, about 5 minutes. Add peas, torn mint leaves, and stock and bring to a boil. Reduce heat to medium-low and cook, uncovered, 5 minutes. Stir in wine, if using, yogurt, Tabasco sauce, salt, and white pepper.

Transfer to a blender or food processor in batches and blend until smooth. Return to pan to reheat, but do not boil.

Ladle into bowls and garnish each with a mint leaf.

# BAKED POTATO SOUP

**SERVES 6**

**This soup has become a popular choice in many restaurants. It is a good way to use leftover potatoes, or you can bake them fresh. Baked potatoes have a different taste than boiled potatoes, which gives this soup an outstanding flavor.**

In a soup pot over medium heat, melt butter with oil. Add onion, bell pepper, garlic, and celery and sauté until tender, 6 to 7 minutes.

In a bowl, blend 1 cup of the stock with flour and whisk into vegetables. Add the remaining 3 cups stock, salt, white pepper, and potatoes and mix well. Reduce heat to medium-low and simmer, covered, until flavors are blended, about 10 minutes. Add milk and whisk in sour cream. Heat, but do not boil. Ladle into bowls and sprinkle with chives or onion tops.

1 tablespoon butter or margarine

1 tablespoon vegetable oil

1 cup chopped yellow onion

1/2 red bell pepper, seeded and chopped

2 cloves garlic, minced

2 stalks celery, chopped

4 cups chicken stock or broth

1/2 cup all-purpose flour

1 teaspoon salt

1/8 teaspoon ground white pepper

4 baked potatoes (about 1 1/2 pounds), skins removed, quartered lengthwise, and cut into 1/4-inch slices

1 cup milk

1 cup sour cream

Chopped chives or sliced green onion tops for topping

**The combination of sweet potatoes and russet potatoes gives this unique soup an appealing color with a slightly sweet flavor. Top it with a few apple pieces before serving to add a contrasting crispness to the smooth texture. Serve as a first course before a turkey dinner.**

1 tablespoon vegetable oil

1 small yellow onion, chopped

1 clove garlic, minced

2 stalks celery, chopped

2 large russet potatoes (1½ pounds total), peeled and sliced

1 large sweet potato (¾ pound), peeled and sliced

3½ cups chicken stock or broth

½ teaspoon dried thyme

¾ teaspoon salt

⅛ teaspoon ground white pepper

1 cup buttermilk or milk

1 Granny Smith apple, unpeeled, cored, and chopped for topping

In a large soup pot over medium heat, warm oil. Add onion, garlic, and celery and sauté until tender, about 5 minutes. Add potatoes and mix well. Add stock, thyme, salt, and white pepper and bring to a boil. Reduce heat to medium-low and simmer, covered, until potatoes are soft, about 15 minutes.

Transfer to a blender or food processor in batches and process until smooth. Return soup to pot and add buttermilk. Simmer until heated through, about 10 minutes. Ladle into bowls and top with a few pieces of apple.

# POTATO-LEEK SOUP (VICHYSSOISE)

**SERVES 4**

**There are many versions of this favorite French soup, but this is one of the best. It can be served hot or cold.**

In a large soup pot over medium heat, melt butter. Add vegetables and sauté for 3 minutes. Add 1 cup of the stock. Reduce heat to medium-low, and simmer, covered, until vegetables are tender, about 15 minutes. Add more stock, if necessary. Transfer to a blender or food processor in batches and purée. Return to pot and add remaining stock, half-and-half, salt, and white pepper and simmer 5 to 10 minutes longer. Blend again for extra creaminess, if desired. Ladle into bowls and sprinkle with chives.

2 tablespoons butter or margarine

3 leeks, white and light green parts only, chopped (about 2$\frac{1}{2}$ cups)

$\frac{1}{2}$ cup chopped yellow onion

3 medium russet potatoes (about 1$\frac{1}{2}$ pounds), peeled and chopped

2 cups chicken stock or broth

1 to 1$\frac{1}{4}$ cups half-and-half

$\frac{3}{4}$ teaspoon salt

$\frac{1}{4}$ teaspoon ground white pepper

Minced chives for topping

230

# CREAM OF RED ONION AND LEEK SOUP

**Don't be intimidated by the onions in this soup. Slow simmering makes them mellow and mild and easy to digest.**

3 tablespoons butter or margarine

2 large red onions (about 1½ pounds), chopped

2 leeks, white and light green parts only, chopped

2 stalks celery, chopped

2 cloves garlic, chopped

2 cups chicken stock or broth

½ teaspoon dried thyme

½ teaspoon paprika

¾ teaspoon salt

Dash of ground white pepper

1 cup milk

1 cup half-and-half

Chopped parsley for garnish

In a large soup pot over medium heat, melt butter. Add onions, leeks, celery, and garlic and sauté for about 10 minutes. Reduce heat to medium-low. Add stock, thyme, paprika, salt, and white pepper. Simmer, covered, until vegetables are very tender, 30 to 35 minutes. Transfer in batches to a blender or food processor and purée. Return to soup pot. Add milk and half-and-half and simmer, uncovered, until heated through, 5 to 10 minutes longer. Ladle into bowls and garnish with chopped parsley.

SERVES 6

# ROASTED RED PEPPER SOUP

**SERVES 4**

Serve this colorful soup hot or cold, along with bread sticks, for the first course of a festive dinner party. Roasting the red peppers intensifies their flavor and adds a smoky touch. This soup can also be made with yellow bell peppers, or make both and serve the two soups side by side in the same bowl. Just pour them slowly into the bowl at the same time.

In a soup pot over medium heat, warm oil. Add onion and sauté until tender, about 5 minutes. Add garlic and cook 30 seconds longer. Add potato, salt, thyme, red pepper flakes, and stock. Bring to a boil, reduce heat, cover, and simmer 15 minutes. Add roasted bell peppers and cook until flavors are blended, 5 to 10 minutes longer.

Working in batches, transfer to a blender or food processor and purée. Return to pot and add buttermilk. Gently heat to serving temperature; do not boil. Ladle into bowls, top with a dollop of yogurt or sour cream, if desired, and sprinkle with chives.

1 tablespoon vegetable oil

1 large yellow onion, chopped

2 cloves garlic, minced

1 small potato, peeled and chopped

$\frac{1}{2}$ teaspoon salt

$\frac{1}{4}$ teaspoon dried thyme

$\frac{1}{8}$ teaspoon red pepper flakes

2$\frac{1}{2}$ cups chicken stock or broth

3 large red bell peppers, roasted (see page 23) and cut up

1 cup buttermilk or milk

Plain nonfat yogurt or light sour cream for topping (optional)

2 tablespoons minced chives for garnish

**Serve this smooth soup in the fall or as the first course for Thanksgiving dinner. The apples give a surprise flavor and added crunch.**

1 tablespoon butter or margarine

½ cup chopped yellow onion

1 cup sliced celery

4 cups chicken stock or broth

2 tablespoons dry white wine

1 teaspoon salt

½ teaspoon dried sage

¼ teaspoon dried thyme

1 can (15 ounces) pumpkin

½ green apple, unpeeled, cored, and chopped for topping

Freshly grated Parmesan cheese for topping

In a soup pot over medium heat, melt butter. Add onion and celery and sauté until tender, about 5 minutes. Add 1 cup of the stock and simmer, covered, 10 minutes. Transfer to a blender or food processor in batches and purée until smooth. Return to pan and add the remaining 3 cups stock, wine, salt, sage, thyme, and pumpkin. Simmer until flavors are blended, about 10 minutes. Ladle into bowls. Top with a few apple pieces and sprinkle with Parmesan cheese.

# BUTTERNUT SQUASH SOUP

**SERVES 6**

**Baking the squash in the oven is an easy way to cook it. This naturally sweet, velvety smooth soup does not need a lot of seasonings, but curry is often added. Serve as a delightful first course with warm rolls.**

Preheat oven to 400°F. Place squash pieces in a flat baking pan. Pour about 1 cup water around squash. Bake until soft, about 1 hour. Remove to a plate and cool. When cool enough to handle, scoop out squash pulp. You should have about 4 cups. Set aside.

In a large soup pot over medium heat, melt butter. Add onion and garlic and sauté until soft, about 5 minutes. Add squash pulp and 1 cup of the stock and mix well. Transfer to a food processor or blender in batches and process until smooth. Return to pan and add the remaining 4 cups stock and seasonings. Simmer, uncovered, until flavors are blended, about 20 minutes, stirring occasionally. Ladle into bowls and top with crème fraîche, chives, and chutney.

1 butternut squash (about 3 pounds), unpeeled, seeds removed, cut into 4 large pieces

2 tablespoons butter or margarine

1 cup chopped yellow onion

1 clove garlic, minced

5 cups chicken stock or broth

3/4 teaspoon salt

1/2 teaspoon curry powder or more to taste (optional)

1/8 teaspoon ground white pepper

Crème fraîche (see page 27), sour cream, or nonfat yogurt for topping

Chopped chives or finely chopped parsley for topping

Chutney for topping

**This vivid, dark green soup with a swirl of yogurt or sour cream on top makes an enticing presentation.**

1 pound fresh spinach, stems removed

1 cup chicken or vegetable stock or broth

3 tablespoons butter or margarine

3 tablespoons all-purpose flour

½ teaspoon dried thyme

Dash of ground nutmeg

¾ teaspoon salt

Freshly ground pepper to taste

3 cups milk

Plain nonfat yogurt or sour cream for topping

Ground nutmeg for topping (optional)

In a large soup pot over high heat, combine spinach and stock. Bring to a boil and cook, tossing once with a fork, until spinach is wilted, about 5 minutes. Transfer to a food processor or blender and purée.

In soup pot over medium heat, melt butter. Add flour, thyme, nutmeg, salt, and pepper. Stir until bubbly. Add milk and stir until slightly thickened. Return spinach to pot and mix well. Simmer until heated through. Ladle into bowls. Add a dollop of yogurt or sour cream and swirl into soup. Add a sprinkle of nutmeg, if desired.

SERVES 6

# SPINACH AND WATERCRESS SOUP

SERVES 4

**Tender, leafy watercress is combined with spinach to make a bright green soup with a fresh taste. This soup can be served hot or cold.**

In a large soup pot over high heat, bring stock, onion, potato, garlic, and salt to a boil. Reduce heat to medium-low and simmer, covered, until potato is tender, about 15 minutes. Increase heat to medium. Add watercress, spinach, thyme, white pepper, and nutmeg and cook, covered, until greens are wilted, 6 to 8 minutes, tossing once or twice with a fork. Remove from heat and whisk in sour cream.

Transfer to a blender or food processor in batches and purée. Return to pot and reheat, but do not boil. Ladle into bowls and garnish with a sprig of watercress.

3 cups chicken stock or broth

1 cup chopped yellow onion

1 large russet potato ($^3/_4$ pound), peeled and cubed

2 cloves garlic, minced

$^1/_2$ teaspoon salt

3 cups lightly packed watercress leaves

1 bag (6 ounces) baby spinach, rinsed and dried

$^1/_2$ teaspoon dried thyme

$^1/_8$ teaspoon ground white pepper

Dash of ground nutmeg

$^1/_2$ cup light sour cream or light cream

4 sprigs watercress for garnish

**Mushrooms, leeks, and tomatoes make a perfect blend of flavors in this bisquelike soup. Serve for a luncheon with croissants and a fruit salad.**

1 tablespoon vegetable oil

1 leek, white and light green parts only, sliced

1 cup chopped yellow onion

2 stalks celery, chopped

1 clove garlic, minced

8 ounces mushrooms, sliced

1 can (28 ounces) whole tomatoes, coarsely chopped, with juice

1 teaspoon sugar

$\frac{1}{2}$ teaspoon dried thyme

1 bay leaf

1 teaspoon salt

Freshly ground pepper to taste

2 cups chicken stock or broth

$\frac{1}{2}$ cup dry white wine

$\frac{1}{2}$ cup half-and-half or milk

Chopped parsley for topping

In a large soup pot over medium heat, warm oil. Add leek, onion, celery, and garlic and sauté for 2 minutes. Add mushrooms and sauté until vegetables are tender, about 5 minutes. Add tomatoes, sugar, thyme, bay leaf, salt, and pepper and bring to a boil. Reduce heat to medium-low and simmer, covered, until vegetables are tender, 15 minutes. Remove bay leaf and discard. Transfer to a blender or food processor in batches and process until very smooth. Wash pot and return soup to pot. Add stock, wine, and half-and-half and simmer until flavors are blended, about 20 minutes. Do not boil. Ladle into bowls and sprinkle with parsley.

237

# SUMMER SOUP

**SERVES 4**

**Fresh garden vegetables and herbs are the main feature of this soup. Any combination of herbs can be used.**

In a large soup pot over high heat, bring stock, vegetables, and garlic to a boil. Reduce heat to medium-low and simmer, covered, until vegetables are tender, about 10 minutes. (At this point, if you wish, you can transfer the vegetables to a food processor or blender, process until chunky, and return to pot.)

In a bowl, whisk together milk, flour, paprika, herbs, salt, and pepper. Stir into vegetable-stock mixture. Whisk over medium heat until bubbly and slightly thickened, about 3 minutes. Add butter, if using. Cook 1 to 2 minutes longer. Remove from heat, add cheese, and stir until melted.

2 cups chicken stock or broth

1 zucchini, chopped

1 carrot, chopped

1 stalk celery, chopped

½ cup chopped yellow onion

2 cloves garlic, minced

2 cups milk

¼ cup all-purpose flour

1 teaspoon paprika

3 or 4 fresh basil leaves, chopped, or 1 teaspoon dried basil

½ tablespoon chopped fresh rosemary, or ½ teaspoon dried rosemary

1 tablespoon chopped parsley

¼ teaspoon salt

Freshly ground pepper to taste

1 tablespoon butter or margarine (optional)

1 cup grated Monterey Jack cheese

**This creamy soup made without cream or flour is low in calories but is still full of flavor. It can be served hot or cold for a light first course.**

2 large zucchini (about 1½ pounds), unpeeled, sliced

½ cup chopped yellow onion

1 medium russet potato (about ½ pound), peeled, halved lengthwise, and sliced

1½ cups chicken stock or broth

1 cup buttermilk or low-fat milk

½ teaspoon salt

Freshly ground pepper to taste

¼ teaspoon dried thyme

¼ teaspoon dried marjoram

Baked Garlic Croutons (page 57) for topping

In a saucepan over high heat, combine zucchini, onion, potato, and 1 cup of the stock. Bring to a boil. Reduce heat to medium-low and cook, covered, until vegetables are tender, about 20 minutes.

Transfer to a blender or food processor and purée. Return to pan and add remaining ½ cup stock, buttermilk, salt, pepper, thyme, and marjoram. Simmer over low heat to blend flavors, about 10 minutes. Ladle into bowls and sprinkle with a few croutons.

**SERVES 4**

# GREEK CHICKEN SOUP WITH EGG-LEMON SAUCE (KOTA SUPA AVAGOLEMONO)

**SERVES 8 TO 10**

**This is an authentic and unusual recipe given to me by a Greek friend. The eggs give the soup a fluffy, creamy texture, and the lemon gives it a refreshing tang. Serve with a Greek salad.**

In a large soup pot over high heat, bring stock to a boil. Stir in rice. Reduce heat to low and cook, covered, until rice is tender, about 20 minutes. Place the egg whites and yolks in two separate bowls. With an electric beater, beat whites until almost stiff. Beat in yolks. While beating egg mixture, add about ½ cup of the stock-rice mixture, then continue to add a little at a time until about 3 cups have been added. Slowly return this mixture to the soup pot holding the stock-rice mixture and mix well. Add lemon juice, salt, and white pepper and simmer for 5 to 10 minutes.

**NOTE:** *Soup will thicken as it stands. Add more stock when reheating.*

8 cups chicken stock

1¼ cups uncooked long-grain white rice

3 large eggs, separated

⅓ to ½ cup lemon juice (2 lemons)

1 teaspoon salt

⅛ teaspoon ground white pepper

**This is a good summer soup to make when garden vegetables are in season. Buttermilk adds a tangy flavor and a creamy texture.**

1 yellow onion, chopped

2 cloves garlic, minced

2 zucchini, chopped

1 medium russet potato (about ½ pound), sliced

2 cups chicken stock or broth

1 large tomato, peeled (see page 23), seeded, and chopped

1 to 1½ cups buttermilk

1 tablespoon chopped fresh basil, or ¾ teaspoon dried basil

½ teaspoon salt

Freshly ground pepper to taste

In a soup pot over medium-high heat, combine onion, garlic, zucchini, potato, and 1½ cups of the stock. Bring to a boil. Reduce heat to medium-low and simmer, covered, about 15 minutes. Add tomato and simmer until all of the vegetables are tender, about 5 minutes longer.

Transfer to a blender or food processor in batches and purée. Return to pot and add remaining ½ cup stock, buttermilk, basil, salt, and pepper. Simmer for several minutes to blend flavors.

241

# POTPOURRI SOUP

**SERVES 6**

**This healthful soup is puréed, giving it a creamy texture without the calories. You will need 6 cups mixed vegetables; carrots, celery, cabbage, and broccoli are good choices. Include a potato for thickening the soup and an onion for flavor. Try one of the variations listed at the end.**

In a saucepan over high heat, combine the vegetables and stock and bring to a boil. Reduce heat to medium-low and simmer, covered, until vegetables are tender, 15 to 20 minutes.

Working in batches, transfer to a food processor or blender and process until slightly chunky. Return to pan and add milk, salt, pepper, oregano, basil, and butter, if using. Heat gently to serving temperature. Sprinkle with parsley and serve immediately.

**VARIATIONS**

- *Add 1 cup grated Cheddar or Swiss cheese with the seasonings.*
- *Add ¼ cup beer or dry white wine with the seasonings.*
- *Sprinkle each serving with freshly grated Parmesan cheese.*
- *Omit the parsley and top with crumbled cooked bacon.*

6 cups sliced mixed vegetables, including 1 small russet potato and 1 small onion

2 cups chicken or beef stock or broth

1 to 1½ cups milk

½ teaspoon salt

¼ teaspoon freshly ground pepper

¼ teaspoon dried oregano

¼ teaspoon dried basil

1 tablespoon butter or margarine (optional)

Chopped fresh parsley for garnish

242

This was the signature soup at an old inn in Coburg, Oregon, that is no longer in operation. This soup is still famous in the Willamette Valley and has become a favorite in many households.

½ cup butter or margarine

½ cup diced celery

½ cup diced carrot

1 cup diced yellow onion

½ cup all-purpose flour

½ teaspoon dry mustard

5 cups chicken stock or broth

3 tablespoons freshly grated Parmesan cheese

2 cups firmly packed grated Cheddar cheese

1 bottle (12 ounces) beer, allowed to go flat

½ teaspoon salt, or to taste

Freshly ground pepper to taste

In a large saucepan over medium heat, melt butter. Add celery, carrot, and onion and sauté until soft, about 10 minutes. Add flour and mustard and cook, stirring constantly, 1 minute. Slowly stir in stock. Bring to a boil and cook over medium-high heat, stirring constantly, until thickened, about 5 minutes. Reduce heat to medium-low and add cheeses, stirring until melted. Add beer, salt, and pepper and simmer, uncovered, over low heat to blend flavors, about 15 minutes, stirring occasionally.

**NOTE:** *The soup thickens and the texture improves the second day. Warm carefully over medium-low heat, as it scorches easily. Add more liquid if the soup is too thick.*

SERVES 6

# CHEESE AND LEEK SOUP

**SERVES 4**

**Leeks are related to garlic and onions but have a milder and subtler flavor that lends itself to this light, delicate cheese soup.**

In a saucepan over medium-low heat, melt butter. Add leeks, onion, and celery and cook until tender, 5 to 10 minutes, stirring occasionally. Add stock and simmer for 10 minutes. Transfer to a blender or food processor in batches and purée. Return to saucepan.

Blend cream cheese and yogurt in blender or food processor until smooth. Add to soup along with salt and white pepper and whisk until blended. Heat, but do not boil. Ladle into bowls and sprinkle with chopped green onions, chives, or parsley.

$\frac{1}{4}$ cup butter or margarine

2 leeks, white and light green parts only, sliced

1 cup chopped yellow onion

2 cups chopped celery

3 cups chicken stock or broth

1 package (8 ounces) cream cheese, cut up

1 cup plain nonfat yogurt

$\frac{1}{2}$ teaspoon salt

$\frac{1}{8}$ teaspoon ground white pepper

Chopped green onions, chives, or parsley for topping

**This is a convenient soup to make because the ingredients are usually on hand. For a stronger cheese flavor, use sharp Cheddar cheese.**

2 tablespoons butter or margarine

1/2 cup chopped yellow onion

1/2 cup chopped celery

2 tablespoons all-purpose flour

2 cups chicken stock or broth

1 1/2 cups milk

1 large russet potato (about 3/4 pound), peeled and diced

1/2 teaspoon salt

1/8 teaspoon ground white pepper

1 cup packed grated Cheddar cheese

2 or 3 drops Tabasco sauce

Chopped chives or green onions for topping

In a soup pot over medium heat, melt butter. Add onion and celery and sauté until tender, about 5 minutes. Sprinkle with flour. Stir 1 minute. Gradually whisk in stock and milk and bring to a boil. Add potato, salt, and white pepper. Reduce heat to medium-low and simmer, uncovered, until potato is tender, about 20 minutes. Add cheese, 1/2 cup at a time, stirring until melted after each addition. Add Tabasco sauce and stir. Ladle into bowls and sprinkle with chives or green onions.

245

# MEXICAN CHEESE SOUP

**SERVES 4**

**When relatives from New York came to visit, I served this soup and they loved it. Company Cornbread (page 53) went well with these "south of the border" flavors.**

In a large soup pot over high heat, bring stock, vegetables, garlic, and chiles to a boil. Reduce heat to medium-low and simmer, covered, until vegetables are tender, about 10 minutes.

In a bowl, whisk together remaining ingredients except cheese. Stir into stock mixture. Whisk over medium heat until bubbly and slightly thickened, about 3 minutes. Cook 1 to 2 minutes longer. Add cheese and stir until melted.

2 cups chicken stock or broth

2 carrots, chopped

1 stalk celery, chopped

½ cup chopped yellow onion

1 clove garlic, minced

1 can (4 ounces) chopped green chiles, drained

2 cups milk

¼ cup all-purpose flour

1 teaspoon chili powder

¼ teaspoon ground cumin

¼ teaspoon dried oregano

¼ teaspoon salt

Freshly ground pepper to taste

1¾ cups grated Monterey Jack cheese

246

**THREE-CHEESE SOUP**

**SERVES 4**

A mellow blend of cheeses goes into this colorful soup. Other combinations of cheese may be used, but include Swiss for a distinctive nutty flavor. Use the food processor for quick chopping of vegetables.

2 carrots, finely chopped

1 stalk celery, finely chopped

$\frac{1}{2}$ cup finely chopped yellow onion

1 clove garlic, minced

2 to 2$\frac{1}{4}$ cups chicken stock or broth

2 cups milk

$\frac{1}{4}$ cup all-purpose flour

$\frac{1}{4}$ teaspoon dry mustard

$\frac{1}{8}$ teaspoon ground white pepper

$\frac{1}{2}$ teaspoon salt

1 cup grated Cheddar cheese

$\frac{1}{2}$ cup grated Monterey Jack cheese

$\frac{1}{2}$ cup grated Swiss cheese

In a large soup pot over high heat, combine vegetables, garlic, and 2 cups stock. Bring to a boil. Reduce heat to medium-low. Simmer, covered, until vegetables are tender, about 10 minutes.

In a bowl, combine milk, flour, mustard, white pepper, and salt. Stir milk mixture into stock. Increase heat to high and cook until slightly thickened, 2 to 3 minutes. Remove from heat. Add cheeses and stir until melted. Add remaining $\frac{1}{4}$ cup stock if too thick. Keep warm over low heat until serving time.

# CREAM OF ARTICHOKE SOUP

**SERVES 4**

**Fresh artichoke hearts may be used, but they are very time consuming to prepare. Here canned artichokes are used for convenience with the same great flavor.**

In a saucepan over medium-high heat, bring 1 cup stock to a boil. Add artichokes and reduce heat to medium-low and simmer, uncovered, 6 to 7 minutes.

In another saucepan over medium heat, melt butter. Add onion, celery, and garlic and sauté until tender, 5 to 6 minutes. Add flour and stir until bubbly. Add artichoke-stock mixture and stir until thickened, 1 to 2 minutes. Transfer to food processor or blender and process until chunky. Return to saucepan and add remaining stock, half-and-half, salt, and white pepper and simmer, uncovered, until flavors are blended, 5 to 10 minutes longer. Ladle into bowls and float a lemon slice on top.

**NOTE:** *For a richer soup, reduce stock to 1½ cups and increase half-and-half to 1 cup.*

2 cups chicken stock or broth

1 can (13½ ounces) canned quartered artichoke hearts, drained

2 tablespoons butter or margarine

½ cup finely chopped yellow onion

1 celery stalk, finely chopped

1 clove garlic, minced

2 tablespoons all-purpose flour

½ cup half-and-half

¼ teaspoon salt

⅛ teaspoon white pepper

Thinly sliced lemon slices for garnish

# CHILLED

**SOUPS**

Cold soups are fun to make and require very little effort and preparation, but you must allow time for thorough chilling (see page 19). Add a complementary garnish for special effect.

To set the tone for a summer meal, serve an enjoyable chilled soup for a first course or a refreshing, cold fruit soup for dessert. Fruit soups can also be served for breakfast.

# CHILLED TOMATO SOUP WITH FRESH HERBS

**SERVES 6**

**A delightful, light beginning to a summer patio party that leaves room for more to come. Make this soup at least one day in advance to allow the flavors to blend.**

In a large bowl or pan, combine all ingredients except sour cream and cucumbers. Cover and refrigerate for 24 hours. Strain and discard solids. Whisk in sour cream. Serve in mugs with a cucumber spear.

1 can (46 ounces) tomato juice

2 tablespoons white wine vinegar

2 tablespoons lemon juice

1 teaspoon Worcestershire sauce

1 clove garlic, sliced

1 tablespoon sugar

1 teaspoon salt

1 teaspoon dry mustard

3 sprigs rosemary

6 or 7 fresh basil leaves, torn

2 sprigs thyme

Freshly ground pepper to taste

1 cup sour cream

2 cucumbers, peeled and cut into spears

**An appealing and healthful combination of green summer vegetables, loaded with vitamins and minerals, blended together. It can be served hot or cold.**

5 cups chicken stock or broth

2 cups chopped fresh green beans

2 cups chopped lettuce leaves or spinach

2 cups chopped zucchini (about ¾ pound)

2 cups peas, fresh or frozen

1 cup chopped celery

½ cup chopped green onions, including some tender green tops

¼ cup chopped parsley

½ teaspoon salt

Freshly ground pepper to taste

Crème fraîche (page 27) or plain nonfat yogurt for topping

In a saucepan over medium-high heat, combine all ingredients except salt, pepper, and topping. Bring to a boil. Reduce heat and simmer, partially covered, until vegetables are tender, about 15 minutes.

Transfer to a blender or food processor in batches, about 1 cup at a time, and purée until smooth. Season with salt and pepper. Chill thoroughly. Ladle into bowls and top with a dollop of crème fraîche or yogurt.

# ZESTY CHILLED TOMATO SOUP WITH HORSERADISH

**SERVES 6 TO 8**

**This cooling soup is like an aspic in liquid form. Serve it on a hot summer day in chilled mugs for an introduction to a barbecue.**

In a large bowl, combine all ingredients except topping and whisk until smooth. Cover and refrigerate several hours or overnight. Serve in chilled bowls with a dollop of crème fraîche.

**VARIATION:** *Add 1 cup small bay shrimp 1 hour before serving.*

5 cups tomato juice

1 cup chicken stock or broth

1 large tomato, peeled (see page 23), seeded, and chopped

1 cucumber, peeled, seeded, chopped, and drained

6 green onions, including some tender green tops, finely sliced

1 avocado, peeled, pitted, and chopped

¼ teaspoon salt

¼ teaspoon ground white pepper

1 teaspoon Dijon mustard

1 tablespoon creamy prepared horseradish

¼ teaspoon Tabasco sauce

Crème fraîche (see page 27) or plain nonfat yogurt for topping

251

**Here is a refreshing soup to serve as a palate teaser for summer entertaining. Serve with Three-Cheese Bread (page 47).**

1 large cucumber, peeled, seeded, and cut into chunks

2 avocados, peeled, pitted, and cut into chunks

2½ cups buttermilk

3 tablespoons chopped red onion

1 teaspoon lemon juice

2 or 3 fresh basil leaves, torn

Dash of salt and ground white pepper

½ tomato, peeled (see page 23), seeded, and chopped for topping

Fresh basil chiffonade (see page 25) for topping

Crème fraîche (see page 27) for topping

In a food processor or blender, combine all ingredients except toppings. Blend until smooth. Cover and refrigerate for several hours. Serve in bowls topped with tomato, basil chiffonade, and a dollop of crème fraîche.

SERVES 4

## COOL CUCUMBER AND AVOCADO SOUP

# CREAMY CHILLED FRESH TOMATO SOUP

**SERVES 6**

Sweet vine-ripened tomatoes and fresh herbs are the key to the intense flavor of this smooth, creamy soup. Although tomatoes are naturally sweet, sugar is added to cut the acid. Buttermilk gives it an extra tang and reduces the calories. Serve it very cold.

In a large soup pot over high heat, combine tomatoes, onion, garlic, parsley and basil sprigs, bay leaf, and stock. Bring to a boil. Reduce heat to medium-low and simmer, covered, 10 minutes. Remove lid and simmer 10 minutes longer. Remove parsley and basil sprigs and bay leaf and discard. Transfer to a food processor or blender in batches and process until very smooth, about 2 minutes. Put through a food mill to remove seeds, or press through a stainless steel sieve into a clean pan, pressing the pulp against the sieve with the back of a big spoon. Discard seeds. Return soup to pan and whisk in tomato paste, buttermilk, salt, white pepper, and sugar and blend. Simmer, uncovered, until flavors are blended, about 10 minutes. Cover and refrigerate for several hours or overnight. Ladle into bowls and top with a dollop of yogurt and some chopped avocado.

4 pounds (about 10) very ripe tomatoes, peeled (see page 23), seeded, and chopped (use a food processor)

1½ cups chopped yellow onion

2 cloves garlic, sliced

2 sprigs parsley

3 or 4 sprigs basil

1 bay leaf

2 cups chicken stock or broth

2 tablespoons tomato paste

1 cup buttermilk

1 teaspoon salt

⅛ teaspoon ground white pepper

¼ teaspoon sugar

Plain nonfat yogurt or sour cream for topping

1 avocado, peeled, pitted, and chopped for topping

**This favorite summertime soup originated in the Andalusia region in southern Spain. It is a combination of fresh vegetables and is sometimes referred to as a salad soup. Serve icy cold.**

4 ripe tomatoes, peeled (see page 23), seeded, and chopped

1 small yellow onion, chopped

1 small green bell pepper, seeded and chopped

1 cucumber, peeled, seeded, chopped, and drained

2 cloves garlic, minced

¼ cup chopped parsley or cilantro

4 cups tomato juice

1 tablespoon fresh lemon juice

1 teaspoon Worcestershire sauce

2 tablespoons olive oil

½ teaspoon paprika

¼ teaspoon ground cumin

1 tablespoon red wine vinegar

2 drops Tabasco sauce

Salt and freshly ground pepper to taste

Sour cream or plain nonfat yogurt for topping

½ cup sliced pitted black olives for topping (optional)

Lemon wedges for garnish

Combine all ingredients except toppings and lemon wedges in a large bowl. Stir well, cover, and refrigerate for at least 4 hours before serving.

Ladle into bowls and top with a dollop of sour cream and a few sliced olives. Garnish with lemon wedges.

**NOTE:** *For a thicker soup, purée 1 to 2 cups of the mixture in a food processor or blender, and then combine with remaining soup.*

# GAZPACHO WITH FRESH TOMATOES

**SERVES 6**

**In this superb version of the famous Spanish soup, all of the ingredients are puréed. Bread is added for thickening. The flavor is excellent.**

In a flat dish, soak bread in the cold water for 1 minute, turning once. Squeeze out excess water.

In a food processor, combine cucumber, bell peppers, garlic, oil, vinegar, Tabasco sauce, sugar, salt, and pepper and purée. Add half the soaked bread and continue processing until smooth, about 2 minutes. Transfer mixture to a large bowl or stainless steel pan. Add tomatoes and the remaining bread to the food processor and process until smooth, about 2 minutes. Transfer to bowl holding first mixture and mix well. Refrigerate for several hours or overnight. Ladle into bowls and top with sliced olives.

2 slices day-old French bread (about ¼ pound), crusts removed

¼ cup cold water

1 cucumber, peeled, halved lengthwise, seeded, and cut up

½ red bell pepper, seeded and cut up

½ green bell pepper, seeded and cut up

2 cloves garlic, cut up

½ cup olive oil

¼ cup red wine vinegar

2 drops Tabasco sauce

1 teaspoon sugar

1 teaspoon salt

Freshly ground pepper to taste

5 or 6 ripe tomatoes (about 2 pounds), peeled (see page 23), seeded, and cut up

¼ cup sliced pimiento-stuffed green olives for topping

**Too hot to cook? Serve this refreshing soup for lunch with Basic Crostini (page 59).**

2 ripe avocados, halved and pitted

2 cups chicken stock or broth

2 tablespoons lemon juice

½ cup plain nonfat yogurt

¼ teaspoon salt

3 drops Tabasco sauce

¼ cup chopped cashews for topping

Scoop out avocado pulp and put in food processor along with stock, lemon juice, yogurt, salt, and Tabasco sauce. Process until smooth. Transfer to another container, cover, and refrigerate for several hours. Ladle into chilled bowls and sprinkle with nuts.

SERVES 4

# COLD AVOCADO SOUP WITH CASHEWS

# STRAWBERRY WINE SOUP

**SERVES 4**

**Make this soup when juicy, ripe strawberries are at their peak. Serve on a hot summer night for a light, refreshing dessert course.**

In a saucepan over medium heat, combine strawberries, sugar, and water. Simmer, uncovered, until berries are soft, 5 to 10 minutes. In a cup, blend cornstarch with cold water. Increase heat to medium-high. Add cornstarch mixture to berries and stir until mixture bubbles and is clear. Purée in a blender or food processor and then return to pan. Add wine and lemon zest. Refrigerate to chill. Add Cognac, if desired. Serve topped with a dollop of crème fraîche and sliced strawberries.

2½ cups fresh strawberries, stemmed and sliced

6 tablespoons granulated sugar

1 cup water

1 tablespoon cornstarch

1 tablespoon cold water

1 cup dry white wine

2 teaspoons grated lemon zest

1 teaspoon Cognac (optional)

Crème fraîche or sour cream for topping

3 strawberries, stemmed and sliced, for topping

Serve this pretty soup for a brunch first course. It can be made any time of the year, but if fresh raspberries are in season, add a few for garnish. Strawberries are also good instead of raspberries.

2 cartons (10 ounces each) frozen, sweetened raspberries, partially thawed

2 cups plain nonfat yogurt

$\frac{1}{4}$ teaspoon ground cinnamon

In a food processor or blender, purée raspberries. Remove seeds if desired. Add yogurt and cinnamon and mix well. Serve icy cold.

258

# CHILLED BLUEBERRY SOUP

## SERVES 4

**This is a perfect ending to a summer dinner. If possible, chill the soup overnight and serve it in chilled bowls.**

In a saucepan over high heat, combine all ingredients except sour cream and bring to a boil. Reduce heat to medium-low and simmer, uncovered, 15 minutes. Cool slightly. Remove cinnamon stick and lemon peel.

Transfer to a blender or food processor and purée until smooth. Cover and refrigerate for several hours or overnight. Whisk in sour cream just before serving.

2 cups blueberries, fresh or frozen

1½ cups water

¼ cup sugar

1 cinnamon stick or ½ teaspoon ground cinnamon

½-by-2-inch strip of lemon zest (use vegetable peeler)

¾ cup sour cream or plain nonfat yogurt

259

# MIXED FRUIT SOUP

**Make this soup any time of the year. You can use fresh or frozen berries.**

1 cup berry purée (raspberry, blackberry, or strawberry; choose one or a combination; see Note)

1 small, ripe banana, cut up

½ cup dry red wine

1 cup orange juice

2 tablespoons honey

¼ teaspoon ground cinnamon

¼ teaspoon ground nutmeg

In a food processor or blender, blend puréed fruits with banana and wine. Place in a saucepan and add orange juice, honey, cinnamon, and nutmeg. Bring to a boil. Reduce heat to low and simmer, uncovered, 2 minutes. Refrigerate and serve very cold.

**NOTE:** *To make 1 cup berry purée, put 3 cups whole berries in a food processor or blender and process until smooth. Remove seeds by passing purée through a food mill or straining it through a sieve, pressing the pulp against the side of the sieve with the back of a large spoon.*

# CHILLED MELON SOUP

**SERVES 4**

**This cooling soup derives its flavor from juicy, ripe melons. A delightful ending to a summer dinner.**

In food processor, place 3 cups of the watermelon chunks, lime juice, torn mint leaves, and honey and process until almost smooth. Transfer to a large bowl. Add wine, cantaloupe, and honeydew melon. Cut the remaining 1 cup watermelon into ½-inch pieces, add to bowl, and mix well. Cover and refrigerate for several hours. Ladle into goblets and garnish each with a mint leaf.

4 cups seedless watermelon chunks (about 1-inch pieces)

Juice of 1 lime

2 fresh mint leaves, torn, plus 4 for garnish

2 tablespoons honey

¼ cup dry red wine or cranberry juice

½ cup diced cantaloupe

½ cup diced honeydew melon

I had just finished testing my last recipe for this book when I saw a basket of local ripe, juicy peaches on the counter of our local farm stand. I was inspired to make a chilled peach soup, combining the peaches with orange juice, honey, and buttermilk. This luscious, creamy dessert soup was the result.

3 large ripe peaches (about 1½ pounds), peeled and sliced

2 cups orange juice

3 tablespoons honey

Dash of ground cinnamon

2 cups buttermilk

4 fresh mint leaves for garnish

Place half of the peaches, half of the orange juice, and all of the honey in a food processor and process until smooth. Transfer to a large bowl. Place remaining peaches and orange juice in food processor and blend. Add cinnamon and buttermilk and mix well. Combine with other ingredients in the bowl. Ladle into goblets and garnish with a mint leaf.

INDEX

# TABLE OF EQUIVALENTS

The exact equivalents in the following tables have been rounded for convenience.

## LIQUID/DRY MEASURES

| U.S. | Metric |
|---|---|
| ¼ teaspoon | 1.25 milliliters |
| ½ teaspoon | 2.5 milliliters |
| 1 teaspoon | 5 milliliters |
| 1 tablespoon (3 teaspoons) | 15 milliliters |
| 1 fluid ounce (2 tablespoons) | 30 milliliters |
| ¼ cup | 60 milliliters |
| ⅓ cup | 80 milliliters |
| ½ cup | 120 milliliters |
| 1 cup | 240 milliliters |
| 1 pint (2 cups) | 480 milliliters |
| 1 quart (4 cups, 32 ounces) | 960 milliliters |
| 1 gallon (4 quarts) | 3.84 liters |
| 1 ounce (by weight) | 28 grams |
| 1 pound | 454 grams |
| 2.2 pounds | 1 kilogram |

## LENGTH

| U.S. | Metric |
|---|---|
| ⅛ inch | 3 millimeters |
| ¼ inch | 6 millimeters |
| ½ inch | 12 millimeters |
| 1 inch | 2.5 centimeters |

## OVEN TEMPERATURE

| Fahrenheit | Celsius | Gas |
|---|---|---|
| 250 | 120 | ½ |
| 275 | 140 | 1 |
| 300 | 150 | 2 |
| 325 | 160 | 3 |
| 350 | 180 | 4 |
| 375 | 190 | 5 |
| 400 | 200 | 6 |
| 425 | 220 | 7 |
| 450 | 230 | 8 |
| 475 | 240 | 9 |
| 500 | 260 | 10 |

# 262

## recipes for serious comfort food

Cozy, warming, nurturing, like a hug in a bowl,
soups and stews are serious comfort food.

The author of the best-selling *Big Book of Casseroles* now introduces *The Big Book of Soups & Stews*, bringing succulent meats, tender vegetables, and savory goodness with 262 delicious recipes for soups, chowders, stews, and bisques—many inspired by the international flavors of countries like Greece, India, France, and Russia. Enjoyed in every season, everywhere in the world, soups and stews satisfy. From a hot and hearty Oven Beef Beer Stew for a cold night to a cool, refreshing Vichyssoise for a sizzling summer afternoon, there's a recipe here for all occasions. A detailed section on cooking techniques and lots of time-saving tips, plus additional recipes for breads, toppings, and garnishes make *The Big Book of Soups & Stews* the ultimate comfort cookbook for the ultimate comfort food.

MARYANA VOLLSTEDT is the author of more than a dozen cookbooks, including *The Big Book of Casseroles*, *What's for Dinner?*, and *Pacific Fresh*, all from Chronicle Books. She lives in Eugene, Oregon.

ISBN 0-8118-3056-X   $19.95 U.S.

90000

9 780811 830560

PQX791801

*Cover* ... B
*Cover & book design by* Vivien Sung
*Cover photograph by* Quentin Bacon

www.chroniclebooks.com